Seven Unmarked Graves

Seven Unmarked Graves

The Search for My Italian Family

Diane Claypool

First Printing

ISBN (paperback): 979-8-218-50136-5
ISBN (ebook): 979-8-218-50137-2

Cover and interior design by Christy Day, Constellation Book Services.
Cover photo by Robert Claypool, Pontestazzemese, Lucca, Italy, 2010.
Editor: Jessica Vineyard, Red Letter Editing, www.redletterediting.com

Printed in the United States of America

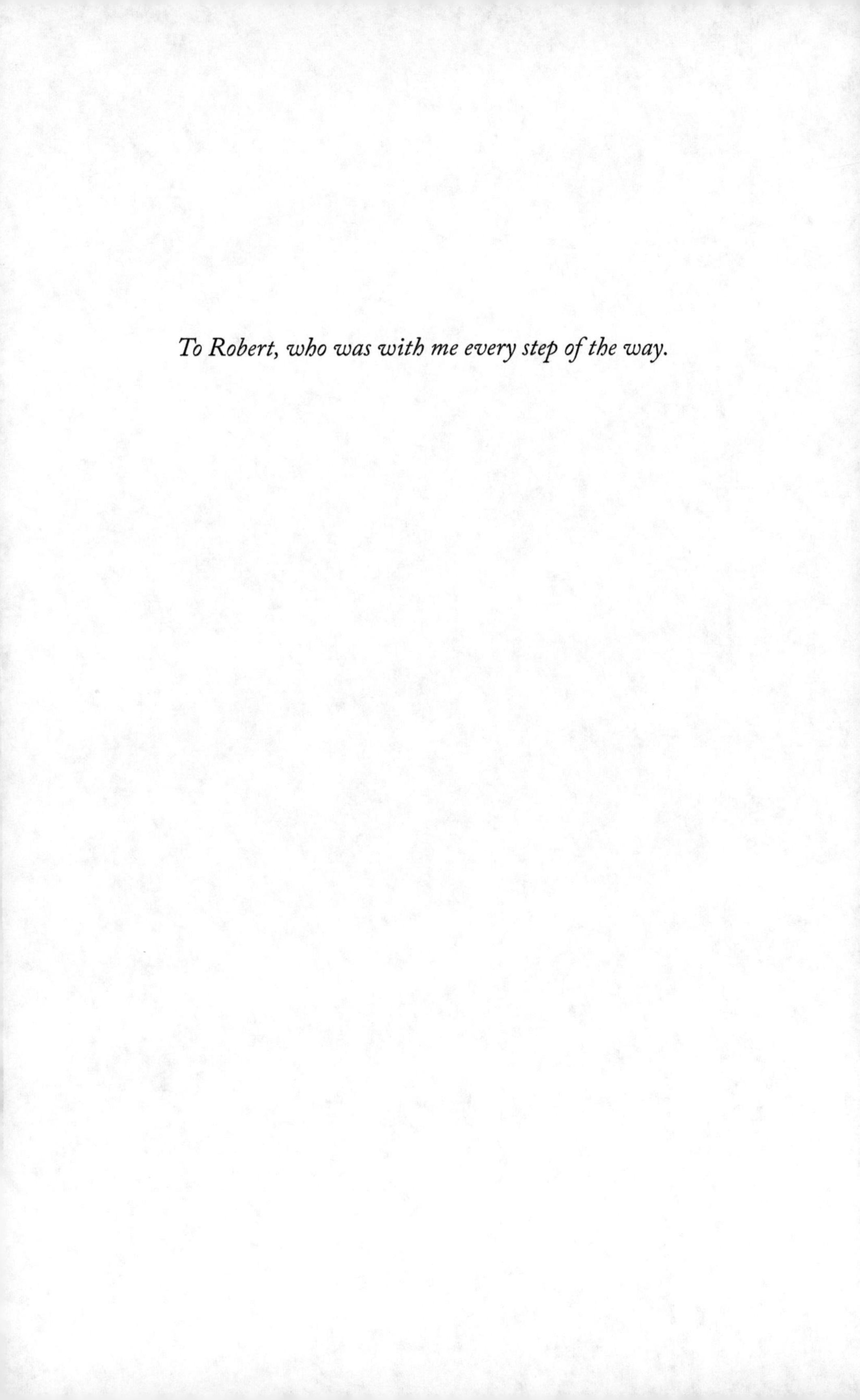
To Robert, who was with me every step of the way.

Contents

My Italian Family Tree

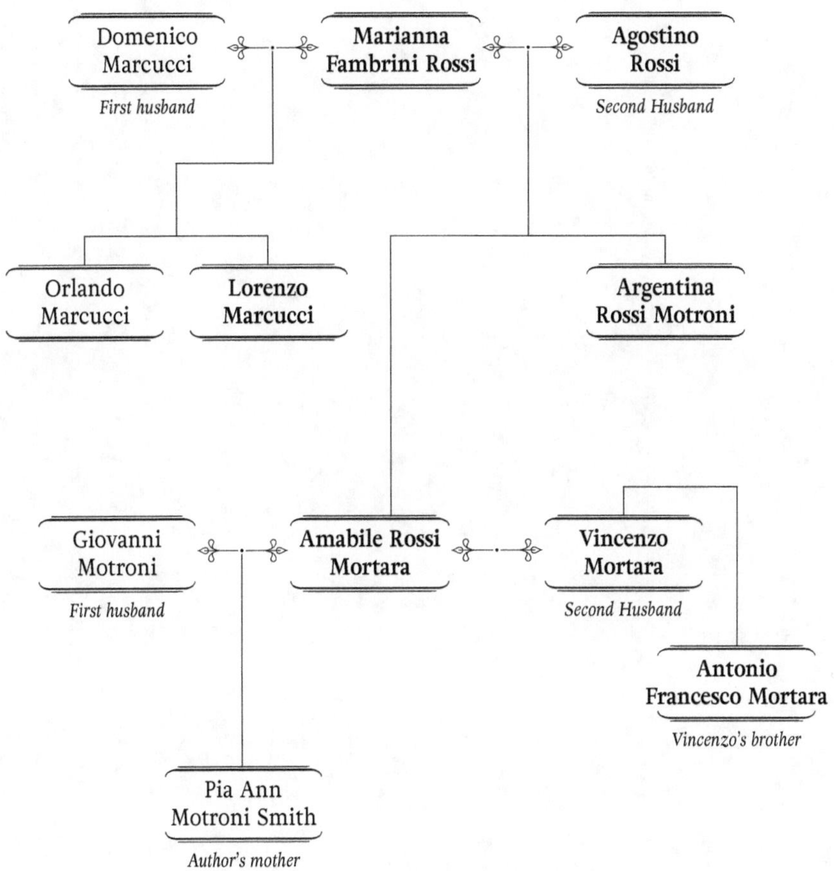

The names on the seven gravestones are in **bold** type.

Acknowledgments

This book could not have been written without the generous assistance of others. I have to start with my husband, Robert. You were my rock throughout our travels. Thank you for your loving support and wholehearted devotion to exploring new territories.

Thank you to Harry Bosworth, "keeper of the records" of my family. You opened the door to my path of discovery, and you were there with us at the finish line.

Heartfelt thanks to Professoressa Monica Rountree. You made learning fun. You infused our classes with everything Italian—meals, music, and magic. And you continually reignited a big spark of enthusiasm on my journey.

To the three wise women of Archivio Storico, Lucca: Maria, Cristina, and Mariella—*molte grazie*:

Maria Chiaro, you opened locked archive doors with your telephone calls and letters of introduction and gave me a treasured book that uncovered the secret past of a uniformed family member. I will always remember your winning smile and your kind assistance. Thank you for all you did to help us.

Cristina Marinari, you followed leads, pulled census binders, provided documents, and explained the duties of a customs officer—vital clues to a forgotten past. You have my heartfelt thanks for all your efforts.

Mariella Morotti, you retrieved records and personally escorted me through bureaucratic barricades in other archive offices. I will never forget your intervention and support. I couldn't have managed without you. Thank you.

Dotoressa Laura Busti, thank you for welcoming us to research in Archivio di Stato, Lucca. Those census records uncovered the hidden lives of my family members. Your assistance made it all possible.

Daniela Marchi, thank you for welcoming us to your villa and introducing us to your friend Mila. None of this story could have been told without your able assistance.

Mila Antonini, how can I ever thank you enough? You were there when I needed you most. You drove us to remote Brancoli villages and provided astonishing glimpses into a forgotten past. You found Tuscan homes once occupied by my ancestors, a lost village, and a living relative with a fantastic memory. You are my forever friend.

Gabriella Gabrielli, thank you. Not once, but twice, you personally found vital keys to my ancestors' lives in Piazza di Brancoli. I am eternally grateful that you joined the search for my family.

Bruno Bottari, *grazie, grazie*. You held the key to the church in Farnocchia. You trusted us with access to a treasure trove of family records, and you paved the way to discovery. I am grateful beyond measure.

Ubaldo Cecchettini, thank you for entrusting me with a borrowed copy of our shared family history. Your generosity is appreciated more than you can imagine.

Mario Orzali, thank you for providing an invitation to the Orzali Family Reunion. Your published research was vital to my search for missing links in a convoluted family history. It was important for me to meet with you and my other family members at an awesome event.

To Pasquale and Maria Bruna Naccarati, thank you for hosting the Orzali Family Reunion. You personally escorted us through ancestral sites in Lucca, two banquets, a castle, an ancient church, and your lovely home. We are forever grateful.

To Marjorie Werner Picchi, thank you for inviting us into your home. Your beautiful watercolor brushstrokes illustrated the villages of Brancoli. And you related your husband Fosco's story of wartime Italy, which provided new, important insights into my family history.

To all the archivists at Archivio Diocesano in Lucca, thank you for your assistance in translating troublesome text in the archbishops' records. We couldn't have done it without you.

To Stein Steinfeld, thank you for filling in the blanks in a shared family history. The information about the Motroni family in San Francisco could not have been accurately described without your input. I am grateful for your help.

To Richard (Marcucci) Wilson, thanks to you and Barbara for your gracious hospitality. You helped me locate a lost portrait, and you provided photos and legends of the lost Italian village of Ponte Rotto. I could not have managed without your assistance.

To Elias Hruska, stepson of Vincent Mortara, thanks to you and Maria for welcoming us into your home. You located and helped me translate Vincent's diaries, critical keys to a forgotten past. I am forever grateful for your kind assistance.

To my mentors: A special thanks goes to Judi Drais (dec.), who introduced me to "Writing Your Life" and provided the setting for other writers to join in. Additional thanks goes to Molly Tinsley, who led a writer's group in my living room and helped me prepare this story for print.

Thank you to Jessica Vineyard, my editor and my friend. Your professionalism, persistence, and patience honed and polished a rough draft into a story worthy of publication. I am grateful I found you.

To Christy Day, who designed the book cover and interior of this book, thank you for stepping forward to assist me in the last stages pre-publication. I am so very grateful for your expertise.

1

The Meeting

I stood at my parents' kitchen sink, up to my elbows in dishwater.

"I received a phone call this morning about my father," Mom said. She reached into a cabinet to retrieve a towel. "He's dying, and we need to go to Mountain View tomorrow."

I braced soapy hands against the kitchen countertop to keep from falling, my knees suddenly wobbly. What was she saying? I adored her stepfather, Vincent, but he lived in Redwood City.

"Mountain View? Why Mountain View?"

"That's where John is." She opened a drawer. Silverware clinked into a tray.

I turned to stare at her. "Who's John?"

"My father, John Motroni."

"What are you talking about? I thought John Motroni was dead."

"Well, he's not." She swirled the towel across a plate and placed it on a shelf. "We lost contact a long time ago. And now, out of the blue, I find out he's dying."

"I have another grandfather! Why didn't you mention this before? You didn't think it was important?"

"There was nothing to tell. Don't get snippy with me."

I twisted the dishcloth and twisted it again. "Good grief, Mom, I tell you everything. Even my love life." My voice grew louder. "The rare times—like maybe two—that you brought up John Motroni, it was always in the past. You never told me he was alive!"

"Calm down! Don't make a mountain out of a molehill." Mom folded the dishtowel over a rack inside a cabinet door. She untied her apron, draped it over her arm. "I hadn't heard from John in ages, and that's all there is to that. I need to change now. I have a Ladies Aid meeting this afternoon."

Alone with my thoughts, I watched water spin down the drain, and felt part of my life spin away with it. Ladies Aid? Unreal! What about Daughters Aid?

My mother was my best friend. We had discussed every imaginable topic, including sex, drugs, and Elvis Presley. This was the first time Mom had revealed another life separate from me, and secrets she didn't share.

Early the next morning, I rummaged through my closet. How do you dress to meet your grandfather for the first time? Mom had once told me, "He was such a dandy." I thought that was cool. Maybe he wore a top hat and tails, like Fred Astaire waltzing around with Ginger Rogers.

I tried on several outfits, agonized over choices, and threw discards onto a growing pile on the bed. Nothing seemed right. I finally rehung the rejects, chose a simple black and red plaid skirt, a white blouse, and a buttoned, red cardigan I would toss over my back like a shawl, its sleeves draped over my shoulders. Maybe he'd look at my clothes and ask if I was in college, and I'd be able to say I was a sophomore, and he'd beam with pride and say, "But you are just seventeen. So young!" Then I muttered, You ninny; he's probably comatose. I twisted my stubborn curls into a ponytail and headed out the door.

It was 1957, one year out from having passed my driver's test, and my parents gave me ample opportunity to practice behind the wheel. I opened the driver's door, but Mom stopped me. "No, this time I'll drive," she said.

When we were in the car together it was always nonstop conversation. Not today. I couldn't tell whether Mom was fretting about her father or concentrating on traffic, but she didn't talk. I had expected more—an explanation for her years of secrecy or some preparation for what we might see at the end of the road. But I was traveling with a mute stranger. I turned on the radio and filled the dead space with KSFO music and chatter for the two-hour drive south from Healdsburg, through San Francisco along Shoreline Boulevard, then El Camino Real to Mountain View.

We drove east about twenty minutes through busy traffic. I reached down to change the radio station, and I looked up to a different landscape. Tree-lined streets looped around low-rise, Mediterranean-style buildings with white stucco walls and red tile roofs. Stone walkways meandered through expanses of lawn studded with pepperwoods and palms. Straight ahead, a white clock tower with red tile trim soared over an attached two-story building. There were no other moving cars in sight. I didn't dare ask my silent mother what we were doing on a college campus, afraid she'd spin around right there in the middle of the road and head home.

Mom parked the car near a two-story mansion with an arched portico on the right side. White chimneys rose on either side of the house, each accented with a diamond-shaped red tile inset that matched the roof. Within the gabled front porch, Art Deco leaded-glass panes surrounded a massive door. This didn't look like a hospital, where I'd expected to find my dying grandfather sandwiched between bleached bedding.

Mom pressed the bell, and within seconds the door was opened by an attractive woman about my mother's age. She was elegantly dressed in cream-colored silk and beautiful brown cashmere, accented by her glossy brown pageboy hairstyle. My mother's clothes and my own seemed too casual and "country." The poised and polished woman was wearing my mother's colors, but she was Saks Fifth Avenue, and we were J. C. Penney. Who was this woman? John's girlfriend? His daughter? Was John rich?

My mother held out her hand. "Hello, I'm Pia Smith."

The woman in cashmere grasped Mom's right hand and covered both their hands with her left. "I'm so glad you could come. I don't know if he'll know you. His memory is failing. He's in the garden. Please come this way."

We followed her around the building, past its tall, dark, rectangular windows. Our shoes clicked on a wide stone path that wove through a manicured lawn and skirted abundant flower beds.

"John, you have visitors!" our guide called out.

An elderly man stood alone near a polished stone bench in the shadow of a palm tree. He stepped into sunlight as we approached. He had an older version of my mother's oval face—high forehead, probing brown eyes, and straight Roman nose.

Slender like Mom, well groomed, he wore classy tan slacks and jacket, his brimmed hat set at the same jaunty angle as Frank Sinatra's. He held himself erect without cane or crutch and seemed amazingly fit for a dying man. He recognized the cashmere woman and smiled. Then, still smiling, he looked at my mother and me, but his eyebrows moved toward the center of his face.

"John, do you remember me? I'm Pia, your daughter, and this is Diane. She's your granddaughter."

Was this really happening? Mom had introduced herself to her father, calling him by his first name! How could she be so emotionally detached from her own father?

John gazed at us with no hint of recognition. Then he turned to the woman in cashmere and spoke. "My brother Ralph was here yesterday."

The cashmere woman leaned close to my mother's ear and murmured, "Ralph died long ago."

Mom tipped her head downward before she gave a couple of nods. She looked directly at John's polished shoes as if she couldn't bear the sight of his face anymore.

Silence. Too long. I squirmed.

The mysterious woman said, "John seems tired."

He didn't look tired to me.

"Yes, perhaps we should go." Mom turned to leave.

"I'll be back a little later, John," the cashmere woman called out.

She and my mother started back toward the mansion. I stood there a few moments, glued in place, and then I followed. Nothing made sense. We had just driven forever to get here, and we weren't even going to stay five minutes! I wanted to talk with my grandfather, hear about his brother, touch his hand, or just sit quietly by his side. Why didn't my mother speak up? Why was she deferring to this woman? Maybe she welcomed the opportunity to leave. But why?

I paused to look back at the smiling man. He had stepped into the shadows again. He had never heard my voice.

We stopped at the front door of the mansion. Mom retrieved a piece of paper from her purse and unfolded it. She handed it to the cashmere woman, who scanned it and nodded.

"Yes, this will do." She smiled, said her polite goodbyes, and stepped inside the stately house, paper in hand. With a clunk of the latch, she was gone.

At that moment I knew I wouldn't see her or my grandfather again. I was a shadow on a stage, moving with actors who exchanged information from a script known only to them while I silently followed, wondering what they would do next and how it would end.

On the way home I asked Mom, "When was the last time you saw your father?"

"Long, long ago," she said. "My parents separated when I was ten years old. End of story."

We drove in silence. This time I didn't turn on the radio. Something in her tone signaled that she might tell me more if I didn't ask questions. I waited. The air crackled with tension. Finally, she spoke.

"Right after they split up, I went to San Jose to visit my father. He lived in a men's hotel. The next morning, he needed to go to work. He told me to stay in his apartment. 'Don't open the door for anyone,' he said. God only knows how long I was alone in that room."

"You must have been terrified," I said.

Mom didn't answer. As tall buildings and palm trees whizzed by my window, I wondered what had happened. She must have heard loud voices, perhaps an argument, maybe some banging on thin walls. I imagined footsteps echoing down the hallway, pausing at her door.

"I wasn't harmed," she finally added, "but it was the most frightening day of my life."

Maybe John's transgression—leaving her locked up in an all-male hotel—had barred the prospect of future visits. I pictured her mother's explosive reaction: *What could he have been thinking? Irresponsible! As God is my witness, that will never happen again!* That one horrifying incident could have severed frayed threads in an already strained relationship between absent father and impressionable daughter.

A couple of months passed with no further mention of John. One rainy December morning, Mom and I were laughing as we watched Toodles, her Pomeranian pup, race into the kitchen and slide into the food dish. The phone rang. Mom answered it, and her smile disappeared. After a brief conversation, she replaced the receiver in its cradle.

"That was the woman from Mountain View," she said. "John's gone. He died of a stroke."

I scanned Mom's face for a hint of emotion. She was serious, but not grief-stricken.

"That woman must have cared for him very much," Mom said. "John was buried with her wooden rosary in his hands. She said she hoped I wouldn't mind. I told her I was grateful."

"Tell me more about my grandfather," I said.

"He was from Italy," my mother said. "His American name was John, but his Italian name was Giovanni. The last time I saw him I was only ten years old. I really don't know anything about him."

"Giovanni Motroni," I murmured. "Why did we visit him on a college campus?"

"I think he worked there," she said. "I've told you everything I know."

I suspected she knew more, but I sensed my mother's discomfort just mentioning his name. Why had she opened the door with that drive to Mountain View? Maybe she wanted something—recognition, open arms, tears of joy. But he didn't remember her. That must have been a devastating moment. I didn't want to cause further pain with my questioning. John had never been a part of my life, and it seemed pointless to probe further.

Five years after John's death, my mother passed away from complications of tuberculosis. I inherited a ring from her, an exquisitely cut, large oval amethyst set in white gold filigree. Ages ago, when I was a young girl, Mom told me the amethyst originally came from her father's cufflink. "He lost the other one," she'd said. "John had this ring made for my mother."

I held the ring in the palm of my hand, a gift from John, passed down from my grandmother to my mother to me. That was all I had from his life. It was all I knew about my mother's father. I couldn't have dreamed that five decades later, John Motroni's ghost would lead me on a convoluted chase through eight years, two countries and a foreign language.

2

———————————

The Journey Home

As a second-generation American, I grew up straddling two cultures, loving both but never belonging completely to either one.

On my father's side, the reserved Brits spoke volumes with few words. "Children should be seen and not heard," Dad would say. In that world, I spent weekends and summers with my parents on a four-hundred-eighty-acre ranch, off the grid. Home was a chalet on a knoll—creek and forest on one side, plum orchards on the other—no electricity, no phone, evening meals by the light of kerosene lamps. Dad's brother had a trout farm and fish hatchery about a mile away on similar-sized acreage. His son, Bob, was about my age, but our ranch duties kept visits to a minimum.

In those rugged Mayacamas mountains of Northern California, I survived mostly under Dad's guidance. "Why aren't you looking down when you walk? That root you just tripped over could have been a rattler!"

In those vast wooded hills, I wore jeans, rode horses, tracked animals, dodged rattlesnakes and poison oak, fished for trout, helped gather fruits and vegetables, and sometimes explored away from watchful eyes.

"Take the dog and watch your feet!" Mom would shout as I ran down the front stairs, giddy with the call to adventure. Alone, wild and free, I was learning self-reliance.

Fourteen miles away from the ranch, our "valley house" was nestled with two others on a three-acre parcel. Mom's extended Italian family—her mother, stepfather, and two uncles—lived there, too. During my single-digit years, they were generously attentive and kind to me, hand gestures punctuating our conversations. Nine months out of the year, five days a week, it was school, dancing lessons, and piano practice. Puffed up by a growing collection of gold paper stars on my exams, I was learning self-discipline. In this home, I wore dresses and skirts, never jeans.

"Girls wearing boys' clothes. Ridiculous!" my grandmother "Noni" would say.

Now, nearly a half century after I'd grown up and moved away, an invitation to my fiftieth high school class reunion prompted a return to my valley childhood home. My husband, Robert, and I followed freeways and winding canyon roads from Ashland, Oregon, to the outskirts of Healdsburg, California, three hundred fifty miles and a lifetime away.

We pulled into the familiar gravel driveway. All three houses were still there, where I once lived with the Italians: the ranch-style home built by Dad, the midsize stucco house for my grandparents, and a cottage shared by two great-uncles.

We stepped out of the car and into an oven. I'd forgotten the sweltering summers in this valley. As a young girl, I would dart unseen into the basement, open the chest freezer, extend my arms to each side, and hover over the top like a flightless bird.

Invited by the current owners, we opened doors to my early childhood—memories of wringer washers and treadle sewing machines, fresh-washed clothing stiff from the line, the sweet aroma of Italian seasoning, my father's black lunch pail, and the unmistakable odor of roofing tar.

Dad came home from work the same time each day, his brown, curly hair damp with sweat, his eyelids at half-mast over steel-gray eyes. His body was a wedge, with slim hips and wide shoulders sculpted by manual labor. While supper was cooking, he'd shower, then crumple into his rocker and hide behind a newspaper, a glass of wine by his side, an invisible "do not disturb" sign over his head. A day of pounding nails on housetops consumed his energy, but at the dinner table he'd come back to life. Dad always had a funny story to tell about the day's events, usually involving goofy animals. I didn't always understand his humor, but I loved hearing Mom laugh.

In my early childhood, before Dad built the big house, we lived with Noni in her two-bedroom home next door. She seemed elegant, like one of those glamour photos in Life Magazine. Some mornings I'd watch her reflection as she sat at a vanity desk. Her tray held a brush, comb, and mirror, all trimmed in silver. She'd brush her long, dark hair up to the top of her head and fasten it with combs, large curls held in place with hidden bobby pins. Evenings were my turn at vanity. Noni would brush my hair a hundred times, the bristles sending shivers down my spine.

My grandmother protected me from life's bumps. When Mom chased me to deliver a couple of swats for one of my many transgressions—throwing a ball in the house, wandering too close to the highway, or disappearing too long on the property—I'd race to Noni and hide behind her skirt. She was so slender that parts of me were easy to spot.

"*Cosa hai fatto*—what have you done?" she'd ask.

"*Niente*—nothing!" I always said that. It was one of the few Italian words I knew, and I used it often.

Moments later my breathless mother would arrive, and the two women would engage in bilingual bickering. My grandmother always won, and, other than a wagging index finger and a fierce frown from Mom, I was spared from further punishment.

Italian meals at Noni's house were big events: the finest vegetables picked from our garden by Uncle Lori; mounds of yellow polenta with chunks of mushrooms—coccola and porcini foraged by Uncle Frances; or pasta topped with marinara sauce, simmered with savory seasonings; free-range chicken from the pen; plates of fruit from carefully tended trees and vines.

The family unit split up during World War II, first when my father was a lineman stringing emergency phone links in Nevada, then when Dad and my step-grandfather, Vincent, were away, busy painting incoming US warships in San Francisco.

At times, a random hobo would arrive at our door asking for work. Noni always had a fence that needed mending or a garden to weed. In exchange, the hobo would be served a hot meal and a few coins on our front stairs. When he left, Noni would grasp the dish and utensils with tongs, place them in a burlap bag, and hammer them to bits before depositing them in a garbage bin. I never knew the reason, but the most plausible explanation was to ward off evil spirits or disease.

In 1945, my father and Vincent moved back home, the war finally over.

Noni's basement carried the rich, sweet odor of earth, held in place behind a retaining wall. In a large, two-door cabinet, mason jars rested shoulder to shoulder in colorful rows, after-season reminders of a bountiful harvest, nourishment to sustain us through winter. In one corner, tied to an overhead beam, braided leaves supported bulbs of onion and garlic. On a wooden worktable, a tray of labeled brown envelopes held the best seeds, saved for spring planting.

Outside Noni's house, a vine-covered pergola stood beneath a giant oak tree. In that magic space, leaves whispered secret messages from my imaginary friends, and shadows danced across the picnic table. On sunny days, my parents, grandparents, and two great-uncles gathered there with me for an evening meal. I was too young to understand the rhythmic murmurings of dinner conversations, but sometimes, when voices raised, I'd wait for the silverware to jump. Vincent drove his points home by thumping his fist on the table. Everyone joined in with noisy responses. Not always peaceful or tranquil, my extended family filled their surroundings with hot debate, warm reassurance, and vibrant laughter. That was a time when I was mostly Italian.

Everything changed a couple of weeks after my ninth birthday, the night Noni was admitted to a local hospital. For endless minutes I sat alone, my feet dangling from a bench in a pea-green corridor, the acrid odor of bleach in the air. Noni didn't belong here. She belonged at home, with her blue iris and red roses, and the pond with goldfish and water lilies just outside her door.

Vincent appeared from one of the rooms at the end of the long hall, his strong, stocky body and suntanned skin easily recognized. I jumped down and ran to meet him. "Bo," as I called my step-grandfather, took my hand in his. "Mommy and Daddy will go home later. You're riding with me, Topina." He always called me that. It meant "little mouse."

I crawled into the brown four-door sedan, with its musty scent of old furniture. We joined other headlights on the highway, and Bo began to sob—big, wracking moans and gasps from deep inside, tears streaming down his face.

I patted his arm. "It's okay, Bo. Noni's coming home soon. You'll see."

He cried so hard I barely made out what he said. "No, Topina. She's never coming home." I understood what that meant. Noni was gone, and I'd killed her.

A few months before, she was washing dishes, and I'd sneaked up behind her with a "Boo!"

She had jumped and turned to stare at me. "Don't do that! You could kill a person like that."

Now I'd never see her again. I couldn't tell anybody what I had done. I gazed out the window into the night, and darkness swallowed me whole.

After that, I carried around a big ache in my chest, but I didn't cry. It was a long time, maybe weeks, before I couldn't hold my terrible secret back any longer. It burbled to the surface and erupted into convulsive sobs of confession.

Mom wiped away my tears and held me close. "You didn't kill her. Noni had heart trouble for years. Remember me hiding her cigarettes? Doctor Dunlavy told her to stop smoking. During the war he even made sure she had extra ration coupons for grapefruit. But then she had that auto accident. It was just too much. Believe me, sweetie, you didn't kill her." She rocked me back and forth.

I felt a huge weight lift off my body and cried even more, weeks of teardrops falling onto my mother's clothes. That was when I knew I could tell her anything. That day, Mom became my best friend, and our bond would continue as a solid lifeline through my growing-up years.

After Noni died, the rest of my Italian family vanished. A couple of years earlier, Noni's half brother, my great-uncle Lori, had passed away in his cottage just across the driveway. Bo disappeared by moving to a San Francisco apartment. Mom said he had a broken heart, and I thought he might die, too. But he lived on, eventually remarried, and moved to Redwood City, where he painted houses to support his second wife and her two children. His brother, my great-uncle Frances, packed up and traveled a hundred miles south to join him. We saw them so rarely after that, they might as well have moved to Mars. The few Italian words I'd learned moved away with them.

Then there were four empty chairs at the dinner table and a couple of vacant houses on the property, which Dad turned into rentals. The cuisine changed, too. My British American father hated zucchini, and he wasn't too keen about pasta. Traditional beef roast was nice, and apple crumble was lovely, but I missed the warmth and spice of the Italians.

As I walked through their homes, I'd felt my family everywhere. I had seen their faces, heard their voices, and, beyond the tears, I'd remembered laughter. Now, more than a half century and a lifetime later, I brought myself back to the present and held my husband's hand as we headed to the car, leaving the old property for the last time.

Robert eased the car onto the highway toward Healdsburg, ten miles away. In my grandparents' time, scattered farms with pastures, orchards, and a few vineyards defined this region, but what I saw this day shook me from my sleepwalk down memory lane. Repetitious rows of grapevines had replaced acres of rolling pastures that would explode each spring into broad-brush vibrant hues of purple lupine and golden poppies. My one-room schoolhouse had been saved from a wrecking ball and was relocated, bell tower and all, about a mile up the road to serve as a tasting room for a local winery. The vastness of this grape industry defied logic. Were there that many wine drinkers in the world?

Weary after a day of driving through two states, reliving my childhood, and enduring the searing heat, we stopped in Healdsburg and checked into a restored Victorian Inn, a relic from the late 1800s.

"I wonder if we could visit Olive Hill Cemetery tomorrow," I said to Robert. This wasn't part of the original plan, but with images of my family swirling through my mind, it seemed so right.

3

Olive Hill

An arched sign between two white columns marked the entrance to Olive Hill Cemetery, an old site of gravestones, oak trees, and scattered evergreens. Robert parked the car, and we followed one of the paths, my feet rocking on small sticks and stones. I scanned gravesites for a familiar tombstone as we stop-started down the slope, and then I saw it: a rose-colored granite block with lilies-of-the-valley etched on each side of her name, *Mabel Mortara*. I stooped to clear away leaves and twigs from Noni's headstone, tipped at an odd angle and too heavy to move.

A flood of memories emerged from long-forgotten crevices: a child's view of the kitchen and Noni at the white stove, slowly stirring a simmering pot of minestrone, the sweet aroma of Italian seasoning permeating the house. She looked graceful even when she cooked—or maybe especially when she cooked—in her dark skirt and white blouse, a white apron protecting her clothes. No matter how busy, she always found time for hugs.

Noni's stone held only her name, no dates. Bare land extended on both sides of her grave; there were no other markers. We were surrounded by tombstones and monuments of all sizes and descriptions. But here, stretches of earth were strewn with clumps of pale-yellow grass, a gnarl of weeds crawling away from the bases of two scrub oak trees, poison oak surrounding another, one scrawny evergreen, and Noni's unfinished stone.

I turned to Robert. "I came here with my parents each Memorial Day to rake and weed and place flowers. There are other members of my family buried here; I'm sure of it. Maybe five or six others. Some of them died before I was born. Mom told me that the older graves were marked by wooden or metal plaques, but they were destroyed by fire."

"What about the rest?" he said.

"Who knows? Remarriages, lack of money, long-distance moves. Whatever the reason, I've lost my family twice. I don't even know where they're buried."

Robert took my hand, and as we walked up the path to the car, he broke the silence. "We have to take care of this. People need to be remembered."

I stopped and stared at him. "What an odd thing for you to say. I heard those words once before. My step-grandfather, Vincent Mortara, and I were here visiting Noni's grave, the only one with a headstone. Bo said, 'This isn't right. People need to be remembered.' Now he's buried here too, but there's not even a little plaque to mark his place."

I recalled his voice as if it were yesterday. Bo had asked me what I wanted for my fifth birthday, and I said I wanted the moon. I knew that was impossible, but Bo played along.

"How can I get that for you, Topina? It's so far away."

"Well," I said, "you could get a very tall ladder."

He laughed, twirled me around, and danced with me in the moonlight. And the moon was mine, all mine.

Of course, I'd have to find a way to mark Bo's grave. But what about the others? I turned back to Robert. "This is overwhelming. I don't even know the names of some of these people. I couldn't possibly order gravestones. I wouldn't know where to begin."

Once through the cemetery, we drove a short distance along Canyon Road and turned south toward the town of Geyserville. I spotted a sign that read "Bosworth & Son," boldly advertised over an old wooden building.

"Park the car! Pull over right there." I pointed to an empty space next to the curb.

"What's going on?" Robert said.

"Bosworth. Obed Bosworth." I repeated the name, struggling for recognition. "I think Obed Bosworth coordinated burials up at Olive Hill, but he passed away decades ago."

We climbed out of the car and approached the store. With a quick turn of the door handle, we stepped back in time onto a well-worn plank floor. The interior carried the aroma of old wood, new leather, hardware, and hay. Aisles brimmed with neatly arranged jeans and jewelry, saddles and hats, boots and books, tools and feed. A balding man leaned against a large desk. Tall and slim, wearing denim and a plaid shirt, he blended comfortably into the century-old structure.

"I'm looking for the keeper of the records for Olive Hill Cemetery," I said. "My family is buried there, but the markers are missing."

"I—am the keeper—of the records," he said.

I was drop-jaw stunned. Obed's son, Harry Bosworth, introduced himself and led me into a storeroom filled with old file cabinets, books, and records from a time when this building served as buggy shop and mortuary. We started with my grandmother's name. Harry picked up an old burial register and gently turned pages, the edges rumpled by time. "Here it is."

I stared at *Mabel Mortara* on the top line and scanned the rest of the report. *Died of heart disease October 15, 1948, age fifty-nine. Parents: Marianna Fambrini and Agostino Rossi.* A wealth of information in just a few lines.

Harry stretched up to pull more funeral reports and invoices, information about Bo, and my great-uncles, Lorenzo "Lori" Marcucci and

Frances Mortara—all people I'd known and loved. How did Harry know where to look?

He retrieved an invoice dated 1911 for Agostino Rossi, Noni's father.

"Died at age fifty-nine. Heart disease." I read aloud. "The casket cost thirty dollars, and the family hired a hearse for ten dollars. No extras. Must have seemed like a fortune back then."

He reached into the stacks and pulled out another document for Marianna (Fambrini) Rossi, Noni's mother. Someone had scribbled "Old Lady" at the top of the page. At age seventy-nine, she had outlived her husband by decades.

Harry found the last funeral record, dated 1920: *Mrs. Ralph Motroni— Argentina Motroni.*

"Her parents were Mabel's parents," I said. "This was my grandmother's sister. Died at age thirty-four of toxemia in Mabel's San Francisco home. I think that's a complication of pregnancy. No mention of the unborn baby. What a sad story." I pointed to an entry on the second page. "What does that mean?"

"It means the family dug her grave."

"Hard times for these people. Really hard times," I said.

In one afternoon, Harry Bosworth had located one hundred thirty-three years of my family history—documents for seven family members, all born in Italy, all buried at Olive Hill. A few certificates listed birth years. I was dizzy with discovery.

Harry began copying my family's funeral records. "The locals thought the Italians were crazy planting grapevines on these steep hills," he said. "Everyone knew they'd fail. Look how that turned out." Local vineyards with old familiar Italian names spelled success: Pedroncelli, Seghesio, Rafanelli, Passalacqua, Asti—the list went on and on.

Harry wouldn't accept payment for his efforts, but a quick elbow to my spouse's ribs sent the message: *Buy something.* As we left the general store, Robert wore his handsome new hat of lined, woven straw with a leather band. I carried a stack of papers and a newly purchased memoir describing the lives of Italian settlers in this region.

Back in the car, I leafed through pages of the past. "My family history could have been lost in another generation. How would my grandkids know to begin at Olive Hill Cemetery? Or a general store in Geyserville?"

"We have to do something about the missing gravestones. It's the right thing to do," he said.

I smiled. "It's the impossible thing to do. Too many graves."

Robert was silent. I gazed at him, my husband and best friend for a quarter century. I'd watched his handsome features get better with age, seen his laugh lines etched more deeply by ready smiles and an easy disposition, touched his dark hair turned now into salt-and-pepper curls. I knew and loved this man, but he still surprised me with acts of kindness and generosity like this.

We retraced Canyon Road toward the neighboring town of Healdsburg. A few twists and turns later, I pointed to Pedroncelli Winery on our right. "My mother lived here when she was a girl. Must have been the early 1900s. She said John Motroni may have planted some of those vines."

I'd saved an old label from that winery, with its sketch of wooden houses in the middle of a vineyard. My mother might have lived in one of those dwellings, replaced over the years by more grapevines and a tasting room. If only I'd asked more about her family, their stories. Now there were no living relatives to fill in the blanks.

4

―――――――――――

The Reunion

The next day, we met with my former Healdsburg High School classmates for a picnic and shared stories on the bank of the Russian River. I recognized most with hugs and handshakes. With others, I was glad we were wearing name tags.

We'd grown up together in the "fabulous fifties," when hormones ran unchecked and premarital sex was taboo. Decisions regarding behavior were based on the answer to a pivotal question, "What would the neighbors think?" It was the era of dial telephones and record players and barely breathable strapless gowns and the struggle for perfect grades and Friday night football games and piano lessons and choir practice and rides in a baby-blue '55 Chevy. I attended all dances because I wore a boy's class ring on a gold chain for most of my high school years. Its owner and I first met on a yellow bus in my freshman year. From the first hello, we chose seats-for-two on the half-hour daily commute—plenty of time for laughter and light conversation and the random lightning bolt that coursed through my body when our thighs accidentally touched.

I scanned the crowd and found Eddie Micheli standing by a picnic table with his wife. A decade had passed since I'd seen him at the last reunion. Handsome as ever, his hair was thick with white curls. His blue eyes met mine as he walked through the crowd toward me. He smiled and held out his arms, and we shared a warm embrace. I wondered if he still had the class ring with a distinctive groove on each side of the band, permanently etched by four years on a gold chain. It seemed odd, seeing him in this setting, overlooking the river where we once swam together as teenagers. We had taken separate paths, but our friendship would span a lifetime. Today's encounter was another high point in a dizzy dance through time.

Robert and I had plenty of time to talk on the long drive home to Oregon, and conversation drifted to seven unmarked graves and my discoveries at the Bosworth General Store.

"How much do you know about your ancestors?" he said.

"I could name my grandparents on both sides, all from Europe. It didn't occur to me as a child to ask about their history. I've learned a little more about some great-grandparents, but I don't know anything about their lives."

"That's it?"

"There is something else. Eddie Micheli. From the class reunion. I remember a lunch at his grandparents' house in Healdsburg when we were still in high school. Eddie and I were wearing matching gingham shirts. Pink. I'd picked out the patterns, purchased that outrageous material, and put them together. Strange thing to remember. Anyway, Eddie's grandfather was asking me about my grandfather, John Motroni. I didn't have much information to share, as I'd never known the man, but Eddie's grandfather mentioned a connection with my ancestors. He said, 'Way back, a long time ago, in the old country, the Micheli family was related to the Motroni family.' I was a teenager, so that message didn't mean anything to me at the time, and I never followed up."

"I can't imagine living in a world where I didn't know my roots," Robert said.

"You have an advantage," I said. "One of your ancestors hitched a ride on a royal bloodline with documentation back to Charlemagne. Your parents' bookshelves are packed with records and photo albums and diaries for both sides of your family. You have their history, their stories."

"I want that for you," he said. "When we started this trip, it was all about your class reunion. That feels like a side road now, a detour from what we were meant to do. We need to mark the graves at Olive Hill."

"Tombstones. That sounds expensive. And there's another problem. Some birth years are missing, and the rest might be wrong. Noni couldn't have been fifty-nine when she died. I did the math. She would have barely passed her fifteenth birthday when my mother was born. That's probably why the dates are missing on her headstone. We have some clues, but not enough for engraving."

"Well, with a little research we can figure it out for all of them."

"You must be joking! Three of those people died before I was born, and the rest disappeared from my life when I was nine years old."

"I think we found information at the Bosworth store for a reason," he said. "They need to be remembered."

"That's crazy, Robert! How can I remember people I never met? And only a child's view of the others?"

His voice was calm. "It's not crazy. It's your family. We should find out everything we can about them. It's important. I think your grandfather Bo would have agreed."

Something tugged at my soul: a broken connection, untold stories locked in a forgotten past. I groaned. "Six tombstones? And engraving for the seventh? And sleuthing my family history? What are we getting ourselves into?"

5

Searching for Noni

I knew so little about my Italian grandmother, just my childhood memories. Where could I find the rest of her story?

"Let's try the Family History Center," Robert said.

The Mormon Church was open Thursday evening, and he offered to drive. A spire soared above Medford's rooftops, leading us to the Church of Jesus Christ of Latter-day Saints. We circled the large brick structure but saw no sign for a genealogy library.

The Siskiyou Mountains in the distance faded to muted shades of velvet blue as we slowly inched around the building once more, the sun setting over evergreens at our backs. We skirted the south side of the church, its high row of windows and two sets of glass doors dark and uninviting. Shrubs on a narrow ribbon of lawn cushioned the somber building from its black asphalt parking lot. We turned down the east side, and Robert pointed to a brown six-inch-square sign high on the brown brick wall. Skinny gold letters spelled out "Family History Center." No wonder we'd missed it. We approached the covered entrance. Would a group of missionaries try to convert me on the spot if I entered their territory? I took a deep breath and opened the door.

The well-lit room was lined with filing cabinets and bookshelves. Three computers rested on tables near the door, a couple of microfilm readers were parked in the back, and a printer workstation sat idle. A receptionist asked us to sign our names and arrival time in the register. I marked "no" in the "Mormon" column, fully expecting messages about Mormonism. I couldn't have been more mistaken. A smiling blond volunteer introduced herself, and we moved together to a computer table with three chairs. She signed on to Ancestry.com and directed me to follow the prompts with any pieces of information that might be helpful. Robert took a seat by my side.

I was drawn to the screen with the notion that if I located my grandmother, I'd find the rest of my family. Maybe Noni could be found through her first husband, John Motroni, the mysterious grandfather I'd seen one time in a beautiful garden long ago.

I typed in *Giovanni John Motroni*, birthplace *Italy*, residence *California*, spouse's name *Amabile* (Ah-*ma*-bee-leh)—my grandmother Mabel's Italian name.

"Oh, there she is!" My pulse was racing. I pointed to the screen so Robert could see her name in the middle of a census record: *Amabile Motroni*.

The volunteer helped me decipher the 1910 Geyserville, California census. Giovanni Motroni was listed as a farmer, with his wife, Amabile, and daughter, Pia. They owned their home and land on a county road, at the current site of Pedroncelli Winery. From the sketch on the old wine label, I saw their house nestled in the middle of a vineyard. I imagined them tasting the grapes, cutting clusters from the vines, and loading full boxes onto a dray wagon. They must have heard the rumble of wheels, the creaking platform of the wagon bed, the clatter of horses' hooves as they followed the winding Canyon Road to Geyserville, where their grapes would be crushed at the local winery.

I refocused on the monitor. California was listed as Noni's birthplace, but that couldn't be right. She was born in Italy. I was sure of it. She disappeared after 1910, then popped up again in 1930 as Mabel Mortara, born in Italy, with a new name, a new birth year, and a new husband. We were still missing decades of her American life. Maybe Giovanni "John" Motroni could provide more clues.

In the 1920 census, John was living alone in a room at the St. Charles Hotel in San Jose. I scanned through all seventeen boarders at that address, all males. This was probably the same hotel where Pia, a terrified ten-year-old, stayed alone in a locked room waiting for her father to come home.

In that record, I located John's naturalization date: 1913. The researcher said the document might list John's birthplace in Italy. She printed a Freedom of Information Act request form for John's citizenship records. On my return home, I mailed it with a modest fee to the US Department of Homeland Security. I hoped that his place of birth might be the same as Noni's.

After weeks of waiting, the package finally arrived. I tore open the envelope and leafed through page after page of pepper dots and inky smudges, most of the information obliterated. I turned back to a comment in the cover letter: *The quality of the image is dependent on the condition of the original document when it was filmed.* The original must have been caught in a downpour without an umbrella.

Giovanni "John" Motroni was slipping further away. I rummaged through a kitchen drawer for a magnifying glass and pored over each blurred line. One word was barely discernible. I wrote what I thought I saw: John's birthplace, *Lucca*.

I scrambled for an online Italian map and found Lucca, capital of the province of Lucca, in the region of Tuscany. Images tumbled into view: a walled Tuscan town, wooded mountains and plains, vineyards and olive trees, rivers and lakes, a western seashore, and Apuan Alps. Six hundred eighty-five square miles of pure magic. What prompted John to leave home?

Another week dragged by before I could return to the Family History Center with the possible name of John's birthplace. US Census records had revealed he was born in July 1869. A researcher suggested ordering birth records for the region.

"From Italy?" I asked.

"No, from Salt Lake City." She pointed to the computer screen. "We're in luck. The Mormon Library has birth records for Lucca. We can order the microfilm. We'll call you when it arrives."

Days later, I received the call and raced off to the genealogy center to review film that included the year 1869. I placed the thick roll on the spindles of the reader and began the tedious task of reviewing every single document, one by one, in Lucca's registry of births: *Ufficio dello Stato Civile, Archivio del Tribunale di Lucca 1866–1929.* I couldn't translate Italian, so I couldn't identify the year of birth, which was not listed numerically but was spelled out in long, loopy letters and impossible to read.

After an hour of searching the columns for my grandfather, eyes burning, I finally found an entire page for Giovanni Jacopo Motroni. I made six working copies of Giovanni's birth record and set them aside, a tantalizing mystery to solve later.

Back home I couldn't stop thinking about the document. I pulled a copy from the file one more time and showed the page to Robert. "What am I supposed to do with this? Other than my grandfather's name, I can't understand a single word."

To crack the code, I enrolled in a beginning Italian class. Curiosity is contagious, so Robert joined me for the fall term as we began our *uno, due, tre* . . . steps on the journey to find Giovanni.

Our instructor, *Professoressa* Monica, was a stunning beauty who spoke English, Italian, and Spanish fluently, sometimes in the same sentence. A petite package in heels, flowing blond hair and elegant attire, with an ebullient personality and a charming sense of humor, she turned what could have been a drudge class into a weekly evening of entertainment. She regaled us in Italian with humorous tidbits about her teenage daughters and her handsome fiancé, and I grew to care about them, too. I was motivated to learn the language just to understand her anecdotes, which always erupted into laughter. In her class, we sang Italian songs, shared Italian food, and watched Italian films. Monica Rountree personified the passion for life I remembered from childhood. She ignited an even bigger spark of drive and enthusiasm to find my family. Now I was fully committed to the quest.

I asked if she could translate Giovanni's birth record. She explained that the old handwriting would be very difficult to interpret, as she couldn't recognize some letters, so Robert and I studied together and laughed at our fractured phonics. I ordered a book from the Ancestry Library, *Italian Genealogical Records*, a primer to decipher ancient documents in loopy longhand.

My second-year Italian class began with complicated conjugations. Robert said, "No more." He had fly rods to build and fish to catch while I fished for clues to my family history. I joined a couple of Italian conversation groups that met weekly and launched solo into Monica's advanced evening classes.

After six terms of Italian and armed with a magnifying glass and a stack of reference books, I worked on translating John Motroni's birth certificate with Robert's help:

Giovanni Jacopo Motroni
Born 25 July 1869 / Gignano di Brancoli, Lucca, Italy
Father: Costantino Motroni / Paternal Grandfather: Agostino Motroni
Mother: Maria Pieroni / Maternal Grandfather: Pietro Pieroni

So there it was. We'd finally located the village where John was born. I searched an Italian map and found the village of Gignano (Jeen-*ya*-no,) a small farming community at the end of a zigzag road, perched high in the steep forested hills north of Lucca. Had Noni been a neighbor?

My quest took me to the Rogue Valley Genealogy Library, less than three miles from my front door. With the help of an able staff, I could prowl through a wealth of data banks; best of all, the building was open Saturdays. But Noni remained elusive; random finds here and there, conflicting birthdates, her hometown not listed. I was running out of options.

December 2006 ushered in a snowy day and a trip to the attic for holiday lights and ornaments. I trudged upstairs and opened the door to boxes of memorabilia wedged between bookcases, chairs, lamps, luggage, and camping gear. I didn't know what I was looking for, but it wasn't Christmas decor. I opened cartons until I found Mom's photo albums. I sat on the dusty floor, books on my lap, and turned to the first page of my mother's life.

In the first photo, my grandmother Amabile held infant Pia in her arms.

Citrus fruit in the background provided a clue to its location: this was probably Los Angeles, Pia's birthplace. She was dressed for baptism, a day of celebration and family unity. But something was odd about the picture: Amabile had a storm-cloud face. A ladder in the image pointed to the tip of a polished shoe. Fingers touching the shoulder of Pia's fluffy gown were protruding from a man's jacket. What was going on here? I studied the print more closely. A slightly jagged edge ran down the right side of the photo. Pia's father, John Motroni, had been neatly cropped from the picture with a pair of sharp scissors.

I lost all sense of time prowling through photo books, sepia prints, and black-and-white images from the last century.

Robert poked his head through the doorway. "Any progress? I thought you were looking for lights."

"I was sidetracked. This is weird. I've turned every page of Mom's albums. Twice. Not one single family photo includes my grandfather. I can't find him anywhere." I reached into the bottom of the box. "Wait. What's this?"

I pulled out a dark brown folder, slowly opened it, and took a deep breath. "I recognize him. It's my grandfather, John Motroni."

In the photo with her father, ten-year-old Pia wore an engraved gold locket. That same locket was stored in my jewelry box. I knew that ornate letters, *PM*, filled the face, and that the back was inscribed *From Mama to Pia, 13-9-13*, the date of Pia's seventh birthday. Old black-and-white photos of Pia's grandmother and mother were inside the locket, but no picture or inscribed name of her father. I believed this photo of Pia and her father was taken shortly after her parents separated in 1916.

I carried the photo to my desk and thumbed through my "Motroni" file. In a 1920 San Jose census record, John was single, age fifty, a boarder in the St. Charles Hotel. I recognized the name of one of the other boarders; John's neighbor was the photographer listed on the front of the photo folder, his photo studio on Market Street just a few doors away.

In 2007, after repeated attempts through Ancestry.com, I finally found the California death certificate of John "Matroni," his last name spelled incorrectly. I ordered a copy, but information was sketchy: names and birthplaces of father and mother were listed as "no record." John's occupation was documented as a retired laborer from Italy. He had never remarried, but his marital status of record was *widower* instead of *divorced*. Why? Noni had married another man after John. My mother was identified as the informant, but she wouldn't have made a careless mistake like that.

John was interred in a secular cemetery, Oak Hill Memorial Park, in San Jose, California. A search through pages of funeral records requested from Oak Hill revealed that Pia Ann Smith, my mother, had purchased John's burial plot. No other name was mentioned. Where did the cashmere woman fit into all of this?

I spread out all the documents on the kitchen table. Armed with a laptop, magnifying glass, notebook, and pencil, I began writing clues, scratching them out, starting over. I must have reviewed John's death certificate a dozen times without understanding all the information on the page. Robert pulled up a chair and joined me while I rambled on about that long-ago trip with my mother to meet my grandfather, John Motroni, on a college campus.

"None of this makes sense. Mom said that the woman from Mountain View called to tell her John had passed. But to the best of my recollection, we drove east out of the city limits of Mountain View to meet him. I've searched the Web, but I can't find a college in that area to match my memory. Where is it? I couldn't have made that up."

Robert picked up the magnifying glass and pored over the death record. "John's last residence was in Agnew," he said.

"I didn't see that," I mumbled. "Agnew. Not Mountain View. Was that where I met him?"

I angled the screen so Robert could see as I searched for "Agnew or Agnews, Santa Clara County." I was dumbstruck as Web links unraveled the secret Mom couldn't reveal, even to her daughter. A careless remark might have yielded disastrous results—raised eyebrows, whispered innuendos, gossip. My mother was well respected in the farming community where we lived. She had worked diligently for decades to maintain her solid reputation. She wouldn't have dared to risk its destruction with scandal. *What would the neighbors think?*

"Agnews was no college campus," I said, my voice barely above a whisper. "Agnews State Hospital was an asylum for the insane." We both sat in stunned silence, eyes glued to the laptop, as I scrolled through the story.

At the time of my visit with Mom in 1957, Agnews was a model of progressive ideas that residents could be treated as outpatients instead of being locked up. Whenever possible, patients lived independently in cottages along tree-lined streets, their treatment offered in separate build-ings formally placed within landscaped gardens of palms, pepperwood trees, and vast lawns. There was a working farm on the property, and a train station. Patients found jobs in the village of Agnew. The two-story building I'd seen at the base of the clock tower was a psychiatric and medical care facility.

In the 1960s, federal funding stopped for most state-run "insane asylums," directing more reliance upon community treatment programs. The 235-acre village of Agnew was eventually absorbed by the City of Santa Clara. The central campus was purchased by Sun Microsystems, later acquired by Oracle, and the cottages moved to another location to be used as low-income housing.

I pointed to an online photo of the superintendent's mansion. "That's it! That was the cashmere woman's house."

"Maybe she was the superintendent's wife," Robert said.

"That's possible. It was the 1950s. Not likely that a woman would be superintendent or medical director. John probably worked there, tending those beautiful flowers. No wonder she knew him so well." I pointed to the screen. "I was standing right there, in front of that mansion. Mom handed the cashmere woman a folded piece of paper. It probably held some details for John's future death certificate."

I picked up the document again. "He died of a stroke," I said.

"But why was he admitted to a psychiatric facility?" Robert said.

"The certificate states he had cerebral arteriosclerosis—hardening of the arteries of the brain. Diminished blood supply would have affected his memory. Maybe he wandered off and couldn't find his way home. That could be the reason why he was taken to Agnews."

I'd wondered why the mystery woman thought John was dying; he looked so well when we saw him. But now, after thirty years of reviewing medical records as a healthcare manager, I suspected John had suffered transient ischemic attacks—temporary symptoms of headache, confusion, abnormal sensation, lack of coordination—red-flag warnings of a future stroke.

"I'd like to believe that the last segment of my grandfather's life was pleasant," I said. "There must have been something likable about John. He was more than just the gardener for the superintendent's wife. The cashmere woman knew him, cared about him. He was buried with her wooden rosary in his hands."

I'd now learned this much about Giovanni "John" Motroni: 25 Jul 1869 — 3 Dec 1957. The dash symbolized the missing story of John's life, the key to finding the rest of my family.

An immigration date on a 1900 census record led me to an online ship manifest. John's American journey had started at Ellis Island.

6

Ellis Island to San Francisco

They call her "The Lady," and the first time I saw her I was too awestruck to speak. In 1989, my daughter, Zoe, and I boarded a tour boat from New York City to Liberty Island to stand at the base of the statue. We climbed twenty stories to her crown, 354 steps in silence, ample time to consider all that she represented. Tears rolled down my face as I gazed down at the sea. I imagined weary travelers uprooted by turbulent times, crammed on the deck of a ship, cheering and crying for joy as the Statue of Liberty came into view—a symbol of freedom and a better tomorrow.

I didn't know it at the time, but my grandfather's story was recorded there, waiting to be discovered. Two decades after my visit I would find his information on the Web, in the archives of Ellis Island.

Research through *Britannica.com: Italy* revealed that near the end of the nineteenth century, Italy was caught in the grip of social chaos and economic upheaval. Poverty, volcanic eruptions, earthquakes, and floods all spurred Italian emigration. Over a forty-year period, roughly one-third of Italy's population had emigrated to North and South America. Between 1880 and 1920, more than four million Italians came to the United States. I reviewed *Ellis Island: American Memory Collections* from the Library of Congress. By poring over online documents and jumpy black-and-white film footage, I followed my grandfather's footsteps in this new land.

On March 12, 1894, the ship *Kaiser Wilhelm II* steamed into the Port of New York. Twenty-four-year-old Giovanni Motroni, a steerage passenger, was directed to a ferry—little more than an open-air barge—and shuttled across the bay to Ellis Island. A paper with numbers on it was pinned to his clothes, his label cross-referenced with the manifest page and line for identification. Eleven days after Giovanni had boarded in Genoa, Italy, he stepped down onto American soil.

On the dock, men in uniforms pointed fingers and yelled commands in a language he couldn't understand. He moved quickly with other confused people toward a castle. There, he was jostled into the Baggage Room, where all immigrants left their bundles and suitcases. With a bump here, a shove there, he was directed to a steep flight of stairs where new arrivals were watched for signs of illness. A wheeze, a cough, a shuffle, or a limp up those stairs would result in a big blue chalk mark on clothing, the code for further medical inspection at the top. Some immigrants turned their chalk-marked jackets inside out in a futile attempt to avoid further scrutiny.

On the second floor, Giovanni entered the Registry Room. Multiple languages cried out in a deafening din and echoed through the great hall. People waited in long lines, slowly inching forward. Doctors checked for sixty different symptoms that might indicate a variety of diseases or disabilities. Giovanni endured the most dreaded inspection done by the "button hook men," who examined each newcomer for trachoma by turning the eyelids inside out with finger, hairpin, or button hook to check for inflammation. Any signs of illness or contagious disease meant detainment for observation and care, or worse, deportation. Twenty percent of all immigrants were detained, half of those for failing medical exams, half for legal reasons: stowaways, anarchists, criminals, or those judged to be immoral. One in a hundred immigrants was deported, returning to the city of departure on the same ship at the expense of the cruise line.

Giovanni must have worried about his future. What if he didn't pass inspection? He stood for agonizing hours, his fate waiting at the end of a serpentine line. The medical exam lasted only a few minutes, but it took an average of five hours to complete the process at Ellis Island.

The last stop was the legal desk, where Giovanni was interrogated. From there, he faced the "Stairs of Separation." The stairs on the right led to rail stations, the center stairs to detention areas, and the left stairs for New York City. He was not detained. Once he was back on ground level, Giovanni collected his belongings and made his way to the Ferry Building, where he purchased a train ticket to California.

For the next eight days, he crossed the continent by rail and arrived in San Francisco on March 20, 1894. There is little evidence to describe Giovanni's cross-country trip, but it's unlikely that he could have afforded a plush passenger seat with a view. Giovanni probably shared a wooden bench with other immigrants.

Six years after his arrival in the United States, Giovanni was listed in the 1900 San Francisco census under his American name, John Motroni, employed as a gardener and renting an apartment on Balboa Street. Four years later, he moved into an apartment on Fillmore Street with his older brother, Luigi (Louis), who had immigrated earlier. Louis owned a florist shop, and he invited John into a partnership in 1904. They advertised in business directories as Motroni Brothers, Florists. At thirty-five years of age, John Motroni was settled and earning enough to support a wife. He found Amabile (Mabel) Rossi in San Francisco.

When Giovanni sailed away from his native land in 1894, Amabile was about nine years old. I wasn't sure of her age, but in one record she was nineteen in 1904 and sharing an apartment on Stockton Street with her younger sister, Argentina. Both young women had listed their occupation as "tailoress." Did they work long hours in a factory? Did Amabile yearn for a better life? How did she feel being pursued by a man almost twice her age? Was she flattered by flowers and swayed by the promise of security and safety? I may never find the answers, but this much I know: Amabile said yes.

John Motroni and Mabel Rossi married on April 7, 1905. According to the San Francisco Directory for that year, they took up residence at 2661 Clay Street, in the Pacific Heights District, just around the corner from John's florist shop. They must have had high hopes, beginning their new life together in that vibrant city by the bay.

7

Earthquake

One year later, at 5:12 on the morning of April 18, 1906, John and Mabel were awakened by a brief tremor. Twenty-five seconds later, a catastrophic upheaval battered their house and the entire region.

Thinking now of that devastating event, I imagined a violent surge of force strong enough to hurl their bed against the opposite wall. They might have held the bars of the headboard, bare feet looking for traction on a floor that was moving in waves. Frequently shaken loose from their hold, they'd grab again, the building rumbling into a roar as the shock grew stronger. Bookcases toppled, pictures fell from walls, dishes crashed.

Sitting at my desk, I counted off sixty agonizing seconds. That's how long my grandparents' house pitched and heaved as walls groaned, glass shattered, furniture flew, and wreckage replaced order everywhere. I tried to imagine myself in their place. During my thirty-five years in California I'd survived smaller tremors that moved furniture, rearranged pictures, and hurled glass objects to the floor. All had filled me with fear and sent me staggering away from windows, ready to dive under the nearest table. The 1906 San Francisco Earthquake was a monster by comparison. John and Mabel must have wondered if they would come out alive.

What were my grandparents feeling when the rocking finally stopped? They were from Italy; they knew about earthquakes—and aftershocks.

Disoriented and frightened, they would have rushed from their home and joined the crowds of people who had escaped to the street in nightclothes, the dazed and wounded, some responding to cries for help. Miraculously, John and Mabel's house and Louis Motroni's house were still standing, side by side. In fact, many of their neighbors' homes in Pacific Heights had withstood the quake amazingly well. Most of the houses in the low-lying areas of the city were shaken from their foundations and reduced to piles of broken beams, twisted iron, smashed bricks, and splintered glass. According to *Eye Witness to History.com*, *The San Francisco Earthquake, 1906*, modern analysis places the Great Quake at 8.25 on the Richter scale.

John and Mabel would have returned to their home to change clothes and clean up the rubble. Three hours later, an aftershock hit hard enough to drop Mabel to her knees, the safest place she could be to keep from falling over. She was four months pregnant.

From their doorstep, they had a clear view of fires down the hill toward the Embarcadero. Several dark plumes of smoke in the east converged to form a giant black cloud. Water lines broken, there was no way to stop the cataclysm. A voracious inferno began to advance across the city toward them, swallowing everything in its path, leaving black rubble and smoke in its wake. Some desperate Italians were on top of their houses, wetting their roofs with stored wine from their basements. In other parts of the besieged city, the fire chief, a fireman, and one police officer were killed by imploding walls and falling chimneys.

Within an hour of the initial earthquake, a messenger had arrived at Fort Mason on the north side of the city. General Funston, commander of the Presidio of San Francisco, had ordered all available troops to report to the mayor at the Hall of Justice. As the fires raged, almost two thousand federal troops arrived on the streets, including horses and riders, without martial law having been declared. Three hours after the quake, San Francisco was under military occupation.

Amid the chaos, John and Mabel saw survivors dressed in layer upon layer of clothing, making their way on foot to the ferry docks or to military tent camps, quickly erected and scattered throughout the city. Many people carried large bundles on their backs; others clutched suitcases and dragged heavy trunks. One dazed woman, captured on film, was carrying only a domed birdcage, its floor missing, the bird gone.

I pored over statistics and photos of the brutal aftermath. Fires burned more than 28,000 structures, leveling more than three-quarters of the city—twenty-five square miles. Of the city's 410,000 residents, an estimated three thousand died in the earthquake and resulting fire.

Four days after it began, the fire finally went out on the western front at Clay and Franklin, seven blocks from my grandparents' home on Clay Street. Their house was spared, but the conflagration would destroy something else. The Motroni brothers quarreled. They knew the florist business couldn't support one family now, let alone two, when the citizens of San Francisco would need every available dollar for basic survival. Who would have money to buy flowers? Maybe Louis saw an opportunity to stay and rebuild together. Rebuild what? Where? Ridiculous! John may have insisted on leaving for a fresh start in some new city. That would have infuriated Louis after all he'd done to make his brother a partner in the florist business. Whatever the reason, their relationship was finished. According to a family member, Louis never mentioned his brother's name again in his household.

My grandparents joined thousands of people who fled on ferry boats across the bay to the Oakland pier. Some were injured, some had lost loved ones, most had lost their homes. All were putting one foot in front of the other just to endure. Did John and Mabel have second thoughts about their decision? *This is madness! How will we survive?* They were leaving a standing home to start over in a strange city, with no forwarding address, no income, no job, and a baby on the way.

I imagined the teeming train station. *All aboard!* The announcement would scarcely have been heard above the clamor. Crowds must have pushed my grandparents forward into a packed train car. What did they find inside? Moving this mass of people would have required impromptu seating, maybe stacked boxes or suitcases or trunks in the aisle between wooden benches. I can't imagine that non-paying travelers would have enjoyed the plush first-class comfort of passenger cars. Once they were inside, the closing doors sealed their fate; no turning back now. With a roar of the engine, the hiss of steam, and the piercing scream of a whistle, the train chugged out of the station.

John and his pregnant wife were two of the three hundred thousand refugees carried away, free of charge, from the ruined city. According to the *Southern Pacific News Release*, August 1906, they traveled 370 miles south to Los Angeles on the Southern Pacific railway in one of the largest evacuations in history.

8

California Roots

Several hours after boarding the train in Oakland, my grandparents arrived at the City of Angels. They must have been exhausted and still in shock, and now they had to find shelter. The competition must have been horrific. Miraculously, they located a little house on Summit Avenue, probably a small, shared space, and according to the *Los Angeles City Directory*, 1906, John landed a job on a ranch. My mother was born five months after their escape from San Francisco.

I believed that Mom's birth certificate might reveal more clues about her parents, such as my grandmother's age and birthplace—hopefully something more than "Italy." On the website Ancestry.com, I entered *Pia Ann Motroni* and her date of birth, place of birth, and parents' names. There was no birth record. Elbows on the desk, head in my hands, I stared at the monitor. Then I remembered advice from a researcher: *Less is best.* I returned to the keyboard and entered three items: *Pia Motroni / Los Angeles, California / 1906*. Still no birth record.

The message from Ancestry.com read: *Matches below are less likely to be for your ancestor but still might be helpful.* I scanned down the screen and found an odd listing: Lena P. Motroni, born September 13, 1906. That was the right date, but the name didn't match. I decided to order the certified copy of birth anyway. What did I have to lose except twenty dollars?

It was a strange decision, but the gamble paid off. Weeks later I received my mother's birth record.

> *Lena Pia Motroni.* Date of birth: September 13, 1906; Female, White, Legitimate
>
> Place of birth: 864 Summit Ave, Los Angeles, California [the family residence].
>
> Father: *Giovanni Motroni.* Age: 36; born in Lucca, Italy; Occupation—contractor.
>
> Mother: *Amabile Rossi.* Age: —; born in Lucca, Italy.
>
> Attending physician: F. P. Hoy, MD

My grandmother's age wasn't stated, but I finally had her place of birth: Lucca, Italy. I stared at the document, desperate to make the pieces fit. Maybe this wasn't my mother's certificate. However, a subsequent census record for this family revealed that my grandmother had only one delivery, one living child. That same 1910 census listed their little girl as Pia, the name I'd watched Mom sign with a big, beautiful flourish of cursive penmanship. Maybe she didn't know she had another name.

I noticed other peculiarities in the birth certificate. Mabel hadn't stated her age, and John had a new occupation—contractor—that had nothing to do with flowers or gardening. More research revealed that one year later, John and Mabel were on the move again, this time north, with infant Lena Pia.

On one of our many trips through California, Robert and I had stopped in Santa Rosa to search Sonoma County land deeds. We learned that in 1907, Amabile Motroni paid a ten-dollar gold piece as down payment for forty-eight and a half acres of land on what is now Canyon Road, Geyserville—the current site of Pedroncelli Winery. The mortgage was cosigned by Giovanni and Amabile for the amount of $1,508.34, more than forty-nine thousand dollars in today's money. With the stroke of a pen, my grandparents had become ranchers.

The 1910 Geyserville census listed my grandparents as living on their property with their daughter, Pia, and Lorenzo Marcucci, Amabile's half brother. Just down the road lived extensions of their families, all from Italy. Orlando Marcucci, another half brother of Amabile's, lived nearby with his family. Ralph Motroni, Giovanni's brother, lived with his wife, Argentina, Amabile's sister, in an adjacent home. One by one, the men had endured the challenges of settling in a new land, a new culture, a new language, and they'd scrimped and saved to pay passage for the women and children who followed.

I found a photo in Mom's album of the Marcucci-Rossi-Motroni family, taken about 1914. Pia and her younger cousin had matching outfits, right down to their flared skirts, flouncy sleeves, and high-strapped shoes. The smaller girl was the daughter of Ralph and Argentina Motroni. I couldn't locate any other information about this child, and she didn't appear in any subsequent census records. It is likely that she died young.

Long after the deaths of all my relatives in the photo, I'd asked my father, "What can you tell me about John Motroni?"

"I didn't know much about him," Dad said. "He was a smart guy, found work wherever he went. He was a farmer for a while. Grapes. Oh, and he was a Druid—joined while he was living in Geyserville. That didn't go over too well with your grandmother."

A Druid! Now that was a strange piece of information. Secret organizations were not approved by the Catholic Church, and certainly not the Druids, who followed Pagan ritual.

John probably enjoyed his monthly meetings with other men, camaraderie with his Italian friends who met in Cloverdale, shared wine, and raised their voices in song. How could anyone argue against virtues for the guidance of man written by Merlin, the ultimate Druid?

Seven Precepts of Merlin:

1. Labor diligently to acquire knowledge, for it is power.

2. When in authority, decide reasonably, for thine authority may cease.

3. Bear with fortitude the ills of life, remembering that no mortal sorrow is perpetual.

4. Love virtue – for it bringeth peace.

5. Abhor vice – for it bringeth evil upon all.

6. Obey those in authority in all just things, that virtue may be exalted.

7. Cultivate the social virtues, so shalt thou be loved by all men.

I couldn't find fault with noble concepts so eloquently stated, but Giovanni's membership must have been a subject of hot debate with his Catholic wife. I imagined fireworks. Multiple clues hinted that the union of John and Mabel Motroni was not one of bliss; early photographs of my grandmother reflected an unhappy face. The wide gap between their ages set the table for turmoil. Throw in one massive earthquake, forced relocation, and a new baby; tension must have built like a smoldering volcano. Their marriage fragile, John's membership in the Druid Order was a wedge that split them even further apart.

In 1910, John and Mabel Motroni sold their home and vineyard. Three years later, still in Geyserville, John applied for United States naturalization, listing his occupation as Real Estate Dealer and Insurance. Two years later, in Santa Rosa Superior Court, he was granted citizenship.

Meanwhile, San Francisco was flourishing. The city had emerged like a phoenix from the ashes of 1906 and offered opportunities for a fresh start. Announcing its amazing recovery and success to the world, it hosted the Panama-Pacific International Exposition at the Palace of Fine Arts in 1915.

That same year, John and Mabel returned to San Francisco and found an apartment on Polk Street, and John opened a florist shop a few doors away. His new venture meant a struggle for survival in a competitive market, but he couldn't have foreseen an even bigger problem. The world was engaged in "the war to end all wars," and a desperate need for coal mandated the closure of nonessential businesses, including greenhouses. The Great War would end in 1918, but John's name had already disappeared from the "Florists" section of business directories, his shop closed. I could almost hear the last threads of a tattered marriage rip apart.

I remembered a booklet I'd inherited from my mother called *Official Publication, Sculpture and Mural Paintings: Panama-Pacific International Exposition at San Francisco 1915.*

I retrieved the long-forgotten pages from the attic to get a glimpse of San Francisco for that particular year, and to marvel at the exquisite artwork. But what captured my attention was a handwritten message, dated 1918, on the front flyleaf.

I'd learned enough Italian by now to understand what it said; it was a poem to Pia Rossi in celebration of her twelfth birthday. I stared at the name; it should have been Pia *Motroni*. Why would my mother use her mother's birth name? The poem was signed by Vincenzo Costelli (born Mortara)—my step-grandfather Bo, the man who gave me the moon. He had adopted his alias following his arrest, trial, and eighteen-month jail sentence for causing civil unrest as a union organizer for West Virginia coal miners. None of these people were using a valid last name!

I returned to Ancestry.com and typed in *Mabel Rossi*. Up popped the 1921 San Francisco Directory listing Mabel Rossi, *widow*, as living at 4011 Irving Street; her daughter, Pia Rossi, lived at the same address.

I located John Motroni in a 1920 census. He was living in a men's hotel fifty miles away in San Jose; marital status, *single*. John was still very much alive when I met him thirty-seven years later in the village of

Agnew. Census records in the years between showed John working as a gardener in cities near San Francisco, always listed as single.

Clearly, by 1916, whether they considered themselves widowed or never married, John and Mabel had separated. Given the culture of those Catholic Italians, that must have been a social earthquake. They came from the same region in Italy, shared the same language, and settled in a new country with their relatives close by. But their marriage had fallen apart, and it was not an amicable parting. My grandmother had reclaimed her birth name, Rossi. John was henceforth cut from all family photographs and never mentioned again in Mabel's household.

In the 1927 directory, Mrs. Mabel Mortara was listed as living with her twenty-one-year-old daughter, Pia Motroni, on Union Avenue in San Francisco—still more name changes.

I may never learn what my grandmother's life was like with John Motroni, but this I know about Bo, my step-grandfather: Vincent Mortara adored Mabel and Pia. Warmth and affection radiated from his poem to little Pia. I translated his Italian poem as follows:

> *To Pia Rossi, 12 September 1918, San Francisco, California*
> To this beloved child, kind and whimsical,
> Dreamer of Muses and precocious writer;
> Wishing her pure and great and long-lasting
> Glory, and with this glory, within her true story
> She must strive for peace and happiness.
> Wishing that you, blessed and beloved child,
> Might live with the mother you adore.
> This day, this gift is sent to you from a faithful heart,
> A tribute for your twelfth journey.
> *Yours, Vincenzo Costelli, with kind and beautiful thoughts.*

"Wishing that you, blessed and beloved child, might live with the mother you adore." The hint of a custody dispute echoed between the lines and had revealed much more. It had unveiled my grandmother's new identity, the reason for missing records, the changes in age. Mabel had something to hide. I began to piece together her story.

In Italy, divorce was illegal until 1970. If a couple separated, child custody was always granted to the husband. My grandmother didn't understand American law, but she would have done anything to protect her child, to keep Pia away from John and his residence in a men's hotel. Mabel Motroni disappeared into San Francisco by using her birth name, Rossi, and declaring her husband deceased. She had no records, no proof, but who would question it? Documents had disappeared in the 1906 disaster. To avoid suspicion, Mabel simply stated that her daughter's last name was Rossi. She must have realized the risk of being recognized in that city by the bay. Did she look in store windows at her reflection, in constant fear of seeing the Motroni family in the crowd of people behind her? And what about ten-year-old Pia? I imagined her mother's words: *If anybody asks about your father, tell them he died.* That lie must have been a terrible burden for Pia to bear. Secrets, fear, and guilt replaced a father who would disappear from Pia's life for forty years.

My grandmother had started a new life as Mabel Rossi, widow. Vincent's poem indicated that he was co-conspirator in her new identity. Noni had managed divorce—Italian immigrant style.

9

———————

European Dreams

Two years after our visit to Olive Hill, Noni's stone was still unfinished; so far we had just her name, Mabel Mortara. Between census records and her death certificate, her birthdate ranged from 1884 to 1890—and I hadn't made much progress with the rest of my Italian family. I'd even taken a chartered bus trip to the Family History Library in Salt Lake City, where I made a few discoveries about my British family, but I found no new information about Noni. I felt I was looking in the wrong country. Maybe Italy held more clues.

Once more, I returned to the attic to prowl through a box of my mother's memorabilia and carried interesting bits and pieces to the growing mound of paper on my desk. Maps of Italy were sprawled open among century-old photographs: a sepia church in Diecimo, a villa labeled "Ponte Rotto," a cotton factory in Piaggione, a body of water bordered by steep woods. Why were these photographs saved? What had they meant to my family?

I contacted my cousin Richard (Marcucci) Wilson to track down a large photo of a uniformed family member, Domenico Marcucci. His photo had once occupied a space behind a gilt-framed painting of roses in my parents' living room. Many decades ago Mom told me he was the first husband of Noni's mother, Marianna Fambrini, whose same-sized photo hid nearby behind a matching gilt-framed painting. Domenico's photo had been forwarded to the Marcucci family, and Richard was my first contact to locate it.

Robert and I spent the following weekend in the California home of Richard and Barbara Wilson. Domenico's 16" x 20" sepia print was located under their bed. As we prowled through Richard's photographs, he shared the legend of a lost village named Ponte Rotto, home of our ancestors. Noni had once lived there with her family.

We left my cousin's home with much more than I had hoped to find, photos of Domenico and Ponte Rotto captured in my camera.

I had some clues to my ancestors but little information about their lives. Maybe, just maybe, I could find the answers in Lucca. I was still immersed in Italian classes, swimming through a swamp of irregular verbs and exasperating conjugations. Would I be ready to speak the language of Lucca after just two years of study?

Decades ago, when I was unmarried, I had booked a solo two-week ship's passage to Tunesia, Spain, Italy, and France, and had spent a bit of time in Rome, grateful for a guided tour.

Years later, Robert and I visited Italy, sightseers following a bobbing yellow pom-pom on a baton held high above our guide's head, weaving through the streets of Florence, Rome, Pompeii, and Sorrento. Language barriers were eliminated, points of historical significance explained, and opportunities provided for photo shoots, but the drawbacks were significant. We moved in a herd, interacting only with other English-speaking day-trippers. I longed to break away, meander over to a shop, chat with owners, and gawk at exquisite Maiolica pottery, its intricate designs dating back to the Renaissance. When we entered the Pantheon and our eyes were riveted 142 feet upward through an aperture in the dome, I gazed into eternity. Four minutes were not enough for me to contemplate the universe. Similarly, seven minutes at the Fountain of Trevi only allowed us to jockey through the crowd of tourists, take one photo, and toss a coin backward over our shoulders into the pool. That, we were told, would ensure a return trip to Rome. But there was no time to be awestruck by exquisite sculpture. Robert pointed to a baton waving in the air. *"Avanti!"* Forward—follow the yellow pom-pom.

Now I wondered if we could navigate Italy on our own. We took classes in Italian Renaissance art, prowled through travel books, and searched the web for housing and archive sites. I obsessed about the province of Lucca, the home of my grandparents. I had discovered that Giovanni was born in the village of Gignano di Brancoli. Amabile had once lived in Ponte Rotto, but she could have begun her life in any one of Lucca's thirty-five districts—some with village houses perched high in the Apuan Alps or the Apennine Mountains; others with valley homes nestled in cities by rivers or lakes. The region covered 685 square miles, extending to the Ligurian Sea. I wanted to find my grandmother's home, trace her history, talk with her people. Daring to dream this journey, we sketched plans for Europe.

Lucca, the capital of the province of Lucca, is a market town located between Florence and Pisa. One guidebook advised spending a day in Lucca Centre, which would provide ample time to walk on the wide oval wall, take photos of red tiled roofs below, visit a museum, snag a souvenir, and return to the train station. Instead, we planned a four-week stay in an apartment we found on the website VRBO, Vacation Rentals by Owner. I imagined strolling along stone streets in the villages where my family once lived. Breathtaking artwork, beautiful music, gorgeous scenery—the romantic lure of Italy filled my dreams.

I filled a small album with regional maps, old family photos, and a scrawny family tree listing just the names and sketchy dates of seven Italian ancestors.

We planned a month in England and Wales to follow my father's lineage through cathedrals and coal mines. As a bonus, we planned to visit the Claypoole Manor House, home of Robert's ancestors in Northborough, England. Then it would be off to Italy for another month.

I was nearing the end of my career in health care administration. For the first time in two decades, it was finally possible to take a vacation longer than nine days. When it came time to retire, my generous physician-employers presented me with an astonishing gift: Eurail and Brit Rail unlimited train passes for two. That was the crowning touch. We were going to Europe!

10

The Crossing

I woke suddenly to the bed swaying beneath me. It took me a moment to get my bearings. Yesterday morning we'd boarded a Eurostar train in London to travel under the English Channel. In Paris we'd found a sleeper compartment in the Thello, an overnighter clattering its way southeast through the Alps to Florence, Italy.

I cursed my fate and switched on the light to peer at my oversized ankle. I'd fallen in England, pitching forward onto cobblestones and turning my lower leg into a painful, throbbing mass. It wasn't just a blow to my ego; now Robert was lugging around most of our baggage. I tried to sweep "bad omen" thoughts from my brain as I envisioned hobbling around Italy for the next month. Returning home early was not an option, not for this trip of a lifetime.

The attendant rapped on the door with a message—one hour to our destination. I wrapped an elastic bandage over the purple bulge and gingerly unwound from the lower bunk. A few splashes from our tiny sink, a quick repack, and soon our "breakfast" was served to our compartment—hot coffee and a cold croissant. The attendant returned our passports, collected last night so we could sleep through the border crossing. Robert complained of feeling cold, pulled on his overcoat, and huddled on the edge of the bed.

"I didn't sleep very well last night. Too noisy," he murmured. "I don't think I'd ever take this train again."

We arrived in Florence a little after six in the morning and hailed a cab to the Palazzo Machiavelli hotel, where we stowed luggage for later check-in. While Robert dozed in a lobby chair, I scanned regional newspapers, recognizing about every fifth word. I felt totally unprepared for Italy. How would I ever navigate us through this foreign language?

Mid-morning, Robert stretched upright. "I just needed a little more sleep," he said.

Church bells rang at odd intervals as we searched for a *tabaccaio*. In Italy, those tobacco merchants sold cigarettes, postage stamps, postcards, and bus tickets out of a street-corner kiosk. Travel passes in hand, I struggled with searing leg pain as we climbed aboard a cross-town bus for Archivio di Stato, one of Italy's 103 state archive offices.

We entered a sun-filled room, and I hobbled toward a smiling librarian behind a large information desk. To my relief, she spoke English.

"I'd like to find the birth record of my great-grandfather, my Noni's father," I said.

The librarian handed me a request form, its instructions printed in Italian. With my rudimentary knowledge, I was able to fill in the blanks with information gleaned from that general store in Geyserville, California: Agostino Rossi, born 1852. I'd found his birthplace, Farnocchia (Far-*nok*-ya), in immigration records.

We waited as the librarian keyed information into a computer. I squeezed Robert's hand. This was our maiden attempt to locate my ancestors in Italy.

"I believe I've found it," she said. "Agostino Rossi, born 24 February 1852, in Farnocchia, to Domenico Romualdo Rossi and Maria Irene Bottari."

I took in a deep lungful of air to compensate for shallow breaths. Could it have been this easy? Robert and I exchanged a high five, our palms slapping together in one loud sound of victory.

The archivist promised to mail the document to our home address in Oregon. She explained that the records from Farnocchia were stored here in Florence, but the remainder of my research for the villages surrounding the walled city of Lucca would need to be done in Lucca.

"This is going to be a breeze!" Robert said. I imagined one-stop-shopping for my family history at a central archive office in Lucca, where they would smile and speak to me in English and make my dreams come true. What could be easier?

Giddy with accomplishment, I leaned on Robert's arm to lessen the weight on my painful ankle as we trudged down the street Via Guelfa to find food. Other than a few snacks and this morning's cold croissant, we hadn't eaten since yesterday morning in London. A small *osteria*, Tozzo di Pane, came into view. We had discovered this little tavern on our tour through Italy three years earlier, and I remembered delicious meals and the gorgeous men who ran the shop. I wasn't disappointed. Today's lunch nourished my soul: savory *ravioli* and *insalata verde*, topped off with a rich, creamy *cappuccino* served by a tall, handsome waiter with a sexy voice and captivating smile. *Buonissimo!*

I caught a glimpse of a party in the adjoining patio and scooted my chair to get a better view. A little girl was surrounded by balloons and smiling family members. Our waiter checked frequently with the birthday girl, watched as she opened her gifts, and received her hugs and squeals of appreciation. I remembered my own early Italian family life, its exuberance and joy of celebration.

We meandered along side streets exploring small shops and vendors' kiosks, but by mid- afternoon, Robert was complaining of headache and chills. We checked into our hotel room, where he fell into a deep sleep. I limped through Florentine streets to forage for food and returned with a couple of pizza slices and fresh fruit. Robert roused long enough to take a few nibbles and promptly fell asleep again. The next morning he announced he was feeling better; he'd just needed to catch up from a restless night on the train.

We toured Florence by bus to pamper my ankle. There were breathtaking statues and fountains at every turn, and a commanding hilltop view of the Duomo. Higher than a football field, nearly 150 feet across, its massive red tile dome roof dominated the landscape. We ended in the Acadamia Museum, gawking at Michelangelo's magnificent marble statue of *David*.

That night a fierce downpour hammered the roof. Our hotel room walls pulsed with light from the outside stairwell. Terrifying cracks and booms rattled windows in their casings and reverberated in empty glasses resting on marble tabletops. I longed to cuddle into Robert's arms, but he slept through it all.

The next day, golden walls and red tile roofs sparkled and shimmered in the morning sun. We strolled along wet cobblestone streets, my ankle much improved, with decreased swelling and fewer stabs of pain shooting up my leg. My frozen left elbow, another result of the fall in England, had loosened up a bit, allowing about ten degrees of movement. My mood ebullient, I savored every moment of our last day in Florence.

After a visual feast of fabulous Renaissance works in the Uffizi Gallery, we boarded the train to Lucca, where we would stay for the next four weeks to find my mother's family.

11

Outside Lucca's Walls

Petite, attractive, auburn-haired, our villa owner, Daniela Marchi, met us at the Lucca train station and greeted us in English. We climbed into Daniela's little car and meandered through the streets outside Lucca Centre, a walled city within the city. She pointed out the *supermercato* where we could shop later to stock our pantry. We stopped beside a large two-story dwelling with umber walls, red tile roof, and bright red geraniums spilling from planters. This would be home for the next month.

My delight far outweighed the sharp pains in my calf as I limped upstairs. Our apartment was even better than its online photos: cheery yellow with bright blue accents, it held a kitchen/ sitting room, bedroom, and bath. A manually retractable double wire was hung outside the bathroom window to dry our laundry—a centuries-old custom for the locals. Daniela punched buttons on a handheld wand, and outside blinds moved up into recesses in the wall. Only in Italy could high-tech reside so comfortably with antiquity. Daniela explained that she lived right next door in the same dwelling, readily available if we needed anything—but then she added that she was leaving now for a few days in Rome. No problem, we assured her. We could manage.

That evening, Robert's usual ruddy complexion took on an ashen hue. He rested while I limped a block away to a small market for simple dinner items. He was feeling no better after a meal, and we turned in early. In the middle of the night, I woke to a furnace sleeping beside me. I dove through luggage for emergency meds and found something to reduce fever. Despite my efforts, Robert coughed and moaned in his sleep throughout the long night. My internal critic attacked. *What could you have been thinking, dragging him all over Florence? Two museums? You had to see two museums?* My ankle throbbed. Our dream vacation was turning into a nightmare.

The next morning, dictionary in hand, I scribbled a monologue in Italian describing Robert's illness. I mentioned fever, cough, rattle, yellow sputum, a three-time history of pneumonia, antibiotics prescribed in the past, and his doctor's advice to seek medical attention immediately if symptoms returned. I asked Robert if he could walk to the *farmacia*, a pharmacy we'd spotted the day before. We needed to start there for directions to a physician.

We plodded a half block and stopped. Robert, who routinely pushed his limits on a treadmill or bicycle, was gasping for air. He placed his hands on his hips and bent over, elbows akimbo, to take a few labored breaths. Fear crawled into my head and set up residence. Robert's last battle with pneumonia had been waged in an intensive care unit. We trudged four long blocks with frequent pauses, then under the train station, and up the ramp to the piazza. There it was, the neon green cross of the *farmacia*.

With a silent groan, I nudged Robert into place in line, about ten people ahead of us. Finally it was our turn. Robert leaned his back against a side wall, head down, color drained from his face.

"Do you speak English?" I asked the man behind the counter. He shook his head no. I retrieved the note from my pocket and read it aloud in Italian. The pharmacist asked me to clarify once more whether Robert had yellow sputum and what antibiotic had been prescribed in the past.

"*Sì*," I answered, "azithromycin," and thought, *Oh God, I don't know the Italian name for that. What if they don't sell it in Italy? What if he doesn't understand what I just said?* The pharmacist beamed and exclaimed "Z-pak!" He asked whether I wanted three days or five.

"*Cinque giorni.*" Five days. Z-pak was the brand name for azithromycin. No doubt we'd be handed a recommendation and dispatched to a doctor's office.

I recognized the five-day carton of azithromycin scooting across the counter toward me. That's when I learned that Italian pharmacists dispense antibiotics without a physician's prescription. I could have kissed him! Repeating "*Grazie, grazie mille!*" many times would have to suffice.

Back in the apartment, Robert was settled, meds taken, fluids at hand. I hated leaving him alone, but we needed groceries. The *supermercato* wasn't more than ten blocks away, so I set off with two daypacks. I realized my mistake midway through the trek, as pain stabbed my ankle. The market was more than a mile from the apartment.

Outside the *mercato*, I watched a customer deposit a euro into a slot in the handle of the wheeled market basket. Presto! That unlocked a cart from its chained moorings, the euro to be automatically refunded when the cart returned to the lock.

I copied other shoppers. I covered my hands with disposable latex gloves, placed fruits and vegetables in plastic bags to be weighed, and pressed a picture of the item on the scale keypad. A label printed with the price magically appeared from a slot, to be removed and stuck on each bag. I read Italian package ingredients and wished I'd brought my pocket dictionary. Just locating low-fat milk and yogurt was a chore. Trying to identify simple food items took far longer than I had imagined. I worried about Robert, alone too long.

The trek home was slower with the added weight on my angry ankle. All progress made in my recovery had been reversed. A quick jaunt had turned into a two-hour journey of agonizing pain.

As I neared our apartment, I heard an ambulance scream out of a dead-end street off Via Mammini. That was our street! What if it was for Robert? Terrified, I turned at our driveway, hauled myself up the stairs, and shoved the huge key into the ancient lock.

Robert met me at the open door. Our words tumbled over each other. "Thank God you're here!" "Did you hear the sirens?" "I thought your ankle gave out." "I thought it was for you!" I slid the daypacks to the floor, and we held each other close.

That afternoon we reclined in sickbed, watching old American TV Westerns with Italian voiceovers that didn't match moving lips. I expected at any moment to hear Chuck Norris say "*Buona sera, y'all.*"

We'd traveled all this way to search for my family in this gorgeous area of Tuscany. Now here we were, stuck in this room—ice packs for my ankle and antibiotics for Robert. Four long days later, we finally dared to venture out, with high hopes of finding my ancestral records in the archives of Lucca.

12

Lucca Centre

I bound my ankle with an elastic wrap and tugged at the base edges to get my shoe on. Robert was much improved, and I could shuffle along, fortified with pain meds, the compression bandage bulging beneath my wide-cuffed pants.

Four blocks from our apartment, the sidewalk ended at an enormous aqueduct supported by red brick arches forty feet high. Here the street split, with each lane of *Via Vincenzo Cosani* passing through an arch, and no room for pedestrians.

We waited for a lull in traffic before darting to the other side, tricky with an uncooperative ankle, then followed along the gigantic structure toward the round pump house, and beyond to Lucca Centre. Our footsteps crunched on a path of marble chips, perhaps the discards of brilliant young artists learning from the works of Renaissance masters. I could almost hear the hammer and chisel of Michelangelo as he released *David* from the marble mass.

The neighborhood sounds of children's voices filled my head with images of Noni as a child, running and hiding from her sister as the two played among the giant arches of the aqueduct.

Two blocks farther, we followed a ramp under the train station, emerged near the *farmacia*, wove three more blocks, and braved traffic in pedestrian crossings where cars rarely paused.

We gaped at imposing walls surrounding Lucca Centre, the old town within Lucca. Originally built by the Romans, then modified in 1650, double walls rose forty feet to enclose ancient, fortified tunnels. On top of the walls, a tree-lined, avenue-wide promenade encircled the town for nearly three miles. We strolled through Porta San Pietro, one of six portals into the heart of Lucca Centre.

As a little girl, Noni probably stood on those walls and gazed down on red rooftops. In my mind's eye, she ran along the walkway with her arms outstretched, long, dark hair blowing in the breeze.

The very essence of Italy resonated through my entire being. An emptiness in my soul was somehow filled by standing here, on this piece of Italian soil. Every cell in my body knew I had returned home.

13

—

Brick Walls

Finding my great-grandfather in Florence's state archives had been simple—it took just a few moments for Agostino Rossi to pop up in an index and his birth registration located; mission accomplished in less than fifteen minutes. What could be easier?

Before we'd flown to Europe, I'd written to Lucca's Archivio di Stato. An archivist had responded in Italian that I could search for family members in their *censimenti*—census records—for the years 1809 and 1823. The original letter was stored at home, but I had typed an English translation on green paper, folded to fit in my pocket. The library loomed ahead.

Lucca's sixteenth-century golden-colored palace, Palazzo Guidiccioni, stretched to form one wall of the piazza, its massive front door surrounded by classical columns and a balustrade, its four ground-floor windows defended by stout iron grids. Two flags flew over the arched entrance: the familiar green, white, and red bands of Italy, and the royal blue European Union flag, studded with its circle of twelve gold stars. We entered the *palazzo* and climbed three steep flights, my ankle sending stabs of pain on every one of the fifty-four steps.

The central area soared two stories above polished library tables flanked by substantial wooden chairs. A man and a woman darted about, checking papers, cross-referencing information in large tomes, racing back to computers for *sotto voce* Italian mumbles and animated hand gestures, tapping items on a screen with index fingers. The tall, attractive woman was polished and professional, her slim frame wrapped in smart business attire. Her slender male companion sported a custom-tailored dark suit, white shirt, and tie, his dark hair slicked back into place. A third person, a gray-haired, well-groomed gentleman, stood like a pillar, watching the frenetic activity that centered around him.

Thankfully, we'd thought to pack Robert's white shirt and a couple of ties, along with my fitted jacket and large silk scarf, deliberately avoiding the garish garb of tourists. Here in Lucca, it was all about *la bella figura*—looking good all the time.

For long minutes we were ignored. Finally, the tall woman broke away and asked what we wanted.

"Do you speak English?" I asked.

"*No.*" Her eyes darted back to the computer corner, then to me.

I explained in well-rehearsed Italian that I wished to search for my family in the records. She raised her index finger. *Wait.* She would summon her supervisor. She spoke briefly with the male librarian. The man with the slicked-back hair approached, his eyebrows separated by two deep furrows over his Roman nose on a hawk-like, fifty-something face. His dark, piercing eyes appraised me slowly from head to foot, then back to my head.

I met his gaze. "Do you speak English?"

"*No.*" The dismissive toss of his head might have brushed away a fly, if one had dared to enter these premises. Clearly, my question was too absurd to be taken seriously.

"*Vorrei cercare la . . . la mia famiglia,*" I stammered, "*nel censimento.*" I would like to search my family in the census.

The somber man asked if they were important, noble names.

"*Non lo so,*" I replied. I don't know.

Wrong answer. The very busy man told me the records were not in this office.

"But I received a letter! The records are here. I have the translated copy from Archivio di Stato." I pulled the folded document from my pocket.

He pointed to the green paper in my hands. "That is not from this office."

Self-talk—*deep breath, patience, patience*. Years of planning. Learning a new language. We had come such a long way. "I don't think he understands me," I said to Robert.

Then I asked in Italian, "If the records aren't in this building, where are they?"

The man looked to the ceiling, shook his head slightly, the back of his hand brushing away that invisible fly. "*Perso nella guerra*," he said in a grave tone.

"What did he say?" Robert asked.

"He said they were lost—in the war."

"This is ridiculous. Let's get out of here," Robert said, his voice quiet but firm.

The supervisor's eyebrows shot up. He understood English.

"*Grazie*," I said, not meaning it.

"Arrogant!" Robert fumed as we descended to the street. "He was lying!"

"Something was going on in there that had nothing to do with us," I said. "With all that scurrying around, they didn't have time for us. They couldn't wait to get us out of there. We were the intruders. The Hawk was protecting his nest."

"That's no excuse for bad behavior," Robert grumbled.

Daybreak found me poring over the map of Lucca. "Look! There's another Archivio di Stato in this city. Maybe we visited the wrong building yesterday."

Robert peered over my shoulder. "It's more than two miles away. How's your ankle?"

"I can manage." I had learned to swallow a pill before starting out each morning to explore Lucca Centre, then another pill before the long walk home—the only way I could endure the six-mile daily hike.

We retraced our steps through Porta San Pietro, but this time we turned in the opposite direction and found Archivio di Stato number two, a much less impressive, newer library. I leaned on Robert to mask my limp, wanting to look self-assured, healthy, and confident. I smiled as we entered the building where my family records waited to be discovered. My jaw dropped as I stared at two familiar faces—the same two people we'd seen yesterday at Archivio di Stato number one.

"That's impossible," I whispered. How could those two people occupy two offices on opposite sides of the city? They must have had rotating shifts. We were going to have to deal with them twice!

I approached the Hawk. "May I search the census records here?"

"They don't exist," he said in Italian, his dark eyes boring into mine, as if to say, "Imbecile, we covered this yesterday."

Then I remembered the little album in my purse, created at home and carried to Italy, stuffed with old photos, maps, and incomplete ancestral charts. One picture had stood out—a handsome man in uniform, Domenico Marcucci. This was a small copy of the 16" x 20" portrait that had been located under the bed of his great-great-grandson, Richard (Marcucci) Wilson. If we could match Domenico Marcucci's uniform with a branch of service, maybe we could reconstruct his story.

I pointed to the photo and asked the librarian if there were photographs of uniforms stored here, or perhaps he could direct us to a museum where they might be on display.

"What did he say?" Robert asked.

"Let's go." I waited until we stepped onto the sidewalk. "There are no records of uniforms."

"Why do they call it an archive? What do they keep in there?" Robert's voice raised. "And why are you so calm?"

I noticed a blue vein bulging near his temple.

"Calm? Calm? I'm swallowing rage! I want to scream, stamp my feet, pound on desks. I can't afford to explode. There's a word for a woman with bad manners: *maleducata*. One slip on my part, and the library network in this town would buzz with news about the American *maleducata* storming around, looking for dead relatives."

"Maybe we should try another archive," Robert said.

A couple of blocks over, we found Ufficio Anagrafe, the registry office for the Lucca region, where my green letter had suggested we search for other vital records. At Window #3, with my Italian-English dictionary in hand, I filled out the necessary forms for the birth certificate of Amabile Rossi. I supplied Noni's approximate date of birth and the names of her parents, information gleaned from funeral records found in Geyserville, California. Noni's birth record would disclose where she was born, something more specific than the province of Lucca. I needed the name of a town to begin my search through census records.

The librarian answered my request with a clear Italian message. "If found, the record will be mailed to your home address in the United States. No exceptions."

"But how can I find the right census record if I don't know the town where my grandmother was born?"

The woman at Window #3 told us to go to Window #5 and ask for a *scheda di famiglia*—a family record—that would list ancestors, siblings, and offspring of my grandmother's parents. That would give us dates and names of towns. We would have to pay the required fee for research. It seemed like the perfect solution. I was willing to try anything.

We found Window #5 to make our plea.

The woman behind the counter said, "*No, non è possibile.*"

"What?" I pointed to Window #3 and continued in Italian. "The woman there told us to request a *scheda di famiglia* here."

"Well, I can't help you. I don't understand you," she said. "Try Archivio Storico around the corner."

Back on the street I found a bench and collapsed, elbows on my knees, head in my hands. Yet another archive office! I couldn't face one more disappointment.

I'd planned everything so carefully; our apartment was a brisk walk to the train station, with easy access into the walled city. We'd arrived in Lucca seven days ago, and we still hadn't found a single record. I hadn't foreseen pneumonia, or a trashed ankle, or brick walls.

Robert slid beside me, his arm around my shoulders. "This is a nightmare," he said. "I feel so sad for you."

"It's not over yet," I answered, wondering what I meant by that. Our success rate in Lucca was zero out of four. We needed a miracle.

"Let it go for now," Robert said. "I'm tired of dealing with people with bad attitudes."

Frustration fell away as we wandered down cobblestone streets, savored the earthy aroma of fresh bread baked in a century-old wood-fired oven, prowled through the musty shelves of an antique bookstore, and ogled exquisite designs in handmade lace, which were draped over a small wooden cart that appeared to have been used for at least a hundred years. I had the distinct impression that I was following the footsteps of my ancestors, who probably had visited these very businesses long ago. We meandered home to the setting sun.

Lucca had a mysterious appearance at twilight each day—a subtle, rosy glow, a pink veil that concealed her secrets. In this quiet respite between daylight and dark, I wondered if Lucca was amused by my feeble attempts to unlock her doors to discovery.

I lay awake in the midnight hours, ankle throbbing. I'd crafted well-organized A-to-B plans and safety nets for what-ifs, rock-solid strategies to find my family. But somewhere along the way, I'd tumbled down a rabbit hole. Nothing was working.

My mind played out reruns of our futile attempts. I floundered against a relentless tide of confusion, my inability to speak the language with certainty, with authority. I was drowning in a sea of self-doubt. My coping strategies shattered, tears flowed. I gave up, gave in, relinquished my illusion of control, and waited for despair to spiral further down, for darkness to take over every molecule in my entire being.

Flashbacks swirled through my mind: a five-minute meeting with a mysterious grandfather, the missing markers at Olive Hill, key records found in a general store in Geyserville.

My perception slowly changed. Frustration and hopelessness were gradually replaced by a growing awareness of the impossible notion that I would find my family because my ancestors would find me. All these roadblocks had happened for a reason, and I was not in charge of the master plan. I exhaled, and an odd sense of relief washed through my body. Relaxed, I fell into a deep, peaceful sleep.

14

Fruits, Vegetables, and Archives

Monday morning found us at yet another library, Archivio Storico—historical archives for the Municipality of Lucca. Its decorative, metal-reinforced doors were wide open. A high-ceiling entry led to a second set of thick-glass doors, locked. I pushed a button on the vestibule wall, hoping that was the doorbell. We waited.

"Here we go again," Robert murmured.

Moments later, a petite woman appeared, the transparent barrier preventing communication. She might have stretched to five feet, perhaps a hundred pounds. Shoulder-length dark hair framed her oval face. She pointed to the small grid next to the buzzer. Through that little speaker in the wall, I asked in Italian if we could search the *censimenti* (census records) for my family. We waited. With a metallic clunk, the glass doors parted. To my surprise, we were greeted with smiles.

The dress code was more casual here: sweaters and slacks. We spoke to the diminutive librarian, Mariella Morotti, who had no difficulty understanding our simple Italian. I told her that my grandfather was born in the village of Gignano di Brancoli in 1869 and that was all I knew. Mariella told us that census records of every decade from 1861 through 1881were stored here.

Inviting us to sit at a long table, she then disappeared into aisles of blue steel bookshelves filled with brown binders. She returned with Cristina Marinari, an attractive young librarian, tall and willowy, with long, dark curls tied loosely at the nape of her neck. Both of them carried in huge, loose-leaf binders and placed them on the table. There before us were stacks of census records for the Brancoli region north of Lucca. My eyelids brimmed with tears. Mariella frowned slightly and tilted her head with an unasked question. I pointed to the stacks and answered in Italian. "We've had a difficult time finding any information about my family. You have brought us this—this miracle."

In Lucca Centre, we had visited small markets: a *fornaio* for baked goods, a *macellaio* for meats and cheeses, a *fruttivendolo* for fruits and vegetables. The first time I reached for a tomato, the salesperson shouted, "*Non tocare!*" Don't touch! I pointed to the item, and the merchant selected "the very best one" for our dining pleasure. No handling food before buying.

But here in Archivio Storico, Robert and I turned irreplaceable, fragile pages of history, powdery to the touch. Every folded page measured 11½" x 16". They were unbound, and both sides were filled with information about a dwelling and its occupants. Households requiring multiple pages were held together with a fine straight pin through one corner, or fastened at the crease with beige silk thread, loosely basted and tied in a knot.

We started with 1871, the village of Gignano, turning individual leaves, looking for a two-year-old Giovanni Motroni. We knew my grandfather's date of birth and parents' names from a translated birth record. We each grabbed a stack and began the slow process of research, hovering over each page, careful to keep reviewed records in order. An hour into the search, we hadn't found Giovanni. Suddenly, Robert straightened up.

"Hey, look at this." Robert pointed midway down the page to entry number 9 in the list of ten family members. "I think that's him!"

Motroni, Giovanni, di Costantino, figlio, m, 2, celibe, Lucca, Catolico.
Motroni, Giovanni, of Costantino, son, male, age 2, single, Lucca, Catholic.

Not only were Giovanni's parents and siblings listed, but the census sheet also documented his grandparents, people who weren't even living in this house. We had tapped into a goldmine of information.

I quickly sketched Giovanni's family tree:

Grandparents

Agostino Motroni	*Pasqua Ghilardi*	*Pietro Pieroni*	*Margherita Carli*

Parents

Costantino Motroni	*Maria Pieroni*

Children

Chiara	*Agostino*	*Angelo*	*Samuele*	*Giuseppe*	*Luigi*	***Giovanni Motroni***

Giovanni's parents' names matched the birth record. There it was—the impossible spine-tingling discovery that would lead me to other ancestors, a deeper understanding of their culture, their lives. After our failed attempts in four other archive offices, Robert had found my grandfather and detailed information about his family.

Costantino Motroni, Giovanni's father, was a *possidente agricoltore*—a person of status, a landowner, probably with vineyards and olive trees coveted for regional wine and olive oil. Giovanni, with five older brothers, wasn't likely to inherit the family farm. He might find employment as a *contadino* (farmhand) when he grew up. But a property owner? Not likely in Italy. A boy's future could be predicted by his place in the birth order. Giovanni wasn't at the top of the list.

Maria Pieroni, Giovanni's mother, had "*fu Pietro*" listed by her name. That meant her father, Pietro Pieroni, was deceased at the time of this census. Maria's sister, Anastasia Pieroni, lived with the family and helped with the care of Maria's seven children. She was single, age thirty, with no means of support after her father's death. Anastasia's future must have looked grim, but she was saved by her brother-in-law, Costantino Motroni, who accepted her into the family as a domestic servant.

Armed with this information, we found the Motroni family in earlier census years, and printed even more names and dates of birth for great-great-grandparents into my family tree. We hit a brick wall with Giovanni's maternal grandparents—not that we couldn't find **Pietro Pieroni.** We found several, probably cousins born within a year of each other. Too many parents had chosen to name a son Pietro Pieroni.

In the 1871 census, Giovanni's grandfather, **Agostino Motroni,** a widower, lived with another son, a daughter-in-law, and nine grandchildren. They resided on *Via di Serra*—Street of the Greenhouse. Agostino undoubtedly taught his children and grandchildren how to extend the growing season by protecting plants under cover from weather extremes. At his knee, they learned how to select the hardiest beans, the sweetest melon, the loveliest flower, and to save those seeds for next season's planting. No wonder my grandfather knew so much about gardening and the florist business. He had learned from his grandfather and his uncle, ancient information passed down from the Romans, who used transparent sheets of mica or oilcloth for their greenhouses.

On our next visit to Storico we met the third librarian, Maria Chiarlo, a gray-haired woman with a beautiful smile. She looked sturdy, built to hold grandchildren in her welcoming arms. Over the next two weeks, most days found us back at Archivio Storico searching through three decades of census records in each of twelve Brancoli villages north of Lucca. Every time we located a new piece of information, I logged it into my expanding family tree and filed a copy of the census in my portfolio. We requested records we had seen before to track new clues, new names, new villages. The three archivists, Maria, Cristina and Mariella, became our friends.

Buoyed by our success, I wanted to return to the previously visited archive offices. Maybe my Italian had been gibberish to them. I contacted our proprietor, Daniela. Where could we find an interpreter to help us break the language barrier?

"I would do it, but my English isn't good enough," she said in perfect English. "I'll ask my friend Mila [Mee-la] to do it."

"I'd be happy to pay her," I said. "How much would she charge?"

"No, no, there's no charge." Daniela sounded wounded that I would suggest such a thing. "You cannot pay her. She would do it because she is my friend. I will arrange it."

We took a break and spent three glorious days exploring Como at the Swiss border and visiting lakeside villages by boat. On returning to our apartment in Lucca, we found a note taped by the keyhole. Mila had agreed to pick us up the following morning.

15

Meeting Mila

I answered the rap at our door to see a smiling, vivacious woman about my age. Well groomed, blond hair framing her friendly oval face, Mila Antonini radiated enthusiasm. And she spoke English.

"Daniela said you need a translator. Maybe I can help. What are you looking for?" she said.

"My mother's family was from Lucca, but I know very little more than that. I have no older relatives, no siblings. I tried to find the records of my ancestors at Archivio di Stato, but the librarians probably didn't understand me. Maybe we could start there."

Robert and I climbed into Mila's car, a tiny four-door Toyota Yaris sporting a Lucca decal. Mila explained that she lived inside the walls, and that decal allowed us to drive through the ancient city's portal. Parking was nearly impossible at Archivio di Stato number two, but Mila managed to squeeze the vehicle into a small space by planting one wheel up on the curb.

The Hawk was absent, but we'd seen the female librarian twice before. She escorted Mila to the computers, where she demonstrated how to enter names. The two women spoke rapid-fire Italian. I couldn't understand a single word.

Mila turned to us. "I don't think they can help you here."

I didn't push the issue. Maybe my family records really were lost in the war.

We trudged around the block to Window #5 in Ufficio Comune. I understood Mila's request to research my family, and I understood the woman's response. It simply wasn't possible. The woman behind the desk was unwilling to discuss it further in any language. I wanted to cry. Not even Mila could help.

Mila asked where my family had lived, and I mentioned Gignano, San Giusto, and Piazza di Brancoli, hilly villages found in census records.

"We'll go to the Brancoli region next week to visit those places," she said. "I will drive you."

"That's too much to ask. I'm so grateful for all you've done for us."

"You didn't ask. I will drive you. I want to do it. What are your family names?"

I rattled off Motroni, Fambrini, Pieroni, Cecchettini—names I had found in census records at Archivio Storico. Mila left with a promise to see us next week for a road trip.

Robert and I had agonized over the logistics of visiting the Brancoli region north of Lucca and had decided it was impossible. Neither of us recognized road signs well enough to drive through that mountain maze. A bus ran twice daily, early morning and late afternoon. I pictured us stranded by the side of the road in some remote little jumping-off place, the next town miles away, no food, no water, no restrooms, hoping the bus driver would remember to stop for us on his return trip ten hours later. And now, the unreachable dream of visiting the villages had morphed into a plan! If my ankle had allowed it, I would have danced in the streets.

We wandered into an old bookstore. I asked the proprietor if he had any publications about the Brancoli region. He shook his head no. As we walked out the door, he shouted *"Aspettate!"* Wait! He just remembered. He had done some research on the Brancoli villages, and he would be willing to sell his personal copy of an out-of-print book. He disappeared into a back room and returned with a 1998 publication, *Le Meraviglie di Brancoli e di Moriano,* by Remo Baronti. I thumbed through *The Wonders of Brancoli and Moriano* with illustrated descriptions of each of the twelve Brancoli churches and villages, and a dozen more in Moriano. I gladly paid the steep price, eighty euros, for a treasure.

Next, we found our way to the office of Lucchesi nel Mondo on top of Lucca's wall, where Mila had suggested we visit. This was a worldwide fraternal organization of people with family roots in Lucca. I explained my family connection, in Italian, to three white-haired men.

One stepped forward and said, "I speak English."

I retrieved my album of maps, ancestral charts, and photos, and pointed to a faded snapshot of a large, two-story dwelling with gardens and four front doors. "Ponte Rotto" was written on the back in loopy letters. A family legend shared by my cousin Richard said that this villa, once owned by our family, had been lost to unpaid taxes during the economic downturn and mass exodus from Italy that stretched from 1880 to 1920.

"Ponte Rotto," I said. "That village isn't listed on any map. Have you heard of it?"

"It doesn't exist anymore," the old man said. "I think it was somewhere near Piaggione, but that was so long ago I don't remember."

I closed the little album. I was still overjoyed by our recent successes. Maybe that was enough. The lost village of Ponte Rotto would have to remain a tantalizing mystery.

16

The Women in the Windows

The next day, back at Archivio Storico, Mariella limped across the room. She told us she had fallen in a bike accident and had injured her leg. She pointed to stacks on the library table; what was I going to do with all this information? I told her I needed to tell these stories to my son and daughter and their adult children. I mentioned I was also writing about the search.

She looked at me with new interest. "You are a writer. How many pages have you written?"

"About two hundred fifty," I said. What a curious question. I didn't mention that about half of that number pertained to my ancestors in Wales and England.

Mariella asked if we had visited Ufficio Comune. I nodded yes and told her the tale of our failed attempts, even with an interpreter. Mariella then revealed that she could access information at other municipal archive offices. She offered to accompany me three blocks around the corner and phoned for an appointment.

Robert followed Mariella and me as we hobbled our way down the street. In Ufficio Comune, Mariella asked the woman at Window #5 if she would research my family members.

"No, that isn't possible," came the reply.

Mariella pointed to me and said to the researcher in Italian, "This woman is a writer." The researcher's eyebrows shot up.

Mariella turned to me. "*Quante pagine hai scritto?*" How many pages have you written?

"*Duecento cinquanta,*" I answered. Two hundred fifty.

Mariella turned back to the researcher. With her palm turned toward the sky, elbow pressed to her side, she raised her hand and lowered it with each enunciated syllable. "*Due Cento Cinquanta Pagine!*" Two hundred fifty pages!

With that, Mariella opened a door into the researcher's office and disappeared. I could still hear the two women, but they spoke too rapidly for me to understand. Mariella emerged from the room and stood by my side. The researcher resumed her post in the window and announced that she would research the family of my grandmother, Amabile Rossi. I was stunned. She agreed to mail the documents to my Oregon home, payment to be submitted by Western Union. I offered to pay in advance by Visa, but there were no exceptions to this policy. I gladly filled out all the necessary paperwork.

I wondered why it was so important that I was a writer. Maybe the printed words would cause a reluctant researcher to justify her actions to her supervisor. Maybe people would snoop into her business—a messy proposition. If I'd only known the power of the word "writer," I might have used it weeks ago.

We proceeded to Window #3. I asked that librarian if the birth record had been located for my grandmother, or the marriage record of her parents, Agostino Rossi and Marianna Fambrini. She was working on it, but certificates would have to be mailed to the States. I explained the problem. "I can't look for my grandmother's family in census records if I don't know where they lived."

The librarian looked at Mariella, who nodded in agreement. The librarian agreed to deliver the requested birth and marriage certificates to me free of charge if I returned next Tuesday.

"You are a miracle worker," I told Mariella as we limped back to Archivio Storico. *Grazie* seemed so insignificant, so not enough. Mariella had moved mountains.

17

The Villages of Brancoli

Early the next morning, I decided to learn more about Brancoli, the region we planned to visit with Mila. I sat at the little kitchen table in our apartment and thumbed through reference books for English versions of Italian words.

> *brancoli*: no direct translation in my Italian dictionary
> *branca*: branch or limb
> *brancolare*: to stumble, to grope, to feel one's way in the dark

Those last two words merged into an image. I was groping, stumbling in the dark, feeling my way through growing leaves on my ancestral tree, one little branch at a time.

I unfolded the map of the Garfagnana Valley and the Serchio River, north of Lucca. To the west, the Apuan Alps; to the east, the Apennine Mountains. With my index finger, I traced spiderweb connections between remote, hilly settlements. Finding the homes and stories of my ancestors in that maze would be nothing short of a miracle.

That afternoon, Mila arrived at our door like a blonde fairy god-sister. She led us to her magic coach, her tiny Toyota, to whisk us away to the villages of the Brancoli region. Personable and outgoing, bursting with enthusiasm, she embodied a curious combination of sophistication and wide-eyed optimism.

We followed convoluted roads into the steep foothills of the Apennines, climbing higher and higher, navigating switchbacks only one car wide for two-way traffic. I rode in the front seat and peered over the edge of the narrow highway to the receding valley below. Mila confided that she had never driven this road before. At each blind turn she tapped her horn several times, crossed her fingers on the steering wheel, and muttered, "*Madre mia.*" Our new friend was praying to the Mother of God! This did not bolster my confidence that we would get out of this trip alive.

Robert, who could suffer motion sickness from one brief stint on a porch swing, braced himself in the back seat, his shoulder jammed against the door nearest the mountainside. His face had turned an unnatural shade of gray-green. Suddenly, Mila slammed the brakes to avoid smashing the grillwork of an oncoming car.

"I honked!" she yelled, then backed up a few feet.

My fingers clutched the seat cushion. The other car tilted as its wheels dug into the mountainside, dislodging dirt and small rocks. Mila maneuvered closer and closer to the edge. My heart raced with adrenaline. I looked down—eight hundred feet down—to the Serchio River and wondered how many cars had rolled over that steep drop. I desperately wanted to find the homes of my ancestors, but in that dizzying moment, I wondered if the price of the quest was too high. Mila inched forward one little nudge of the gas pedal at a time. My fingers cramped as I dug them deeper into the upholstery. The other car alongside now, each jockeyed forward, inch by inch. Somehow, miraculously, we managed to pass each other without a scrape.

We zigzagged past small villages, each with its own ancient stone church, most with steep hillsides of olive trees, grapevines, and gardens. We stopped several times to prowl through cemeteries, but I couldn't find a match with my ancestral names. The narrow country road finally ended at a stone-paved cul-de-sac, just enough room to turn around, in the tiny hamlet of Deccio.

"An old man lives here," Mila said. "He made a Motroni family chart from parish records."

She bounded over to a cottage and knocked at the door. She spoke briefly with an older woman who wore a white apron covering her dark skirt and blouse, and soon returned to the car. "He's gone today, out in the fields."

I wasn't disappointed, just amazed. She knew this place without ever having been here before—and she had found the home of some old man who had researched the Motroni family! Mila was an Italian Sherlock Holmes.

I limped across the *piazza* of Deccio. Up four uneven steps, a two-story stone building with a red tile roof rose above the retaining wall. Its wooden door was partially hidden by sheer curtains tied to the frame on either side, the village version of a screen door. I spotted a round white sign rimmed in red sticking out from the wall. There were no words in the center of the circle, just a red symbol of an old-fashioned telephone receiver.

Robert pointed to the sign. "What is that?"

"It's a bar," Mila said.

I imagined tipsy drivers weaving their way down the narrow ribbon of road and wondered if we should plan to leave this place before the bar opened for business.

"People come here from all over for coffee," she added.

Coffee! In Italy, a bar was where you found coffee.

"That sign means there is a telephone here," she said. "That's not so important now. People have cell phones."

"Doesn't the bar have a name?" Robert said. "There's no writing on the sign. How do people find this place?"

"They know it's here," Mila said.

A square gray belfry towered above residences in the foreground. I leaned on Robert's arm to protect my ankle as we climbed to the churchyard for a stunning view. Across the wide chasm, clusters of light-colored buildings and red tile roofs dotted the mountain peaks. Gray bell towers marked the locations of ancient churches perched precariously on steep inclines. The sweeping panorama revealed olive trees flanked by vineyards in impossible locations on terraced hillsides. My ancestors must have relied on faith and sheer determination to tend crops in such difficult terrain.

I remembered Harry's words back in Geyserville: "The locals thought the Italians were crazy planting grapevines on those steep hills." *No, Harry. They weren't crazy. They knew exactly what they were doing. These successful, terraced Tuscan vineyards look just like the ones in Geyserville and Healdsburg, only steeper.*

Back in the car, we followed the ridge back the way we came. In some areas, trees formed a canopy over the dappled country lane. In other places, sharp hairpin turns allowed for a light-headed look down to the ribbon of road where we had just been. We veered onto another artery up the mountain, to an area where the road leveled off. An ancient gray church and bell tower came into view. The structure abutted the road with no room for pedestrian passage between the two. I gaped at a placard with the church's original construction date: AD 794. Those rough-textured, gray brick walls had witnessed baptisms, weddings, and funerals for more than twelve hundred years. My ancestors had probably attended this Church of San Giorgio.

Less than a quarter mile away, a stone retaining wall rose fifteen feet high and stretched ahead for a couple of blocks. Across the road, a guard rail made of metal pipes marked the edge of the abyss. I doubted it could hold back a goat, let alone a car. We rounded the bend, and Mila found a narrow place to park, the nose of her car pointing out into space above a sheer vertical drop.

"This is Gignano," she said. Mila had found my grandfather's village.

"Oh, my God, we're here. We're really here," I babbled. "But where are the houses?"

Across the street, a large white sign was attached to the gray rock wall, and narrow stone stairs wound up to a building perched high on the hill. Red letters on the sign spelled out *"bar / spuntini / Trattoria da Tosca"* (café / snacks / Tosca Diner). Mila approached a couple of men standing nearby and, speaking Italian, asked them where the Motroni house was located. They pointed to a narrow walkway between a high wall and a two-story dwelling. "It's the last house on the lane."

The path took us around a corner to the left and behind the hill, out of sight of the car. Our shoes clattered on gray granite slabs, irregular, geometric shapes fitted precisely together and extending for about a block, wall to wall between gray and honey-colored houses with red tile roofs. I wondered how these people were able to move building materials and furnishings through such a narrow corridor. I imagined donkeys carrying huge loads to their destination. In the space between buildings, small potted trees on winding stairs lined the way to more stone houses perched higher on the hill.

"I think we're looking for a five-story home," I said. "According to the census records, Giovanni's father and uncle lived at the same address. Giovanni and his family lived on two floors, and his uncle's family lived on the fifth floor."

Mila stopped and turned to me. "That's impossible. I guarantee there are no five-story dwellings in all the villages of Brancoli."

Just ahead, the path sloped down to the right and stopped at a light-yellow stucco house. A handsome young man watched us from the yard, as if he had been awaiting our arrival. Tall and slender, he bore classic Italian features: dark hair and eyes.

Mila spoke to the young man in Italian. "We are looking for Signore Motroni."

"I am Signore Motroni," he answered. My heart skipped. He was probably my distant relative.

"Do you live in this house?" Mila asked.

"I just moved in," he said. He pointed across a grassy area to another dwelling about a quarter block away. "That one over there was the original Motroni house. It was purchased by a family from Boston. They come here for a short time each year. The rest of the time it is vacant."

Then Signore Motroni apologized. "*Mi scusate*. Excuse me, I must go now. I am late for an appointment." With that he turned up the path and vanished around the corner of a building.

Mila seemed to accept the whole incident as if this sort of thing happened all the time. I was astonished by Signore Motroni, who materialized out of the ether like a wizard, just long enough to guide us to the home where my grandfather was born and raised. Robert pulled his camera out of its case and began capturing images of Gignano.

We strolled across a grassy area to the house—two stories of gray stone capped with red tile. Ivy crawled up the front wall and hung over the turquoise door. Attached to the Motroni home, a double-walled stone structure with a tile roof ran across the courtyard and connected to a three- story dwelling. I faced the Motroni residence and counted aloud, "One . . . two . . ." then turned to face the house across the courtyard; Mila and I finished the rest of the count in unison: "three . . . four . . . five."

"That explains the fifth floor," I said. "In 1871, these two homes shared the same address."

I remembered my grandfather as an old man, standing by a park bench in a beautiful garden in California. I climbed two steps to the turquoise door, my grandfather Giovanni's door, and turned to see the courtyard. When he was a little boy, Giovanni must have played in that grassy area with his siblings and his cousins. I could almost hear the laughter and chatter of children echoing through the corridors of time.

18

Legends from the Serchio River

We must find an old person with a good memory," Mila said as we wound our way out of Gignano. "There is a woman, Ada Motroni, who might know something about your family. I think she used to live here, but she moved, maybe to San Giusto di Brancoli."

"How do you know that?" I asked.

"It is what I like to do," Mila answered. "I love to solve mystery."

We began crisscrossing back and forth through the mountains, trying to follow confusing signs, only to get lost again and again.

Mila shook her head. "I don't know how to get there. We'll come back later."

We made our way down steep, tortuous roads, a dizzying descent. Once safely in the valley, my pulse dropped to a normal rate and Robert's color returned. At the highway Via Nazionale, instead of turning left toward Lucca, Mila turned right.

"Where are we going?" I asked.

"I have something interesting to show you. I think you will like it," Mila said.

We followed the Serchio River north as it bisected the steep Apennine foothills. Twenty minutes later, Mila parked the car on a graveled area.

"That's Ponte della Maddalena, the Bridge of Mary Magdalene," she said.

She pointed to a medieval stone structure that rose steeply above the center of the river and lunged down to the opposite bank. The arch beneath the apex was built to accommodate the passage of tall boats. I imagined peasants leading oxen and loaded carts, laboring to reach the top and then straining to keep from toppling down the other side.

"I will tell you a story about that bridge," Mila said. "Many years ago, a master mason bargained with the devil to help him complete the bridge on time. In exchange, the devil would claim the first soul to cross the bridge. The mason, feeling remorse about his pact, confessed his sin and sought help from a bishop, who told him how to outwit the devil. The day after the bridge was finished, the mason sent a pig across. The devil, furious at having been tricked, threw himself into the Serchio River and has never been seen in these parts again. From that time on, the bridge has also been called Ponte del Diavolo, Devil's Bridge."

"That's a great story," I said. "Now I will tell you another legend. Once upon a time, my family owned a dwelling in a village called Ponte Rotto. When Italy plunged into economic freefall in the 1880s, taxes rose as high as these mountains, too steep for my family to pay. They left the village they loved and sailed across the ocean to America to begin a new life. But here's the mystery. I was told Ponte Rotto was once located near Piaggione, but it doesn't show up on any map. It disappeared from this land along with my family, never to be seen again."

"How do you know about that village?" Mila asked.

I pulled out my little album. "This is Ponte Rotto," I said, pointing to faded black-and-white photographs, front and back views of the main building. The two-story structure held four contiguous dwellings, an older version of today's condominiums.

"That story interests me," Mila said as we started back the way we came.

Ten minutes later, Mila slammed on the brakes and skidded to a sudden stop on a dirt strip by the bank of the Serchio River.

"What's wrong?" I asked.

"Look!" Mila pointed to the end of a building across the street, an ugly, mottled gray wall. On half of the building, the side closest to us, rust-colored stucco had peeled off in patches, exposing gray stone and brick beneath. Numerous holes revealed internal metal rods. Big bites in the roof had been chewed off by countless storms. But the other half of the building was totally remodeled, with pristine plaster in shades of yellow. That side sported a new red tile roof.

"What are you looking at?" I asked.

"Ponterotto!" Mila exclaimed. "There. Look at the sign on the wall."

"What? Where?" I struggled to understand what Mila was talking about.

I peered at a rectangular shape on the end of the building, gray on gray, but the letters were nearly impossible to read. I saw a "P" and a bunch of smears like melted crayon. The sign ended with what might have been "TTO."

"Really? Do you really think so?"

"I tell you, that's it," Mila said as she climbed out of the car. "Look over here." She pointed down to a crumbled rock formation at the edge of the bank. "That was once the support for a bridge. Ponte Rotto means 'broken bridge.'"

As Robert began snapping photos of the two-story building, the curtain moved in an upstairs window. We were being watched.

"I'm not sure," I said. "This doesn't quite match the front doors in my photo."

Mila bounded across the highway to the renovated end of the building, Robert and I tagging behind. Two middle-aged women were chatting in a grassy spot as they tossed grain to free-range geese and chickens. With their heads down, they threw furtive glances our way.

"*Buona sera*," Mila called out with a big smile and a friendly wave. She strode up to them and started an amiable Italian conversation explaining who we were and why we were taking photographs. "Show your photo," Mila said to me.

I opened my album to a faded image of Ponte Rotto. One sturdy woman hovered over the photo, nodded her head, and gave a vague "*hmm-hmm.*"

"Will she allow us to see the back of the building?" I asked Mila. More rapid-fire Italian conversation followed.

"Yes, yes," Mila said. "Come."

The five of us trekked around the corner, and two more women emerged from their dwellings to join us. I pointed to my backyard photo, taken by a relative long ago, and we began comparing rooflines, which weren't the same. My old snapshot showed distinct roofs, each one defining a separate two-story home. On the right side of the photo, a woman stood on a second-story balcony, near a little closet that jutted out from the dwelling.

Robert pointed to a paved patch of earth that climbed straight up a steep hill. "May we walk up there to take a photograph?"

More Italian discussion was followed by, "Yes, yes, go."

I leaned on Robert, and the two of us side-stepped up an impossible incline. Twisting moves on my ankle caused agonizing pain that almost brought me to my knees. But I needed to get a couple of steps higher for a better perspective. Robert snapped photographs of the building, before-and-after images of amazing transformation.

It was hard to believe we were looking at two halves of the same building. The partially renovated two of the four units sported immaculate apricot and beige walls, cheery and bright. Newly created balconies brimmed with greenery and red flowers.

The other end of the building was a disaster. Holes and cracks marred ugly gray walls, exposed gashes through brick and stone. But that roofline appeared to match my photo. A dilapidated closet clung to the outside of the second story. The door was missing, and a toilet was visible.

"A privy with plumbing," Robert said.

"I couldn't figure out why there was a little closet out there on the balcony in my old photo," I said. "That was a bathroom. Oh, my God, this is Ponte Rotto!"

We returned to the bottom of the hill, and I babbled to Mila, "Look at my photo, the little closet." Then I pointed to the second story of the unfinished building. "There it is! Can you believe it? That was the privy. Mila, this villa really is Ponte Rotto!"

"Yes, yes, I told you," she said.

"When this makeover is complete, I wonder whether any trace of the original Ponte Rotto will remain," I said. "Maybe you found this place just in time, before the closet disappears, before a paintbrush wipes out the last remaining letters on the wall."

I turned back to my little album. "This photo was with the Ponte Rotto collection." I pointed to the snapshot of a steep mountain and water below, with houses at its bank. "My family must have seen this view every day. This is the Serchio River." I turned to one of the women. "What do you call this place?"

"Piaggione," she said. I wondered if she knew it was once called Ponte Rotto.

Back in the car, I blurted, "I don't believe it. How did you see it, Mila? How did you know? If you hadn't taken us to Devil's Bridge, this wouldn't have happened. You are Wonder Woman."

Mila was beaming. "Now we should visit the town center of Piaggione," she said.

Minutes later, Mila parked in front of a small church striped with horizontal marble bands of pink and white. Classical columns framed the portico. Three arches were repeated on the second level, which was topped by a peaked roof and cross.

"My grandmother and her parents probably attended services here," I said to Mila.

I hobbled across the lawn to join Robert, who was snapping images of a large bronze statue of Christ holding a lifeless soldier. Robert pointed to the sides of the marble base. "Look at this—names of World War I casualties."

I read a stirring tribute to the people who had sacrificed their lives—soldiers and civilians, men and women. War came to everyone.

We circled the statue as I read aloud. "Motroni, Ghilardi, Caselli, Rossi—those are my family names." Images flashed through my mind: farmers shouldering rifles instead of hoes, women's white aprons spattered with blood. I felt an overpowering sense of loss, too heavy. I had to turn away.

We reached Mila's car, and I retrieved my album to show her one more sepia photograph of two-story buildings arranged in a semi-circle, mountains in the background. On the bottom of the photo was printed "Fabrica Cottone Piaggione." A cotton factory.

"We will find it," Mila said. And, of course, we did.

At the cotton factory, we drove around abandoned buildings, their cracked windows grayed by spiderwebs, weeds growing between the pavers. Once a bustling manufacturing center, the place was now deserted.

"What a shame that is," Mila said, as we headed out toward Lucca. "Such a waste."

"I think the cotton factory spawned other industries: clothing design, pattern production, sales," I said. "When I was a little girl, my grandmother Noni made patterns for my clothes with freehand sketches on brown tissue paper. Noni's training as a 'tailoress' may have started there."

I remembered Noni draping paper over my shoulders. "Do you want a Peter Pan collar or points?" she'd ask. I'd stand on a kitchen chair, twitching and squirming impatiently as Noni marked a hem for my skirt or pinned a tuck for a shoulder seam. I still have a child's hooded cape—navy-blue velvet with white satin lining—made of leftover fabric from Noni's dark skirts and shimmery blouses.

"Now we will celebrate," Mila said, as we drove through a portal in the wall of Lucca Centre. "Ah, here is my apartment. We're not supposed to park here, but there is no other place." She aimed the Yaris diagonally, one wheel on the curb, into a space large enough for a bicycle.

She entered the foyer and started up the stairs. "I'm on the third floor. We'll take the elevator," she called back as we trudged up high-rise steps that curved skyward. "Almost there," she shouted midway through the climb. "How do you like the ride?"

There was no elevator. No wonder she was so fit; she lived in a training camp for Olympians.

Mila opened her door to a small sitting area decorated with comfortable pillows, a center table, and Rino Mariani, her handsome boyfriend. Mila was full of surprises. Tall, tan, and trim, with full white hair and a mustache, this man, probably in his sixties, could have been a supermodel. We reminisced in two languages about our day as we nibbled on nuts and crackers and raised our goblets of sparkling Prosecco in celebration.

Later, Mila dropped us off at our apartment with hugs, a kiss on each cheek, and plans to meet next week. Nothing, I thought, could possibly top this day.

19

Lost Records

The next morning, Maria Chiarlo opened the glass doors for us at Archivio Storico. We chatted amiably in Italian about her neighborhood, which happened to be where our apartment was located.

"You've probably reviewed all the Brancoli census records we have here. I have something for you," she said.

Maria disappeared into an inner office and returned with a book in hand, larger than a paperback and twice as thick. *Guida all'Archivio Storico Comunale—Guide to the Municipal Historical Archive*—was filled with beautiful color photos of documents and sketches of the history of Lucca, all stored here in this building.

"It is for you," she said.

"*Grazie! Quanto costa?*" How much does it cost?

"*Niente.* This is my gift for you. Have you visited Archivio di Stato?"

"We tried. Several times. The man there told me my family's records were lost in the war."

Maria's brow furrowed into a frown.

"*Perso nella guerra,*" I repeated. Maybe she didn't understand me.

"I know the director there," she said. Good thing I hadn't made any snide remarks about the Hawk. Maybe he was the director.

"You will need some papers." Maria headed for her office as Robert and I pored over her book. The copyright date was 2007, just last year. The first page listed eight contributing editors. Among them were Maria Chiarlo, Cristina Marinari, and Mariella Morotti, our friends here at Archivio Storico.

A few minutes later, Maria returned. "I made copies of these inventory pages. For the Brancoli region, you should look in the *Sesto* and *Parrocchie di Campagna* volumes."

Maria stamped and signed the copies and handed them to me. I stared dumbly at red seals and signatures. I had no clue what she was talking about.

"I just made a phone call," she said in Italian. "Please present these documents at Archivio di Stato. You have an appointment. They are waiting for you."

What do you say when locked doors fly open, when impossible dreams are realized, when thank you is not enough? "*Grazie, grazie mille,*" was all I could manage.

Clutching the banister in one hand and stamped papers in the other, I ignored my screaming ankle as Robert and I climbed three stories in the Palazzo Guidiccioni. We entered the familiar high-ceilinged central area of Archivio di Stato, Lucca's state archive office. I looked for the Hawk, whose piercing eyes would target me for the verbal kill. Instead, in a total turnaround from our first two visits, we received a warm welcome from a smiling woman with curly brown hair. She ushered us through the adjacent library chamber, beyond the long information desk, and into a small meeting room lined floor to ceiling with books. There we were greeted by a round-faced gentleman with white hair and silver-rimmed glasses. He opened his hand, palm up, and waved it over the table, where several volumes had already been placed. He repeated words I recognized, Maria's words, "*Sesto*" and "*Parrocchie di Campagna.*" He opened books and explained that these were the ones we would need.

At a loss for meaningful utterances, I nodded and mumbled "*Grazie, grazie*" as I handed Maria's signed papers to the gentleman.

We followed the smiling woman back to the library chamber, where she placed a couple of tomes on a table. She asked us to place paper bookmarks between the pages to be copied. A tall female librarian carried in more volumes and placed them before us. I recognized her from prior visits. She seemed reserved, detached as usual.

The first book, *1809 Parrocchie di Campagna, Comune di Sesto*, was covered with a light-gray textured cardstock that resembled thick papier-mâché. Curled brown tabs of paper peeked out from one edge. Each narrow band, teased open, revealed a letter in alphabetic order. Tan pages were divided by family, three families per page, with *capo di famiglia*—the head of household—listed first. Family members, their ages, relationships, and occupations appeared in chronological order, the youngest last. Behind a curled "M" we found my Motroni family. *Possidento, contadino, bracciante*—landowner, tenant farmer, laborer. My family had been intimately involved with the land, tending crops on those rugged hillsides for over two centuries.

Robert pulled the second book from the stack, *1823 Statistica Nominativa Personale, Tutte le Famiglie dello Stato di Lucca*. Thicker than the 1809 volume, a worn and torn brown paper book cover concealed its hard binding. The tan interior followed the same format as the 1809 version, but information was crammed in small cursive as though paper had been at a premium, with ten families per page.

As Robert and I turned fragile pages, names of my ancestors jumped off the census records. Carli, Caselli, Cecchettini, Fambrini, Ghilardi, Motroni, Orzali; the roll call was staggering. We worked, heads down, paper strips flying between pages. All of the Pieroni families received a bookmark—one of them had to be an ancestor of my Pietro.

Bleary-eyed, we closed the books a couple of hours later. The information clerk gathered bookmarked volumes and escorted us through an unmarked door. What was this? An elevator! Thank God for the clerk who wanted to ride. I didn't have to navigate those agonizing stairs again.

On the ground floor, we followed the clerk into a little office. He placed our volumes on the desk, where a blonde secretary was seated. She spoke in Italian and said she would copy the bookmarked pages onto a CD and mail it to our home in Oregon. We paid a modest fee.

I practically floated as we crossed the piazza. Then I spotted the tall librarian coming our way. On three prior encounters with her, we had walked away empty-handed from Archivio di Stato. But not today. I had found my family. I bore her no ill will.

Our eyes met. I smiled and gave the appropriate greeting, an enthusiastic *"Buona sera."* Good afternoon. Her eyes registered shock, disbelief. She turned away as if she didn't hear.

"What was that about?" I asked Robert.

"Who knows? Doesn't matter," he said.

I was puzzled by her response but tried not to let it bother me.

Like a stream with leaves and logs bobbing along and swirling in eddies, the byways in Lucca Centre were shared by bicycles, pedestrians, and an occasional automobile or small delivery truck, moving in both directions, all weaving to avoid each other. As we walked down a narrow cobblestone street with no sidewalks, an old green bicycle bumped past us, chains and fenders jangling. We watched in horror as the rider narrowly escaped colliding with a car that failed to stop at a blind intersection. The cyclist made a sharp turn, the bike wobbled, and he fell to the pavement. He rose, righted his fallen bike, and bowed to the driver with the melodramatic movements of an actor at the end of a standing ovation.

"Complimenti," he said loudly. The driver surely heard, *My compliments on your splendid driving—you almost killed me, you idiot.*

At that moment I realized that I had delivered the ultimate insult to the librarian with my naive *"Buona sera."* She probably heard, *Thanks a lot for all your help; I found the records anyway and have a nice day.* Those layers of language hadn't been covered in class. Subtleties of communication in this society could only be learned by a lifetime in Lucca.

That evening, I thumbed through Maria's gift—the guide to the contents of Archivio Storico. Colored sketches of military uniforms grabbed my attention, pages filled with belted jackets and braided epaulets. One hat looked familiar. I opened my little album to compare it to the uniformed officer in one of the photographs, Domenico Marcucci, the first husband of my great-grandmother Marianna Fambrini. His strange hat resembled an inverted bucket with a chin strap, topped off by a round knob over an emblem. I looked back and forth, from album to sketch—it was an unmistakable match. Who could miss that cylindrical hat with a ping-pong ball on the top! At the bottom of the page, *"Divisa della guardia daziaria"* identified the uniform of a customs officer, a government employee who collected taxes on foreign goods.

"Look at this," I called to Robert. "Domenico Marcucci must have been a customs officer!"

The sketch was dated 1870, nearly a decade after the unification of Italy and the creation of this branch of military service under the Department of Finance. We knew Domenico had died or disappeared from records about ten years later, at the age of forty. It was reasonable to conclude that he had served his country in this window of time, and odds were good he was a customs officer.

"Domenico, I've had such a tough time finding anything about you," I murmured. We'd looked for military uniforms in the wrong office. At least the Hawk hadn't lied about that. They weren't in Archivio di Stato. These sketches were stored in Archivio Storico after all.

20

The Road to Farnocchia

One branch on my growing family tree was just a small stub. Agostino Rossi, Noni's father, was born in Farnocchia, a village perched high in the Apuan Alps. We had found scant information about him: an Italian birth certificate and a California funeral record. Agostino's parents, Romualdo Rossi and Irene Bottari, remained a mystery—no story of their lives, no flesh on their bones, just fill-in-the-blank names on my ancestral chart.

Robert and I pored over a map of Italy's northwestern region. The convoluted road to Farnocchia resembled a seismograph mid-earthquake. On the remote chance that we could find Bottari-Rossi records closer to sea level, we set out by train for Pietrasanta, a northwestern coastal city at the foot of the mountains. An hour later, we climbed a few blocks from the station.

In the central piazza, we stopped to gape at a sixteen-foot verdigris and bronze-colored statue of three young children. A label at the base identified "The World for Children." The teenage girl carried a small child in a shawl slung over her shoulders and held the hand of a little boy by her side. Their disheveled hair, haunted eyes, and downturned lips portrayed loss and despair. In a chilling moment, I felt the anguish of Noni's mother, Marianna Fambrini.

Brancoli census records had revealed a tragic story about Marianna's early years. She was thirteen years old when her mother died, leaving behind three children: two young girls and a little boy. The women of San Giusto must have rallied to provide guidance, comfort, and support. But with her mother gone, and her father preoccupied with his work as a laborer, Marianna assumed a heavy cloak of responsibility. Her life unraveled even further five years later, while she was working at a grocery store a few miles away, at Capannori. That year, both her brother and her sister died of unstated causes. I wondered how Marianna found the strength to endure. She and her father were the only two survivors in her nuclear family.

A short distance away, another colossal statue echoed shades of gray-green and earth tones, this one of a young woman embellished with gold earrings, bracelets, castanets, and a don't-mess-with-me dagger at her waist. "Esmeralda" was printed on a small note beneath her bare feet. Graceful arms raised, back arched, hair flowing, her smile captured sheer joy. One knee held high, her twirling skirt arrested mid-turn, folds of sculpted fabric caressed a sensual body.

I'd like to believe that Marianna found such happiness, that she twirled her skirts in a dance of unbridled joy and somehow pulled herself out of the madness of loss to marry her first love, Domenico Marcucci. They once lived with their young sons in a village near Lucca.

The two massive statues flanked the Cathedral of San Martino. At the end of the piazza, a giant poster of Gina Lollobrigida celebrated her acting and her art, with the star's movies scheduled weekly for the next month. As we read and reread the bulletin, we realized that the stunning movie star from the 1950s and 1960s was also a gifted sculptor. The statues in the piazza were her creations. She had once played the role of the gypsy Esmeralda in the 1956 film *The Hunchback of Notre Dame*.

At the opposite end of the piazza, we peered into a little alley, where we saw works in progress by other artists. Countless columns, statues, and busts competed for tight space in an open garage. St. Francis of Assisi, distracted by his bird in hand, stood calmly under the hooves of a rearing stallion. A breathtaking Madonna of La Pietà was flanked by Bobby Kennedy. A Greek goddess found narrow footing between Neptune and the wall. Marble dust covered the stone floor. Propped up by a flimsy kickstand, a blue bike was parked perilously close to exquisite artwork. Shelves and walls displayed scattered heads, hands, feet, fingers, all waiting to be attached to stone people. Like them, I felt incomplete.

I was no closer to understanding the life of my ancestor Agostino Rossi. How did that rough-cut miner capture the heart of Marianna, the beautiful widow of an officer and gentleman? What prompted him to leave the Apuan Alps to find her in a village near Lucca? How did they survive the culture clash? I might never know the answers, but I longed to know more about the man.

I spotted a black-robed priest, and we wove around Esmeralda to join him across the piazza. In my best Italian I said, "*Buona sera*. I'm looking for records of my family. My great-grandfather was born in Farnocchia, and I wondered if the parochial records are stored here."

"*No*," the priest smiled. "*Non sono qui.* They are not here. You might try Pontestazzemese, where they store public records of the region. And the church in Farnocchia might house the parish records." He pointed back down the hill toward the station. "A map is there."

We stopped to gaze at a large geographic diagram of zigzag roads connecting village dots in the Apuan Alps. We hadn't planned a trip into the high mountains; in fact, we hadn't planned anything for this finale. We were scheduled to leave Lucca for Rome in four days.

"We won't have time to look for records, but it might be fun to explore the area," Robert said.

With the threat of rain heavy in the air, we boarded the bus to Pontestazzemese. Stone walls and stucco buildings encased the narrow road, their footprints touching the edge of the pavement. The route meandered along a river into a region of rolling hills, making a gradual climb. Twenty-five minutes later, we stepped down at Pontestazzemese near a narrow bridge connecting two sides of the village. A few commuters made their way across the street to a blue twelve-passenger vehicle aptly named *VAI*—You go.

"*Dove va questo autobus?*" I asked. Where does this bus go?

"*Farnocchia,*" answered the driver.

"Let's go," Robert said, despite his visceral aversion to winding roads.

The road to Pontestazzemese had been easy. Then I flashed back on the map to Farnocchia—the spiky turns, the steep terrain. *Surely we could continue safely on VAI,* I told myself. It couldn't be too difficult if ten other people, all locals, were willing to take the risk.

Robert wedged his body into a corner between the seat and the window as VAI's engine revved. We snaked through fog-shrouded mountains, the serpentine switchbacks carpeted with slippery yellow leaves and framed by roadside rivulets. The driver geared down, rapped his horn, and accelerated through light rain around blind turns just wide enough for one very small bus.

We stopped to let off two passengers at Stazzema and then back-tracked along the same wild ride for a couple of miles. We veered onto another route and climbed around sheer rock and forested bluffs through scattered villages. Outcroppings of rain-drenched ferns studded vertical terrain. I peered through drizzle over a slender guard rail separating us from a fifteen-hundred-foot drop; a forested peak towered on the other side of the chasm. Our driver, a small knot of a man with decades of wrinkles lining his face, barely managed to get his short arms around the steering wheel. I prayed he wouldn't suffer cardiac arrest on the next turn.

We crept around a stone wall with a warning sign: an exclamation point surrounded by a red triangle and "CADUTA MASSI" printed beneath.

"What does it mean?" Robert asked.

I dove into my Italian dictionary. "Here it is: 'massive rockfall.'"

Robert groaned. "Big boulders. Bad news for a minibus."

I imagined this road when it was a narrow ribbon of dirt just wide enough for a pack mule, a scar on a steep mountainside carved out by men with calloused hands wielding axes, picks, and shovels while they dodged avalanches of *caduta massi.*

Robert had assumed his gray-green complexion and was staring out the window. With adrenaline coursing through my veins but no option for fight or flight, I turned to the locals for distraction. Between blasts from the bus horn, I spoke Italian with passengers who seemed perfectly comfortable with our harrowing ride, probably desensitized after riding this road hundreds of times.

We stopped at a village, and I moved to the seat across the aisle from a round-faced man with a ring of white hair. "*Mi scusa, Signore,* we're going to Farnocchia to find information about my family."

"I live in Farnocchia," he said. "What is your family name?"

I told him that my *bisnonno* (great-grandfather) was Agostino Rossi, and his parents were Romualdo Rossi and Irene Bottari.

He answered in Italian, "My last name is Bottari, but Irene wasn't my relative. There are no remaining families by the last name of Rossi."

"My *bisnonno* was a miner in Farnocchia," I said.

Signore Bottari said the marble mine had closed. At one time there were a thousand residents in the village, but their numbers had dwindled to about a hundred. "The older ones are pensioners, and the younger ones drive to their jobs an hour away in the valley," he said.

That explains why Agostino, a miner, left home, I thought. *He must have seen his way of life disappearing along with the marble.*

Signore Bottari talked about the weather here, the winter snow that usually melted within a day. "However, last year the snow was this deep," he said, pointing to his knees.

I wondered how people from these villages traveled this hazardous road on snow and ice. I slipped back into my seat when we stopped to let off an elderly couple. They stood with their bundles in the rain by the side of the road as the bus pulled away, no other people in sight, no village in sight.

"*Dove abitano Loro?*" I asked. Where do they live?

"*Lì.*" There. Mr. Bottari pointed up a steep goat trail that disappeared behind a large boulder. I had a new appreciation for those rugged individuals who managed to survive up there, in a remote area untouched by tourism. They embodied the true grit of my ancestors.

An attractive dark-haired woman seated across the aisle wore professional attire in burgundy and beige: a soft wool skirt, a floral silk blouse, and an embroidered wool jacket. She filled in details about local healthcare, which was managed by one physician, who visited the villages in a circular route every week, her village on Friday. Other than a small co-pay, medical care was free. She said in case of emergency, one could reach a medical school and hospital in Pisa in a little more than an hour if transportation were immediately available. I pictured myself as a patient with a frantic driver careening through these mountains like Mario Andretti. Forget the hospital; I'd die of fright along the way.

A twenty-something passenger in the window seat ahead turned to speak to us—in English. She said she was earning her degree in language at the university in Pisa. She spoke fluent Italian, French, English, and German. She usually drove her car to and from school daily, but it was in the repair shop, and she relied on the bus and train in the interim. She successfully shattered my impression of undereducated villagers.

Farnocchia was the last stop on our half-hour ride. There were no towns beyond this point. The light rain had become a downpour, resonating like a drum roll on the roof.

"When does the next bus arrive?" I shouted to the driver over the din.

"*Questo è l'ultimo per oggi,*" the driver shouted back. This is the last one for today. I checked my watch. It was 5:45.

"You might be able to get a ride on the school bus," a passenger said loudly in Italian. He didn't wait for a reply and disappeared down the steps to ground level.

"I want to get off," I said to Robert.

"You can't be serious. There's no Marriott in Farnocchia. Where do you plan to stay?"

"There's a school bus. Maybe we could get a ride back on that. We're so close."

"There's no guarantee we can get a train connection if we return later," Robert said close to my ear. "And we have an appointment in Lucca's Archive Office tomorrow morning. We're supposed to pick up the information about your grandmother."

The drum roll picked up tempo as VAI slowly turned around.

"The piazza is just around the bend. We're so close. I only want to look," I said.

"It's starting to rain harder."

"We're so close," I repeated.

"Yeah, to closed doors and no place to stay." Robert turned to gaze at me. "This bus ride was just for sightseeing. I see another trip to Italy in our future. Next time we'll plan a few days for Farnocchia." I was silent, still considering my options. Three drenched people entered the bus.

"This hasn't been a total loss," Robert said. "You've learned a great deal about Agostino Rossi on this ride."

I put my head in my hands and groaned. "*So close.*" I straightened up to shout over the roar of thunder. "I know you're right. I'd be *pazza* to get off in this torrent."

We were still on board when VAI headed back through the rain to the valley below.

21

—————

Diecimo

Tuesday—three days from a train ride to Rome. We reported to Lucca's Ufficio Anagrafe, the registrar's office, where the woman in Window #3 had promised to deliver my family records. True to her word, she slid the documents to me across the sill.

"*Grazie, grazie mille.*" We didn't even wait to get outside of the office but plopped down on a bench and began poring over papers about my grandmother, handwritten in Italian.

"Amabile Rossi's birth year was 1884, not 1889," I said. "Her obituary was wrong. No wonder we couldn't find Noni in Lucca's birth records. And we finally have the parish where she was born: San Giusto di Brancoli. Census records wouldn't have helped; they ended in 1881 and didn't start again until the 1930s."

Included in the packet was the marriage record of Noni's parents, Agostino Rossi and Marianna Fambrini. "Odd. This has them marrying in 1908. That was a few years after their two grown girls had sailed off to America. How is that possible? There must have been tremendous pressure from the priest and the villagers to do the right thing."

"Maybe this was the right thing for them," Robert said.

"Raising two daughters out of wedlock? That was sinful behavior in the eyes of the church. Marianna must have chosen a life riddled with guilt and shame. But why?"

"We may never have an answer, but I think this was all about Ponte Rotto," Robert said.

"You may be right," I said. "In the early 1880s, Marianna was a forty-year-old woman with three young sons to raise. What if her husband, Domenico Marcucci, had disappeared? What if she didn't know whether he was dead or alive? Maybe Agostino Rossi fell in love with her and offered to support her and the boys on a nice chunk of land with a river view. According to immigration records, Agostino and his brother, Santi Rossi, owned the villa at Ponte Rotto."

"We know Agostino and Marianna had two daughters, your grandmother and her sister," Robert said. "I wonder what finally prompted their marriage at such a late date."

"Think about Italy's economy; it was falling apart," I said. "Marianna's children had grown up and sailed off to the United States in hopes of a better future, and Ponte Rotto couldn't be saved from back taxes. Marianna had chosen to 'live in sin' with Agostino—for the future of her sons. Twenty-five years later, she married him—for the future of her daughters. Agostino was planning to go to America. If he came into money, his daughters would be eligible for an inheritance, but only if he were married to their mother. I believe Marianna had struggled to protect her children, to put them first at the risk of her reputation. My God, she was brave."

I shuffled through the papers and found the document for Marianna Fambrini's first marriage. The woman in Window #3 had made penciled notes in the margins. As an extra bonus, she had listed the parents of both bride and groom. Marianna's first husband, Domenico Marcucci, the man in uniform, had lived in Diecimo. I stared at the name of the village, then pulled out my little album to see "*DIECIMO—La Chiesa*" printed beneath the sepia print of a church, my last mystery photo.

I pointed to the picture for Robert to see. "Diecimo! That church must have been central to the lives of Marianna's first family. No wonder this photo was saved."

Robert checked his map; his finger traced along the Serchio River. "Diecimo is about ten miles north, just a couple of miles from Devil's Bridge."

"We need to ship books home," I said. "But other than that, this afternoon is wide open. Let's check the train schedule."

Less than an hour later, we stepped down to a two-story railway station in Diecimo. I gaped at what we found inside—shuttered windows, no ticket agent, just two benches across from each other in an empty corridor. There would be no help for the trip back to Lucca.

We hiked up the road and spotted the open door of a trattoria, where clusters of men dressed in jeans and work shirts sat at circular tables and shared glasses of wine. Their hand gestures punctuated animated conversation as they joked and laughed in the language of Lucca. The village women were absent; probably home, cooking delicious concoctions or sharing news with neighbors as they hung clothes out to dry, like chores done a century ago.

We ambled toward the center of town and meandered down a side street. The farther we went, the newer the houses, the more upscale the neighborhood—two-story homes clad in honey-colored stucco topped with red tile; balconies brimming with flowers, lush landscaping. Waist-high walls between buildings held terra cotta pots of cascading vines and flowers so perfectly arranged and maintained that they appeared fresh from the florist. Not a single car moved on any street. An old man stood watching us from an empty schoolyard.

"*Buona sera*," I said. Then in Italian, "Do you know anyone here by the name Marcucci?"

"I've lived here all my life," he said. "Unless they just came here recently, there are no families here by that name."

"*Grazie.*" I must have sounded disappointed. "Could you please tell us where the church is located?"

"*La chiesa è là.*" The church is there. He motioned around the corner.

We skirted the schoolhouse to a street with an unobstructed view. A tall, gray bell tower soared above the rooftops. Arched openings marked the stories, just like my old photo. As we approached, the tower loomed ever higher, five stories above another two stories that formed the church. Master masons must have clung precariously to scaffolding more than seven stories up as they put the final changes on this masterpiece.

We trudged up the empty street to find locked church doors and a vacant parking lot. A plaque at its base dated the church from the late twelfth and early thirteenth centuries. However, another sign stated that the original building was mentioned in records dated AD 919. We were looking at a thousand years of history, and we had solved the puzzle of the mystery photo in my album.

"When Domenico and Marianna were children, they were separated by the Serchio River," I said. "I wonder how they met."

"Maybe they walked over Devil's Bridge," Robert said.

I smiled at the image of two young lovers crossing the bridge to their future.

22

The Archbishop's Records

B ack at "Storico" the next morning, Mariella suggested we look in the 1815 index of parochial population records. Like census records, names and ages of family members in each village were listed. Cristina piled books on the library table for us, and Robert leaned back in his chair to watch as I dove into the stacks.

Mariella walked by us, stopped, turned back, and tapped the tip of her index finger on the table in front of Robert. "*Al lavoro!*" she said. To the work!

He chuckled and picked up yet another tome to review. "No room for slackers here."

I spread my ancestral chart out on the table so we could search for specific surnames, and our task was completed within the hour. Cristina disappeared to copy our bookmarked pages. That's when Mariella told us there was one more archive office to consider. "Have you looked in Achivio Arcivescovile?" she asked.

I couldn't believe my ears. I thought we had explored every hiding place for documents in all of Lucca. "What is that?" I asked.

"The archbishops' records are stored in that building. You should go there," Mariella said.

"Not another library," Robert groaned. "They must spring up overnight."

Mariella told us that church records from the twelve Brancoli villages were here in Lucca Centre. She helped Robert locate the address on his map.

We were running out of time. Our stay in Lucca was ending in two days. Forget lunch. We raced across town for the next archive office, skirted St. Martin's Cathedral, and crossed diagonally to an oblong three-story building with a small bronze sign on the wall near the door.

"'Curia Arcivescovile' [Ar-chee-ves-co-*vee*-leh]. I think this is it," Robert said. He pushed open a set of ornately carved double doors ten feet high, and we entered a cream-colored reception room. I spoke Italian with the man behind the desk and asked for permission to search for my family in parish records.

"You must wait," he said as he pointed to some chairs.

A short time later, another man appeared from an interior corridor and left the building. The receptionist motioned that we should proceed into a hallway around the corner, where we found an undersized elevator with room for two. We stepped off two stories up and located the library, a small chamber fit for kings. A gigantic crystal chandelier held white candles aloft. Grand scale works by Renaissance masters flanked the ornate doorway. Massive gold frames hung on scarlet walls accented in white. I felt insignificant in this room—diminished by soaring ceilings and opulence. We saw five library tables arranged in a U-shape, a pair on each side. No wonder we had to wait; no more than eight people at a time could conduct research in this room.

Two women were seated at the head table. One, a fresh young face with a flawless complexion, approached. She moved quietly, softly, as if she'd had special training in the art of walking correctly among the archbishops' archives.

"*Buon giorno*," she whispered. "The library closes at one o'clock."

We had little more than an hour to explore the records. I spoke quiet Italian with the whisper-soft woman, and showed her my family tree with names, dates, and Brancoli villages. I pointed to blank spaces on the Fambrini and Cecchettini branches. She nodded understanding and retrieved two heavy volumes the size of old Bibles.

We turned ancient pages filled with loopy letters of irregular widths. Each priest had dipped his quill point in ink many times for every entry. Births, marriages, and deaths documented in church registers had also been transcribed in chronological order into these archbishops' records. Every event listed family members: spouses, parents and their fathers, sometimes extending back generations to the great-greats. All entries were written in Italian. This was the mother lode of Catholic records.

"It's really hard to read," Robert whispered.

With my ancestral chart between us, we inched our way down pages, scanning for a familiar name buried within each entry.

"Wait," I whispered. "I think I found something about Marianna's mother. This was Noni's grandmother. She died decades before Noni was born."

I stood, and "Whisper Soft" returned to our table.

"*Potrei fare foto?*" I asked as Robert retrieved the camera. May I take a photo?

She picked up the tome and carried it to another table with better ambient light. "Try here."

> *5 February 1857 Fambrini, Ma. Nonziata, wife of Domenico, of San Giusto di Brancoli [received last rites and passed from this life] at age 52, [buried in the cemetery of San Giusto].*

"Sad," I said. "Her daughter Marianna Fambrini was only thirteen when her mother died."

Time was up. I asked if we needed an appointment to return the next morning, our last day in Lucca. No reservation was needed; we should return at nine o'clock.

At a nearby trattoria, we ordered pizza. Oven roasted over fire and served on a thin crust, the sweet, earthy taste of wild mushrooms topped light servings of savory marinara sauce and drizzled cheese—*mozzarella bufala*—made of milk from water buffalo. Paired with an espresso, nothing would match this delicacy back home. We topped it off with a cone of gelato, a must-have frozen decadence made of cream, sugar, and fresh fruit or nut puree. Despite our daily indulgences for lunch, our clothes fit more loosely—probably because we traveled six miles on foot each day. My injured ankle had finally improved to a slight limp despite a daily battering.

"Why is everything crammed into our last two days in Lucca?" Robert said. "We need to go back to Arcivescovile tomorrow morning, Mila is supposed to drive us back to the villages tomorrow afternoon, I need to pick up my shirts at the cleaners, and we have to pack. This is *pazzo*."

"Let's just trust the process," I said.

"I can't believe you said that. You have at least three separate plans for executing every decision. 'If this doesn't work, there is always Plan B' you always say. You used to be goal-oriented, a bit of a control freak, and here you are, adrift, not a single plan in place. What happened to you?"

"Italy happened to me. If the doors of Archivio di Stato hadn't been locked, Mila would never have been sent to us. If that hadn't happened, we couldn't have visited the Brancoli villages, and we wouldn't have found the lost village of Ponte Rotto. Just think, we might have missed meeting the three wise women in Archivio Storico. I'm not managing anything. Let's just go with it and see what happens next."

Wednesday morning, we returned to Archivio Arcivescovile and were promptly directed into the library. "Whisper Soft" greeted us and retrieved more volumes for us to review. Minutes stretched into an hour with little new information. A critical register was missing from the file and was being transcribed. She said we might find information at the church in Piaggione.

"Thanks, but there isn't time," I said in Italian.

We went back to line-by-line review. Robert nudged an elbow to my ribs. He had covered his page with a letter-sized blank sheet of paper. He lowered it to reveal the heading. Slowly, inch by inch, he teased the paper down. I rose from my chair to see better. Two librarians joined us. We stared at the document, important enough to fill a page. I translated the record.

> *Parish of Piazza di Brancoli. Marriage the 22nd day of April in the year 1841, Domenico, son of Giulio Fambrini of Ombreglio, presently residing in San Giusto di Brancoli, to Maria Annunziata, the daughter of Domenico Cecchettini.*

Marianna Fambrini was Noni's mother, and Robert had found the marriage record of her parents.

"This is fantastic! You filled a huge gap in my family history."

"Let's wrap it up," he said.

The young librarian moved our tome to another table, where Robert took a photo of the document. We closed our volumes, and another soft speaker approached, gray curls framing her smiling face. "Would you like to see another part of the library?" she asked in Italian. We followed her into another room, this one lined with books. In the center of the chamber, a glass case surrounded a yellow parchment scroll. "This one is dated AD 685. There are hundreds of others."

I gasped. "*Non sembre possibile*—It doesn't seem possible. What a treasure!"

"Come. I'll show you another room." She led us into a chamber with soft line drawings painted directly onto walls. We were surrounded by whimsical tendrils, leaves, flowers, and birds, all woven together. "This was once the palazzo of a very wealthy man. An artist was commissioned to complete some works in Lucca. He was staying in this room and painted these walls for his host."

"Beautiful," I said. "Who was the artist?"

"*Raffaello*," she said.

"Raphael?" I tried to wrap my mind around the Renaissance master who had stayed in this room and painted these walls in the early 1500s. This "Grotesque" style was a huge departure from his classical portraits we had viewed in Florence's Uffizi Gallery. These exquisite doodles revealed magical moments of spontaneity, a window into the mind meanderings of a genius.

We left Archivio Arcivescovile in a daze, privileged to have seen far more than we had ever hoped to find.

23

Brancoli Revisited

Mila arrived after lunch to transport us to the Brancoli villages, but this time Robert and I were both shown to the back seats of the car. Mila had another passenger, Gabriella Gabrielli, a dark-haired, slender woman who didn't speak English. She and Mila chatted so rapidly, I couldn't grasp a single word. I wondered why Mila had brought her along today, our last day in Lucca.

We began climbing through the Brancoli mountains on the same winding lane we'd seen before. But compared to the perilous road to Farnocchia, this one seemed easy.

"We should go to Piazza di Brancoli," Mila said. "The Cecchettini family is in Piazza."

"How does she know that?" I murmured to Robert.

"It's Mila. She knows," Robert said.

We drove through a series of horn-blaring twists and turns and then stopped at a confusing directional sign filled with too much information.

"*Va' lì,*" Gabriella said. Go over there.

"No, that's not the way." Mila answered in Italian.

"*Va', va'?*" Gabriella pointed her index finger toward the passenger window.

Mila followed Gabriella's command and turned right. I hoped for the remote possibility that Gabriella knew what she was talking about;

there wasn't room on the road for a U-turn. More switchbacks led to a knee-high rock wall, the only barrier between the car and a tumble to the Serchio River far below. Yellow stuccoed houses, red tile roofs—this was the village of Piazza.

Once parked, we climbed out across the road from a church. Gabriella greeted a couple of men by name. A tail-wagging dog approached her for a quick pat on the head. Gabriella called him by name, too. She blazed the trail down a cobblestone path between two-story buildings and stopped to rap loudly on a set of double doors. No answer.

"It's Gabriella. Open the door." She pounded the panels with both fists. Then she shouted something I couldn't understand.

Slowly, the door opened. Two women stepped out onto the landing. Gabriella introduced me to Signora Cecchettini, who introduced her mother. Gabriella spoke rapid Italian. "*Famiglia . . . America . . . Cecchettini.*" I understood only a few words.

"Show them your photo," Mila said. I pulled out my little album and pointed to a picture of three people: Noni's parents, Marianna Fambrini and Agostino Rossi, flanking a third family member.

Signora Cecchettini let out a squeal and chattered in Italian. "Aaagh! I have that picture in my attic! I didn't know who they were! How do you know those people?"

"*I miei bisnonni,*" I said. My great-grandparents.

"Maybe this isn't the same picture." Her hand went up; her voice lowered. "I could have been mistaken. No, I'm certain this isn't the same picture. I have lots of faded photos in the attic. No one could possibly recognize them."

She had completely derailed her original train of thought.

"*Per favore.*" Please. I showed her my Cecchettini ancestral chart.

"No. No. None of these people are members of my family. I don't recognize a single name," Signora Cecchettini said.

Before we took this trip, we had learned that long after the mass exodus in the late 1880s, some American-born relatives had returned to Italy to claim title to land once owned by their family members. There were rumors of Italians having been displaced from their homes decades after the original owners had emigrated to foreign soil. Signora Cecchettini probably thought I was one of those land-grabbers. She wasn't taking any chances.

Signora Cecchettini and her mother smiled for the camera despite a rippling undercurrent of tension. As we parted company, I had the distinct impression that a copy of my photo was indeed in that attic, and that more clues about my ancestors were stored there.

Gabriella must have sensed my disappointment. "You should meet my daughter and son-in-law," she said. " His last name is Motroni. They live nearby."

No wonder Gabriella was so well acquainted with the people of Piazza di Brancoli; she had family here. I leaned on Robert's arm as we climbed a steep goat path of winding stone steps that skirted retaining walls. At the crest of the hill, the young couple welcomed us into their remodeled stone house. Gabriella and I were related by marriage, probably many generations back—too long ago for Mr. Motroni to fill in the blanks. Near the front door, a sign stated "1733," the date of original construction. I couldn't imagine transporting building materials and appliances up that monstrous incline, no handrails on either side of the stairs.

"Is there a road up here?" I asked.

"Yes, but you have to hike in a long distance to the house," Gabriella answered. I wondered how these people managed that steep terrain in snow and ice and rain. True grit.

Back at the car, Mila asked, "Where would you like to go?"

"Is it possible to return to Gignano?" I said.

24

Discoveries at Gignano

More zigzags were ahead as we headed back toward the valley, but this time we followed a road west through the mountains, then made another hairpin turn and traveled east up steep terrain. I recognized the church by the side of the road and the questionable guard rail of Gignano.

Mila parked at the edge of the same dizzy precipice in the piazza. The village had changed in one short week. Colorful triangular flags were strung in a victorious V-shape, the point fixed below an enormous banner taped to the rock wall. It read "*SI RINGRAZIA*"—a big "thanks" in big letters. Below the greeting, names of individuals and businesses filled all the white space. I recognized Cecchettini and D'Aiuto, my ancestral surnames, on the list.

"They are celebrating the *vendemmia*—the grape harvest," Mila said. "There will be a *festa*. See those three black cauldrons by the side of the road? They light a fire beneath and then drop *castagni*—chestnuts—into boiling water seasoned with laurel and anise."

Mila rubbed her palms together briskly. "You do this to remove the skins," she said. "Mmm-mmm-mmm, delicious. This will be a very big celebration. They will drink wine from last year's harvest, and there will be plenty of food up there." She pointed up curving stone steps to the trattoria perched above the retaining wall.

My mind's eye saw villagers already gathering to celebrate hard-earned success in a place where the fruits of a year's labor could be ruined by a whim of the weather.

"I'd like to see my grandfather's house again," I said.

Mila spoke briefly with two men standing by the wall, telling them who we were and why we were snooping around Gignano.

"I'll bet they already know who we are," I said. "The village is probably buzzing about the couple from America with a keen interest in their houses."

We followed the same granite path we took seven days before. Images of my grandfather swirled through my mind—my five-minute meeting with an old man in a beautiful California garden. I climbed four stone steps to place the palms of my hands on the doorframe of the Motroni house. There was something unusual about the intense energy I felt there, a finger-tingling connection with my ancestors beyond the constraints of time and space. *Does DNA have a memory?* I wondered.

As we turned to leave, Mila said, "I wish we could have found Ada Motroni." This was the woman with the same last name as my grandfather, Giovanni Motroni. I didn't know what to say. I wondered why Mila was so fixated on her. Even if we found this mysterious Motroni woman, there was no guarantee we'd recognize a common ancestor.

We wound our way back to the stone wall, where Mila approached the two men still standing near the banner. "Excuse me, did Ada Motroni once live here?" she asked.

"Yes, she used to live here, but she moved to San Giusto. Her son built a house for her there."

Mila gave a big smile and an enthusiastic "*Grazie!* Maybe we'll find her in San Giusto."

The second man chimed in, "*Lei non sta a casa oggi*—she isn't home today. She went to a birthday party for her granddaughter."

A birthday party for her granddaughter. And Ada lived in another village miles away across the mountain. The network of communication in these villages amazed me. Everyone seemed to know everyone else's business, each intimate detail right down to the minutia of the moment. What an extraordinary way to live. Maybe this arrangement wouldn't be tolerable long term, but part of me longed for big gatherings and traditional *festas* and the family connections I took for granted as a child—seasonal celebrations with relatives filling the house with life.

We climbed into the car, but Mila didn't start the engine. "I am sad," she said. "I wish we could actually speak to Ada Motroni."

"Mila, I cannot ever thank you enough for all you have done," I said. "You drove us to villages all over these mountains. We prowled through cemeteries together. You opened my eyes to the world of my grandparents. You even found the lost village of Ponte Rotto. This was an adventure I will never forget. You are a miracle worker."

"But it is what I like to do. I love to solve mystery," she said.

We eased back onto the road to return to Lucca but couldn't have gone more than a quarter mile when Mila slammed on the brakes and pulled off to the left side of the road, perilously close to the abyss. She stared straight ahead at a mottled pink stucco church. Two small pink balloons fastened to the corner of the building waved in the wind. Several cars rested in impossible places on both sides of the lane, some scant inches away from the drop-off, others tilted with wheels biting the upside of the mountain.

Mila said, "I have to get out. Wait for me."

"Where is she going?" I asked in Italian. Gabriella shrugged her shoulders.

We watched Mila enter the building through a side door. Minutes ticked by as we sat in silence. Then she reappeared, waved her arms frantically, and darted back into the building.

"What does that mean?" I asked.

"She wants us to get out of the car," Gabriella said. We climbed out, not an easy task considering where we were parked.

Mila emerged from the building again, this time with a smiling older woman barely five feet tall, dressed in pastel shades of pink and teal. Her short, auburn-dyed hair glowed in the sun, creating a halo effect around her face. She walked erect, her ancient spine in perfect alignment. Sure-footed, one hand on Mila's arm, the other on her hip, she stared straight at me as they approached.

Mila was beaming. She announced rather grandly, "This is Ada Motroni!"

Everyone spoke Italian, all at the same time, and as words tumbled over each other, Mila introduced me as the woman who had traveled all the way from America to find her family.

"*È una piacere*—It's a pleasure," I said, taking Ada's hand.

Robert retrieved the camera. Patrizia, the birthday girl, joined us and stood by her grandmother Ada's side.

"Show your photo," Mila said.

I opened my album to show Ada photos of my grandfather, Giovanni Motroni. I turned the page to the Motroni branch of my family tree and began to introduce my relatives, pointing to their names: "*Mio nonno*, Giovanni Motroni; *bisnonno*. Costantino Motroni; *bis-bisnonno*, Agostino Motroni . . ."

Ada turned her palm up to the sky and moved her hand up and down as she spoke Italian directly to Mila. "Tell her . . . tell her this is my family, too."

Mila placed her hand over her heart.

The earth moved, stars exploded, and tears filled my eyes.

"My family had a *serra*, a greenhouse," Ada said. She spoke about her family, *agricoltori*-farmers who once lived in the steep foothills near Piaggione in a place called Serra.

Chills rippled down my spine. Ada was describing Domenico Motroni, my grandfather's uncle. Robert and I had found him in census records when he was residing on Via di Serra—Street of the Greenhouse. At his uncle's knee, Giovanni had learned how to select the best seeds, how to enrich the soil, how to extend the growing season by nurturing plants under cover. Giovanni had carried those skills to vineyards and florist shops and beautiful gardens in America.

My mother and Ada shared the same great-grandfather, Agostino Motroni. This woman with an extraordinary memory said she had four sons, two daughters, and fourteen grandchildren.

Patrizia called me to follow her. I was reluctant to leave Ada, but the birthday girl was insistent. I followed a short distance around the side of the pink church. She pointed above the door to a carved relief of two soldiers, kneeling to help a child.

"*Americani,*" she said. "*Americani.*"

"*Grazie per questo*—thank you for this," I said. Americans from World War I were still being honored in a way I couldn't have dreamed possible.

We quickly returned to the reunion group. Our meeting had to be brief because we were delaying the birthday celebration of Ada's granddaughter. In Italy, elders are respected and held in high esteem. All festivity had stopped until this grand lady returned to the party.

Ada turned to me and said in Italian, "I am ninety-four years old. You had better come back soon, or you will visit me in the cemetery."

As we drove toward Lucca, down the twisting path of archival discoveries, ancestral homes, chance meetings with relatives, and new friends who guided our way, I asked in stunned amazement, "How is this possible?"

Mila said, "This is Italy, where nothing is possible, and everything is possible."

25

Encore

Two weeks after we arrived back home in Oregon, I began assembling information for Olive Hill Cemetery. Still missing was information about Lorenzo Marcucci. Also missing was information about the two Mortara brothers, Vincent and Frances. I had confirmed the dates for four of the seven unmarked graves at Olive Hill. Then Robert caught me searching the web for euro exchange rates.

"Tuscany is calling me back," I said.

"We just unpacked!"

"There's so much more to discover."

"You received a huge packet from Window #5 in Lucca. There's no guarantee we could find anything more on the next trip," he said.

"That packet has lots of information about Marianna Fambrini's first husband, Domenico Marcucci. But his disappearance from Diecimo in 1880 is still a mystery. Archivio Arcivescovile is a giant treasure chest just waiting for us. We never did find the right Pietro Pieroni."

"We're flying back to Italy to find Pietro Pieroni?"

"What about that aborted trip to Farnocchia? I wanted to know more about Noni's father, and there we were, in his village, rain pouring down, the last bus of the day leaving, and no place to stay. You did mention another trip."

"I thought we'd have a breather before the next flight."

"We'll have a breather. Tuscany isn't the worst place to visit."

Robert smiled and chuckled. "No, Tuscany isn't bad at all."

The next thing I knew, Robert was bringing home rented Italian films and stacks of Tuscany history books. Meanwhile, I forged through advanced Italian classes and rejoined a couple of conversation groups that met weekly. With a dictionary in my lap, I read Italian literature and printed tiny, translated words all over the pages.

I wrote to Mila about a return trip—perhaps in a year or two, to attend Lucca's Festa di Santa Croce, a big annual event scheduled in mid-September. Mila said that month was filled with plans to help Rino sell his hand-woven baskets for the *vendemmia*—the grape harvest. She looked forward to a few days with us, but the first couple of weeks she wouldn't be available. That actually sounded perfect. Most of the month of September would be devoted to research in Archivio Arcivescovile, the mother lode of vital records penned by priests in the Brancoli villages.

Two years later, after strategizing and saving, we returned to Italy, this time to an apartment inside the walls of Lucca Centre.

On our first night there, we found a restaurant with a hidden garden, above us a vine-covered pergola just like the one that sheltered family gatherings when I was a little girl. Evening breezes caressed us as we enjoyed a romantic Tuscan meal by flickering candlelight.

Suddenly a gunshot exploded nearby, followed by a whirring sound and the rapid flight of birds. We both ducked.

"My God, what was that?" Robert said. No one was running for cover. Conversations had resumed as if nothing had happened.

The waitress smiled as she sauntered by our table. "*Tutto a posto e niente in disordine*" she said—everything in place and nothing out of order—which meant absolutely nothing to us.

"They must have fired a blank," Robert said. "I didn't see any pigeons falling from the sky."

"Bird Patrol," I said. "Welcome back to Italy. Anything is possible."

We started our first morning with a brisk walk to the Forno, a bakery in operation since 1901. The sign said, "*Oggi come ieri . . . il pane dei Lucchesi.*" Today like yesterday . . . the bread of the people of Lucca. And what wonderful bread it was! A hard roll, once sliced, revealed a soft, dark delicacy rich with whole grains and seeds. The owner beamed with pride as he described his *pane* recipe, unchanged for generations, baked in a wood-fired oven. My ancestors might have tasted this same bread when they came to Lucca to sell their wine and olive oil.

Breakfast finished, we strode across the walled Tuscan town, swallows darting above, soft breezes tugging at my sleeves, clusters of Lucchesi exchanging Italian-speak. The long-awaited adventure was about to begin. Finally, we could access parish records for each of the Brancoli villages. At last we could piece together the lives of my forgotten family. We rounded the corner of Cathedral San Martino, and the massive doors of Archivio Arcivescovile came into view.

"We did it! I can't believe it. We're finally here," I said.

Robert reached for the latch. "Wait. What's this? There's a note on the door."

I read it, then read it again, then again. "Oh, no! It's closed."

"That's okay," Robert said. "We'll come back tomorrow."

"No, no, no!"

"What's the problem? What does it say?"

"The archive office is closed—for the entire month of September!"

Back at the apartment, I scratched heavy lines through the planning calendar for the first two weeks of September and stared at it as if some new master plan would materialize before my eyes. Now what?!

Robert wrapped his arm around my shoulders. "Didn't Mila want to see us tomorrow? In her last email, she said she'd be working with Rino at the *Murabilia* garden show. We'll find her! And after that we'll plan a trip to Farnocchia. We'll salvage this. You'll see," he said.

How could he be so jovial when the sky was falling? I was in no mood to be cheery. Robert busied himself elsewhere while I stormed around in silence. Slowly, my funk began to lift with thoughts of Mila. I missed her smile and her wide-eyed enthusiasm. Her extraordinary talent for finding people and places was crucial, especially now, with my family history behind locked doors.

The next morning, we arrived a little later than usual at the Forno. We found the place packed, with more people waiting at the open door. Robert stayed outside while I took my turn. Finally, I stood before the dark-haired, good-looking owner, the pastry case between us. I was confident that I could navigate my way through his language with ease. After all, I had just completed four years of Italian lessons.

"*Buon giorno,*" I said. "*Un panino scuro, per favore.*" A dark roll, please.

The owner said in Italian, "We have many delicious breads and pastries for sale. Why do you order the same thing every morning?"

"*Perché è BENissimo,*" I said.

He frowned. "*Che?*" What?

All transactions stopped. The crowd was hushed. I had made a mistake. Instead of saying his bread was very good (*buon*), I said it was very well (*ben*). I had just failed Italian 101.

He raised one hand and pointed his finger like a baton. "*Buo-NISS-imo,*" he said, his finger slicing the air on the second syllable.

The crowd looked at me.

"*BUO-niss-imo,*" I said.

The crowd looked back at him.

"No-no," he said, wiggling his index finger side to side. "*Buo-NISS-imo!*" He raised his hand and sliced the air again on the second syllable, bouncing it on the down stroke.

The crowd looked back at me.

"*Buo-NISS-imo*," I said.

The crowd looked back at him.

Both hands in the air, he smiled and shouted, "*Brava!*"

The crowd gave a collective sigh of relief and resumed quiet conversation.

"What took you so long?" Robert asked, as I joined him with my package of *panino scuro*.

"Italian lessons," I mumbled.

As we ambled along a cobblestone street, I heard children in a hidden courtyard, their easy chatter punctuated with laughter. The first graders had a better grasp of the language than I did. In Italian, I faltered, stumbled, reached dead ends, tried another way to express myself, to be understood. Like this journey to find my family, each conversation was a series of false starts, some successes only with passionate persistence. But it was in that struggle that I felt most alive.

The annual *Murabilia* was far bigger than I had imagined. I was expecting a few tables topped with local fruits and vegetables. Instead, the half-mile open-air market held more than 250 stalls of plants, yard art, and crowds of aspiring gardeners. We were among the twenty-three thousand visitors who paid a nominal fee to attend the three-day event. Map in hand, we visited countless kiosks and wove through flowers and vegetables, wind chimes and pottery, shrubs and trees, all on top of Lucca's walls. Robert stopped to watch a man weaving baskets.

"That's Rino!" he said.

I recognized handsome Rino's tanned skin and white hair. In the center of his exquisite functional art was Mila Antonini, her floral print pullover blending into the surrounding flowers.

Mila flashed her radiant smile, and a two-year absence vanished with hugs. I wanted to buy one of Rino's beautiful baskets, but Mila said we couldn't ship it to America. She stated that in an ironic twist of international law, bugs accidentally introduced in shipping cartons from the United States wouldn't be allowed to return to their home of origin in the hidden recesses of Rino's baskets. Customers crowded in, so we couldn't stay long, just time for a kiss on each cheek. I gave Mila the address of our apartment, a two-story dwelling inside Lucca's walls. She agreed to meet us there in two weeks.

On Tuesday, we woke to the sounds of pigeons practicing their Italian "Rs" with doleful repetition. No shotgun blast, *grazie Dio*. We planned to travel by train to Pietrasanta, then by bus to Pontestazzemese, where we'd stay a few days to search archive records for Noni's father. The final leg of the journey would be the long-awaited scary minibus ride to Farnocchia.

We reached the station and checked the electronic reader board for our train: one hour to departure. A half hour later, the listing had disappeared. A nearby coffee bar was filled with frustrated travelers. Another hour later the train was canceled, and the next one would put us in Pontestazzemese too late to secure lodging. We hauled our luggage back across Lucca to our apartment. We'd have to try again tomorrow.

On Wednesday, a torrential downpour kept us home, browsing through the extensive book collection in our apartment, the history of Lucca at our fingertips, grateful we hadn't attempted a bus ride through the Apuan Alps in this weather.

On Thursday morning, we rolled out of bed at five o'clock. Baggage in hand, we followed our flashlight beam through two dark courtyards to the outer double doors. Lucca's soft lights guided us to the rail station a half hour away. Our train tickets purchased from a vending machine, we found a bar for coffee. The train arrived late, but at least it wasn't canceled. At seven o'clock we arrived in Pietrasanta, only to discover that our bus to Pontestazzemese wouldn't leave for another three hours.

The central piazza of Pietrasanta looked bare without Gina Lollobrigida's massive sculptures; we'd arrived between revolving art shows. As we meandered down a side street toward an open market, I heard one old man chuckle and say to his friend, "Look at those people packing their luggage through the streets." We were not stunning examples of *la bella figura*—the beautiful way Italians love to present themselves with style.

Finally on our way, the bus followed the winding river course through a steep canyon. Houses were chiseled out of the rock and clung like mussels to outcroppings, their doors perilously close to passing traffic. I held my breath each time the bus passed a car. How could the driver manage to maneuver us through such tight spaces in two-way traffic, with unforgiving rock on one side and a sheer drop to the river on the other? But he did, time after time. Thirty minutes later, we stepped down to the pavement of Pontestazzemese.

We checked into a room at La Pania, a three-story hotel. In its dining room we feasted on *tagliatelle con funghi*, an egg-noodle concoction smothered with wild mushrooms and lightly drizzled with marinara sauce. *Mmm-mmm-mmm*, as Mila would say. Upstairs, we changed into business attire and returned to an empty lobby. The hotel and restaurant staff of two had disappeared.

The brick-red building next to the hotel bore the sign "Municipio di Stazzema" over the entrance. This was where we hoped to find records of my Farnocchia family. A second sign over one door in the lobby said "*Informazione*," but on closer inspection, spider webs around the doorknob gave us a clue that the keeper of information was out on a very long break. We meandered upstairs to closed doors and empty hallways. None of the offices listed on a third sign mentioned archives.

Back on the ground floor, I spotted the glass door into a bank, where two men were talking. In Italy, only one person at a time may enter a bank, so Robert waited in the empty lobby as I stood before the glass door to be granted entrance. As if by magic, it slid open, and I approached the larger of the two men, a wide counter between us.

"*Buona sera, Signore*—Good afternoon, sir. I am looking for my family, and I need to find the archive office."

"*Madama*," he said, "*questa è una banca.*" This is a bank.

Ouch. That was biting sarcasm. *Madama* is used to address a woman of high social status.

"Yes, yes," I answered in Italian. "I know that. But the information office in the lobby is closed. Can you help me?"

His voice lowered, and he enunciated every word as if he were speaking to a small child or an idiot. "*Madama,*" he repeated more loudly, "*Questa è una banca.*"

I believed I'd found the brother of the Hawk in Lucca's Archivio di Stato. The second man stood to one side, observing. Now he walked toward me, perhaps to eject me forcefully out the magic door. I tried one more time with the big guy behind the desk.

"*Per favore, Signore, dove ci sono i ricordi archivi?*" Where are the archive records?

His eyelids narrowed to slits. "*Lì, vada lì, alla porta gialla,*" he said in a gruff voice. There, go there, to the yellow door. He waved his index finger at a tall building across the creek.

I could see no sign of said door but figured it might become visible at closer range.

"*Grazie,*" I said. I felt his angry eyes burning into my back as I waited at the glass door to be allowed out.

"What did he say?" Robert asked.

"It's a *banca*. Oh, and look for *la porta gialla*."

We crossed over the bridge and circled the three-story building; no *porta gialla*. Robert stepped into the empty street and craned his neck to see the third floor. He shielded his eyes with one hand and said, "There it is, the yellow door!"

We scaled the zigzag of four steep flights of outside stairs. I flashed back to my tortured ankle on our previous trip and gave a prayer of thanks to be pain free.

Robert grasped the latch, and the yellow door opened into a room lined with ledgers and books, several card files, and a desktop computer. A slender, soft-spoken man stepped forward to help us. With his classic Italian face, dark hair and eyes, he blended into the brown background of the small library. He didn't speak English, so I requested information for Domenico Rossi and Irene Bottari, Noni's grandparents, in my best Italian.

He checked the 1866 census records for Farnocchia, apparently the oldest ones on file. He checked another location, and another. Then he returned to say, "*Mi dispiace*." I'm sorry.

My Rossi-Bottari family was not listed. "Maybe they moved away," I said.

The archivist shook his head. "There is another possibility. In 1996, a terrible flash flood did extensive damage to four thousand homes in this entire region. Roads were ripped out. Some villages were isolated for days." Tears brimmed in his eyelids. "Thirteen lives were lost. Perhaps your family records perished as well."

Maybe he was so passionate about his job, his inability to meet my request caused visible pain. More likely, that flood had delivered a terrible personal loss.

I couldn't mask my disappointment.

He studied my face, then jotted a note on a small piece of paper and handed me the slip. "This is the name of a priest in Stazzema. He might be able to help you."

I pictured us wandering around another remote village in search of a black robe. My *grazie* was not enthusiastic.

Back on ground level, I peered over the bridge to a crystal-clear stream cascading over rocks and boulders. "How could floodwaters have reached the third floor?" I said to Robert.

"Maybe the records weren't on the third floor back then. Maybe whatever they salvaged was moved to a safer spot after the disaster." Robert paused. "It doesn't get any easier, does it?"

I shook my head. "The archbishop's archives closed in Lucca, and now this. A flood! I really thought it would be different this time."

Robert gave me a reassuring hug. "We'll leave for Farnocchia first thing tomorrow."

The next morning, the hotel dining room was decked out in white linen, with chairs for at least sixty guests. More tables were set in the next room, the trattoria, and even more outside in the covered patio on the creek side of the building.

At breakfast, the innkeeper/waitress asked, "Will you need reservations for dinner tonight?"

We gave each other a look. The hotel lobby was always empty, and last night we saw only one other couple in the dining room. Robert requested the seven thirty slot, and she printed our names in the log. We kept our laughter in check until we were out of earshot. Really? We were the only two guests registered in the entire three-story hotel.

26

Farnocchia

The blue VAI minibus to Farnocchia pulled up in front of the Banca of Pontestazzemese. Robert found a seat near the back and wedged himself against the side wall.

We began the tortuous ascent through the Apuan Alps, these mountains much newer and more treacherous than the rolling western slopes of the Apennines in the Brancoli region. Sharp, spiky protrusions capped sheer bluffs, only a narrow ribbon of asphalt away from deep chasms. The driver maneuvered around each turn by drifting from one side of the road to the other, just to get the van around the corner. He constantly moved his legs and arms: gear down, honk, accelerate, brake, squeeze by another vehicle inch by inch, turn, gear up, repeat. A few village stops and forty minutes later, we arrived at Farnocchia, and Robert exhaled.

We strolled up the road and around the corner, scattered houses on the hill to our left, a forested drop-off to our right, and Franca's Alimentari, the only store in town, straight ahead. Inside, crammed into a small space, shelves brimmed with produce and pasta, blankets and batteries. A glass cooler held meats and cheeses. Three shoppers spoke a sharper, harsher Italian dialect I didn't understand. *What if we came all this way to be stopped by an unexpected language barrier?* When the customers finished their purchases, I approached a male clerk and said in my familiar Italian,

"I'm looking for information about my family." To my relief, he switched from the local dialect and responded in the Italian I knew.

"You should talk to Franca," he said.

A woman appeared from an adjacent room, brown curls framing a smiling face, sturdy body accustomed to stocking shelves and moving goods. I told her in Italian that my great-grandfather Agostino Rossi was born here, and I hoped to find church records of my Bottari-Rossi family.

"Repeat the names, please," she said.

"Agostino Rossi's parents, Romualdo Rossi and Irene Bottari, were all born here."

"There is a farmer who has keys to the church. His name is Bruno Bottari. I will phone him." She disappeared into another room. The ten-minute wait seemed like an hour.

Franca returned to say, "Signore Bottari has agreed to meet with you this afternoon. Come this way, please." She led us outside, where an old man sat on a bench. His clothes hung loosely on a slender frame, his thin white hair surrounding a pale, wrinkled face.

"Please, take a little walk with the *Americani*," she said to the man. "Show them the village." The old man uncurled, stretched his back, and smiled.

"Come this way," he said. It seemed that Franca had the respect of the villagers. We had stumbled upon a community leader, the go-to person for problem solving.

We followed our tour guide to *fare un giro*—take a tour around the village. Farnocchia was perched on a mountainside with steep forests in all directions and set against a dramatic background of rocky gray and white crags soaring in the distance. Getting from one block to another involved walking down the hill, then climbing stairs of limestone or marble to skirt houses bathed in white or pale yellow, all with terra cotta tile roofs. Red geraniums and pink impatiens cascaded from every balcony; pots of blue hydrangea and red rock roses flanked every door. The village was immaculate, as if it had been thoroughly swept and dusted for a photo shoot this very morning. We returned to the piazza out of breath from countless stairs, but managed multiple *grazies* for the old man.

I spotted a skinny sign attached to the wall of the Alimentari: *Bar, Trattoria da Franca.* A side entrance to the building opened to the bar, then a flight of stairs up to the trattoria. We found seats at a table for two as lunch was being served on starched white table linen: trays of antipasto—fresh vegetables, salami slices, olives, and cherry tomatoes—followed by the woodsy taste of wild mushrooms permeating egg-pasta ribbons in a savory-sweet cream sauce, all accompanied by vino. The sumptuous meal ended with a perfect half-dome of chocolate mocha gelato with a white vanilla center, followed by a cup of the finest cappuccino—all this for less than twenty euro for two.

"I think I hear my arteries slamming shut," Robert groaned. "We need to *fare un giro* several more times around Farnocchia."

At the top of the stairs above Franca's Alimentari, we gazed at a black-and-white painting of a marble miner, signed by an artist named Vagilio. The miner's sledgehammer was buried in a cleft of white rock.

"Those wide shoulders and upper body were developed, day after day, by swinging a heavy hammer like that against a wedge," Robert said. "Just imagine the strength it took to split marble."

"We're staring back in time," I said. "My great-grandfather was a miner here in Farnocchia. That could have been Agostino Rossi, the way he looked a century ago."

Back on street level, we chatted with the locals in the piazza and watched the road for Signore Bottari, the man with the church key. Hours dragged by.

Four o'clock. I began to pace. It was less than two hours before the last bus of the day was to leave. We watched two little girls play in the courtyard under the watchful eyes of old women, probably grandmothers and great-aunts. A man tried to organize a hunt for *cinghiali* (wild boar), and there was a great deal of discussion about how many dogs were needed.

Four thirty. The grocery truck arrived, and Franca arranged the next delivery. A couple of Italian tourists bickered over whether their relationship would be sealed in marriage; odds were good that the bachelor would remain single.

Five o'clock. I tried to stay focused on an eighty-year-old woman who was sharing a story about family members who had left long ago for the United States. I paced.

Finally, a couple appeared, sauntering up the road toward the piazza. It was now five ten. Our bus would arrive in thirty-five minutes.

"*Signore Bottari?*"

"*Sì, sì!*" Of course! He conducted a brief interview, asking twice for me to repeat the names of my family members.

"Romualdo Rossi and Irene Bottari, both born here in Farnocchia," I said in Italian.

"You should go back to Pontestazzemese, to the archive office." Bruno clearly didn't want to hand-hold a couple of tourists who might need lots of help translating priests' writing.

"We were there yesterday. There were no records of my family. Apparently, they were lost in the flood," I said. "We're anxious to get into the church, but we need to move quickly. Our bus will arrive at five forty-five."

He paused, nodded. "Yes, there was a flood in 1996 that wiped out most of the buildings in Pontestazzemese. Terrible disaster. Terrible."

Didn't he understand me?

"Notebook. I forgot to bring a notebook," I said to Robert.

Signore Bottari watched Robert bolt across the piazza and disappear into the general store.

"*Va bene,*" he said. It goes well.

It's not going well at all, I thought. *I'm ready to scream, jump up and down, tear at my hair.*

Then Signore Bottari and his wife led me, at an agonizingly slow pace, up the hill to the Church of San Michele. As he unlocked the door, I looked at my watch—five twenty-five. Robert arrived panting and handed me a newly purchased spiral notebook.

We entered a cool sanctuary with a pale, blue-and-white domed backdrop. Paintings extended up the walls and along the curved ceiling. Marble statues and artwork graced the nave and several chapels. Signore Bottari told us to wait, and he disappeared down a corridor. *Oh, no, another delay.* I asked his wife if we might take photos, no flash, and she nodded yes.

Signore Bottari returned with a key and unlocked a cabinet, revealing shelves of ancient registers. "What would you like to see?"

"*Nati, matrimoni, morti,*" I answered quickly. Births, marriages, deaths.

He pulled out five random registers and opened one. The names Rossi and Bottari leaped from the pages. Robert clicked the camera as I wrote rapidly, with time for only three scribbled entries. I looked at my watch—five forty. I placed my pencil and notebook in my purse. In an act worthy of an Academy Award, I calmly smiled. Inside, I was weeping like a child.

"*Grazie,*" I said, "*ma c'è un problema*—but there is a problem. I cannot do it. The bus is coming now."

Signore Bottari said, "*Ma non c'è* un problema—but there isn't a problem. We will meet tomorrow!" He was beaming. "I cannot stay with you in the church. You will have to work alone. You must ask Franca to call me just as soon as you arrive, and I will come."

"*Grazie, grazie, allora domani*—well then, tomorrow!" I shouted as we raced down the hill to meet the bus.

"Did you understand what he said?" I asked Robert as we boarded VAI. "This is huge! Bruno will let us work alone in the locked church. Nothing is possible and everything is possible. I love this country. I love Bruno. I wonder if we're related."

A couple of hours later, back in Pontestazzemese, we entered the large, vacant dining room in La Pania restaurant, its many tables dressed for dinner.

"*Buona sera. Prenotazione?*" the waiter asked. Do we have a reservation?

"*Sì, Claypool, alle sette e mezzo.*" Seven thirty.

He penciled a checkmark in his notebook before leading us through an arched entry to a table for two. One other couple sat at the opposite end of the trattoria. Robert chuckled as he gazed at squares of white linen and tableware filling two big rooms and a covered patio.

Within a half hour, four other couples arrived. Soon, more followed in twos and threes. Over the next half hour, more than a hundred people poured through the doors. After being seated, with shouts and waves of recognition, many picked up their *bicchiere di vino*, sauntered over to another table, and dragged up a chair. With general confusion and milling about—like starlings swirling in for a landing, rising and landing again—diners finally settled in. Waiters wove through the crowd, pizza tray held high in one hand, wine bottle in the other. As people left, more arrived at the packed house, now filled with noisy patrons celebrating life at a gigantic pizza party. The joy, the camaraderie—this was the face of Italy I loved.

The next morning, after enjoying a complimentary pastry and cappuccino, we strolled out to the bus stop. Near the bridge, we counted trout in the clear stream that bisected the village while we waited for the familiar whine of the bus engine echoing up the canyon.

"Look at that fish, no longer than ten inches," Robert said. "He's lying there in that little pocket waiting for a morsel to come through his feeding lane. That channel is roughly eighteen inches wide and no more than sixteen inches deep. Look, he just came out, took that midge, and slid back to his hiding place. And there he goes again."

My spouse, an avid fly fisherman, was more interested in trout feeding behavior and stream entomology than the task ahead. If there hadn't been a "No fishing" sign, he might have found a way to test these waters.

For a brief moment, I wondered if I could endure that wild ride through the Apuan Alps one more time as a full-fledged acrophobic with a travel partner prone to vertigo. But the hope of finding my family records far outweighed my fears, and we climbed aboard VAI, bound for Farnocchia.

Along the way, the minibus slowed, crossed the road, and crept scant inches away from the upside of the mountain. I rose from my aisle seat to see the problem on the other side of the bus. A slide had created a jagged bite in the highway, with chunks of earth and asphalt strewn down the steep canyon. Just yesterday the road was intact. I turned to say something to Robert, who was pressed into the corner, his eyes tightly closed.

Finally, safely deposited in Farnocchia, we hurried to meet Franca at the general store.

"*Buon giorno*. Signore Bottari told us to ask for him. I believe he is expecting a telephone call," I said.

Franca smiled. "That won't be necessary. He's waiting for you at the church."

We darted up the hill and met Bruno Bottari at the entry. He opened the thick wooden door, and we stepped inside.

Bruno gave instructions in Italian. "When I leave, you will be locked in. When you are finished with the books, please put them here on the table to be filed. You may use the push bar to get out, but once outside, you cannot reenter. Do you have any questions?"

"Just one. When we were here yesterday, I noticed multiple entries on the same page written by different priests. Do you know why that was necessary?"

"The Church of San Michele was the parish church with many smaller churches and chapels under its jurisdiction." Bruno waved at books shelved in the unlocked cabinet. "This was the central location for records, so priests came here from surrounding villages to document religious events in these registers."

With a wish for good luck in our research, Bruno left the building at eleven o'clock, the lock on the great doors clanging shut behind him. Once more, he had taken my breath away. This church kept information for the entire region, every entry in chronological order. That meant we could trace family members in surrounding villages without leaving this site. These records held more than I had dreamed possible.

Light streamed through the high windows, illuminating the cabinet and the workspace. We sat alone in the complete silence of the empty church. A marble statue of Mother Mary looked down on us. No doubt my ancestors had been moved by her presence in this very spot. It was strangely reassuring to know she was there as we pored over parochial registers.

I found a great-great-great-grandmother with no last name; birthplace, a Lucca nunnery. I imagined a newborn being placed into a cradle in a foundling wheel outside stone walls. With a push of the handle, the wheel moved like a revolving door, and the baby disappeared into the convent. The bell cord was pulled, and a heartbroken mother retreated into the dark night. I hoped that this infant, raised by nuns, had found love and joy here in Farnocchia.

Four hours later we emerged, bleary-eyed, with photos of documents, notebooks full of family trees, and records of twenty-seven direct ancestors, some reaching back five hundred years. We were stopped by records dated before 1600. Scrawled in blurred Latin, barely legible brown ink on powdery yellow paper, we could go no further.

"How can anything top this day?" I said.

Robert grinned. "I think you said that once before, just before Mila found Ada Motroni."

We strolled down the hill and savored the fresh scent of the forest, leaves whispering the story of what villages were like before the tourists arrived in Italy. No traffic, carefully tended gardens, bird songs, every turn in the road a visual marvel of alpine peaks and valleys; I looked through Agostino's eyes at the world he saw a century ago.

Around the corner, the piazza and general store came into view. Franca Uliva, the woman who had made it all possible, posed for photos. A short time later, Bruno and his wife sauntered up the road to meet us. We gave him our profound thanks and a donation to be used at his discretion. He declined. I insisted. The four of us smiled for the camera. In the photo, the fifty-euro bill protruded at a slant from Bruno's shirt pocket, his way of saying, *I'll tolerate this, but we really don't need your money.*

I turned to Bruno's wife and asked, "*Per favore, come si chiama?*" What is your name? Then came the final surprise. Bruno Bottari was married to Adrianna Rossi.

I grinned and held my arms out wide. "Bottari? Rossi? *Siamo cugini!*" We are cousins!

They laughed and said it was *certamente possibile*—certainly possible.

"*Arrivederci*—until we see each other again," we said, knowing this might be our last meeting. I had hated the thought of coming here, and now I wanted to stay forever.

The bus ride didn't seem as dangerous as before. Robert held my hand as we swayed side to side down the convoluted road to Pontestazzemese.

27

Public Transportation, Italian Style

Sunday morning, we hauled our luggage out to the bus stop and checked the sign: there was an eight thirty-five departure for Pietrasanta. No cars, no buses, no motorbikes on the streets, just eerie silence. Twenty minutes went by, then forty; no familiar engine whine in the canyon.

We peered at the metal sign with odd regularity, as if it could change while we weren't looking. Finally, a man approached on the empty street.

"*Mi scusa,*" I began. "We wait for the bus, but it doesn't come. Is there a problem?"

"No problem, but look here, *Festive* [fes-*tee*-veh]." He pointed at a small, framed box of information within the sign.

"*Festive?* Is today a holiday?"

"Today is *Domenica,*" he said. "This is the bus schedule for Sunday."

"I don't understand. It doesn't say *Domenica.*"

"*Festa, Domenica*—both are *Festive.*" He pointed at the little square again. "One bus leaves today at two o'clock. *Festive!*"

"Now what?" Robert groaned. "The shops are closed, the streets are empty, there's no restaurant, no place to wait for the next bus."

We trudged back to Hotel La Pania and explained our dilemma to the innkeeper. She gave us the key to our room at no extra charge. "It's okay. We don't clean until two o'clock." *Grazie Dio.* Thank God.

A few hikes around the village and five hours later, we boarded the *Festive* bus and snaked through the canyon back to Pietrasanta, with scant minutes to spare for the train to Lucca.

At the unmanned transfer station near Viareggio, we milled about on a crowded platform. Lights were out in the overhead message boards, and there were no train schedules listed. I approached an old Italian couple for directions to the platform for Lucca. A pair of women from Washington hovered nearby. They couldn't speak Italian, and they, too, were trying to reach Lucca. They tagged along as we wove upstairs and back down to another level. Everywhere we looked, not a single electronic sign was lit.

"What has happened?" I asked a man in a business suit.

"*Sciopero* [*sho*-per-oh]*!*" he said.

"Railroad strike," I said. "We're stuck in the transfer station. No train, no bus, no taxi, no service." The Washington duo looked stunned.

"No one is leaving," I said. "I think we should stay here."

Ten minutes, twenty, thirty. We all checked our watches. Finally, forty minutes later a train arrived, a "limited" bound for Lucca. We sprinted down the platform and dove through the door, the Washington women right behind us. Robert gave his seat to an older woman. Late arrivals stood in packed aisles or sat on luggage. Nearly an hour later, we stepped down at the Lucca train station.

"Nothing to eat since that pastry at breakfast. I'm famished!" Robert said. He crumpled onto a park bench near a trattoria and guarded our bags as I waited in the crowd for pizza to go. Then we wound through cobblestone streets, lugging suitcases and dinner for two, with Lucca's dim overhead lights guiding us to the big double doors outside two small piazzas to the condo.

"The flashlight is somewhere in our bags," Robert said. "Do you want to unpack? Or do we try to find our way in the dark? We didn't leave a light on."

"Let's go for it," I said. We had made that trip across the courtyard so many times, I was certain we'd find our apartment.

The massive outer doors to our small piazza clanged shut behind us. We held hands, brailed our way along the walls, toe-tapped across the tiled floor through two jet-black courtyards, found our doorknob through trial and error, and finally turned the key to our front door. Home at last!

28

Archives Revisited

We planned a surprise visit with our friends at Archivio Storico. Lucca's morning sunlight bounced off the glass doors as I pushed the buzzer for entrance. Mariella Morotti greeted us with big smiles and open arms. I practiced Italian as we caught up on two years of news.

"We have a problem," I said. "We can't research the parish records of Brancoli because the archbishop's archives are closed for the entire month of September. Our only other resource is Archivio di Stato for census records."

Mariella retrieved a small piece of paper, jotted a few notes, and signed it.

"Take this to Archivio di Stato. I will make an appointment for you." Like Maria, this wonder woman could unlock archive doors with her signature. We made a lunch date and gave her photos taken two years before, of me with Maria, Mariella, and Cristina, the three wise women of Storico.

We crossed through busy brick streets and cobblestone byways to the opposite side of the walled city. I took a deep breath as Robert pushed open the doors of Archivio di Stato.

I paused. "I'm not looking forward to meeting the Hawk again."

"Maybe he was transferred to some remote outpost, like the top of Mt. Vesuvius," Robert said.

We climbed steep stairs to the third floor. "No wonder the Italians are so slim. Imagine doing this several times a day."

I retrieved the little piece of paper signed by Mariella and handed it to the man at the reception desk. He left briefly and returned with a smiling woman with curly brown hair. I recognized Dotoressa Laura Busti, the woman who had helped us two years earlier. When I stated my name, she said Mariella had called about our coming. A male librarian placed indexes and large volumes of *censimenti*—Brancoli census records for 1809 and 1823—on our library table. He apologized; the secretary was out. It wouldn't be possible to get copies downstairs.

Robert pointed at his camera. "Photo? No flash?"

"*Sì, sì*, no flash!"

"No Hawk," I whispered to Robert.

"Vesuvius," he said.

A couple of hours later, after poring over countless entries, we left the building with more names and dates for my Pieroni-Carli relatives, digital copies in the camera. We had finally found the right Pietro Pieroni, along with his parents and grandparents.

The kind attention on the part of the staff had been a huge turnaround from the rude behavior we had experienced on our arrival two years prior, when we had attempted research here on our own without an ally. We walked back to our apartment, grateful for our discoveries. It seemed that in Lucca, progress was made not by what one knew but who one knew.

That afternoon, after a series of missed appointments and messages to reschedule, Mila finally arrived at our apartment at four o'clock, three hours late but vivacious and charming as ever. She seemed overextended between obligations with her grandchildren in Lucca and her love interest,

Rino, who lived two hours away. We learned that during our absence from Italy, Mila and Gabriella had visited with Ada Motroni, my distant cousin we had found at the birthday party in the pink church on our last visit.

"She is an amazing woman. I like her," Mila said. "I will call Ada to make all the arrangements, and we will drive to her home in San Giusto di Brancoli next week."

Mila continued to deliver surprises. This one left me speechless.

29

Interlude

We opened our bedroom window to brilliant sunshine and break-your-heart soul sounds from a jazz saxophone across the narrow street. A short stroll away, strains of Mozart resonated from a studio piano. Just around the corner, behind a gated courtyard, student voices practiced Puccini. Another twist, another turn, and the triumphant scales of a trumpet filled the air. Lucca was a giant music box with concerts every night.

"How can we moan and groan about hard times in Lucca?" Robert said. "This is fabulous."

In less than twenty minutes, we could walk the entire width of Lucca Centre; thirty minutes covered the length. Within those oval walls, forty churches held exquisite art and history, just a small portion of riches once held in Lucca. Napoleon had carried away untold wealth during his ten-year reign in the early nineteenth century. Museums and mansions allowed vibrant glimpses into the past lives of the *Lucchesi*—athlete and poet, mother and child, peasant and statesman, all suspended in time by larger-than-life sculptures. We gaped at brush strokes of brilliant artists whose passion had captured pain and pleasure, rage and bliss.

At Palazzo Pfanner, open to the public, we explored the mansion still owned by the Pfanner family. In its formal grounds, we wound around waterfalls and ponds, exotic flowers and exquisite statues. We learned there was a beer garden here in the late 1800s. My family might have visited this lovely spot when they carried their wine and olive oil to Lucca's markets. I mind-whispered to my grandmother, "Noni, were you here? Did you press your face against these cool marble walls to escape the summer heat? Did you play in this garden?"

With more time to explore, we rented bicycles and pushed them up the ramp to the top of Lucca's wall. The wide promenade provided a haven for pedestrians, bikes, and baby strollers. We had just started a leisurely ride when a loudspeaker suddenly blared commands in Italian.

"What did he say?" Robert asked.

"I don't know. Maybe we should get off the track."

We had barely shoved our wheels onto the grassy area when we spotted a car zooming around the corner straight toward us. A car—on top of Lucca's wall! Close behind were uniformed cyclists, helmeted heads over handlebars. We had stumbled into a *gara bici*—a bike race. Primary colors streaked by. Just out of sight around the bend, a crowd roared encouragement. More cars, more teams, more cheers, more garbled shouts from loudspeakers; this was going to be a long event. We retreated into Lucca's cobblestone streets to dodge autos, pedestrians, and one horse-drawn carriage on our way back to the bike barn.

The next morning, we boarded the train in Lucca and stepped down in Florence an hour later. To cross the Arno River, we joined the crush of pedestrians funneling onto Ponte Vecchio. The "Old Bridge" supported shops where tourists stopped to gawk at display windows filled with gold jewelry. Bicycle races on top of a wall and a gold market on top of a bridge. Italy defied logic.

Across the river, through a clog of sightseers, the massive gold-colored Pitti Palace begged for exploration. We wandered for hours through an astonishing collection of paintings and sculpture, most from the

Renaissance period—massive works that covered walls and ceilings. Salons were adorned with gold, reflected in crystal prisms, and draped in the finest silk brocade. In the hills behind the palace, Boboli Gardens stretched for 111 acres—manicured lawns and trees interspersed with fountains, reflecting pools, an amphitheater, enormous floral displays, gigantic statues, and wide marble stairs that climbed forever. This was the home of the ruling families of Florence, and later, Tuscany. Their accumulation of wealth challenged my imagination.

The fruits of my family's labor might have been served at their tables: wine poured into crystal goblets; a silver platter of fire-roasted *cinghiale*—wild boar—from mountain forests; olive oil drizzled over vegetables on gold-rimmed plates; sweet delicacies of *dolce farina*—chestnut flour— served on a porcelain tray. The privileged were fed by three tiers of farmers: *padroni, mezzadri,* and *contadini*—landowners, sharecroppers, and farm laborers, people of the earth, my people. They had endured through the centuries. I had found some of them still tending their crops in those steep Brancoli hills. Now, their offspring toured the abandoned estates of royal families.

30

Back to Brancoli

The following Wednesday, Mila and Gabriella arrived at our apartment to whisk us away to the Brancoli region. We stopped in a small town along the way to find *caramelle*, candies, for my cousin Ada Motroni, but the shop had closed permanently.

Buckled in once more, we followed a serpentine ribbon of asphalt as we climbed through the Apennine foothills toward the village of San Giusto. Mila no longer crossed her fingers and said, "*Madre mia!*" at every curve. She didn't check with Gabriella for directions. She honked and paused briefly at blind turns, then powered through. During our two-year absence, Mila had mastered the art of driving on the roads of Brancoli.

"Ada's son built this for her," Mila said. She pulled into the driveway of a large home with a spectacular view to the valley far below, an ancient gray church perched a short distance away. Backed by a mountainside with scattered trees and well-maintained Tuscan houses, this home seemed out of a fairy tale.

Mila rapped at the entrance. The front door opened wide, and ninety-six-year-old Ada Motroni said, "*Buona sera!*" with a wide grin, her short, auburn-dyed hair surrounding a round face etched by decades in the Tuscan sun. Today she wore black and white, her mid-length skirt swinging above bare legs. Her carefully painted, iridescent toenails peeked out of white wedge-soled sandals.

Mila apologized profusely; we had tried to find *caramelle*, but the shop was gone. Ada waved off the problem and led us into a bright kitchen and dining area, clutter-free and spotless. We settled at an enormous round table. I imagined her large family seated here, through joys and sorrows, squabbles and laughter, celebrations marking the milestones of generations. I envied the richness of her simple life. Our five-minute meeting two years ago had not given us enough time to get to know this sweet little lady, who was old enough to be my mother.

"I made coffee for you," Ada said.

"Thank you, Ada, but we just had coffee," Mila said.

Ada argued, Mila rebutted. I saw a new side of Ada: a spirited woman with a loud voice. The heated discussion escalated as I squirmed. I wanted to say, "Let's just drink the coffee, for God's sake." Then the argument was over as quickly as it began, all smiles, sans coffee.

Ada brought out some black-and-white family photos and spread them on the table.

"Look, that's my father, and my sister is milking the cow. She's laughing. She thought everything was amusing. And this one, my big family under the tree, and my mother—that's lace in her hands; she was always weaving lace. That one is me at my wedding, and in this one I was a girl—maybe in my twenties. I have to get more *foto*."

"*Che memoria*," Mila said. What a memory.

Ada smiled and sauntered off to climb the stairs, her wedge-heeled shoes slapping against the soles of her feet. I held my breath as she returned down the polished wooden steps with boxes in her arms. What if she tumbled! But she demonstrated unusual agility for an elderly woman and returned to the table without incident. As we pored over old documents and photos, Ada's daughters, grandchildren, and great-grandchildren wove in and out of her ample kitchen, stopping long enough for greetings.

Two listened in, providing clarification in some discussions. "Yes, Ada's family once had a *serra*, a greenhouse, near this village . . . Yes, our family used to live in Gignano . . . No, we never lived in Ponte Rotto, but it was in the parish of San Giusto."

That last statement opened another door. San Giusto was listed as Noni's birthplace. It was entirely possible that she was born at home in Ponte Rotto, in San Giusto parish.

Mila and Gabriella settled into easy Italian conversation and shared some of their own stories. Mila complained that she longed to travel, but her boyfriend, Rino, didn't want to leave Italy.

Ada responded, "Go on vacation, Mila. You don't need your boyfriend. Take a salami."

Mila's face flushed a rosy glow, and we laughed. Ada wasn't the mild-mannered little old lady I had dreamed up, but a firecracker of wit with a wicked sense of humor, much more fun to know.

We all squeezed into Mila's car and drove to a nearby church, where Ada said we could find family records. Mountains and sky formed a breathtaking backdrop, brush-stroked blue on blue, soft wisps of white rising from the river far below. A sign in the parking lot read, "The church is open from 8.30 to 18.00." Of course, the priest was out today—another locked door.

Mila raised her hands into the air. "The church is always open unless it's closed."

Dusk was closing in. Ada gave directions as Mila maneuvered the car through twists and turns to a house nestled in the hills. "There is a man up there. He made a chart of the Motroni family. Park here, Mila."

"I can't park here," Mila said. "This is in the middle of a fork in the road."

"Park here, park here," Ada ordered.

"But I can't. Cars have to get by. I have to go up a little farther." Mila stopped at a narrow space that caused the car to tilt upward, making its doors more difficult to open against gravity.

"You should have parked back there where I told you," Ada grumbled. Robert held the door as she struggled to get out of the car. "I'm not sure where he is. But he's somewhere here."

We were losing daylight. Mila, Gabriella, and Robert walked toward a lighted cottage, but Ada struck off toward a little building with a darkened window. I followed close behind. She rapped on the door—no answer. She tried again.

"Ada," I said in Italian, "No one is here. It's getting dark. Maybe we should return."

Ada turned and said, "If you can't keep up, maybe you should go to the car."

I was glad she couldn't see my shoulders shake with silent laughter.

She trudged in her wobbly sandals on the dark pathways, with God knows how many obstacles, and peered around sheds and other out-buildings looking for the missing man. Finally, she returned to the house with lighted windows, where Robert, Mila and Gabriella waited near the front door.

"Ah, there you are," Ada said, as if they had lost their way and finally showed up. "We'll try the door. Maybe he is visiting." She marched up to the entrance and rapped. She greeted a white-haired couple, who stepped outside to talk. Ada called them both by name, but the old man didn't respond. She began quizzing him about the Motroni family chart. The old man shook his head, shrugged his shoulders, and raised his palms upward.

"You made the chart," Ada said. "Do you have a copy here?"

The old man smiled and repeated the shoulder shrug.

The woman by his side said, "Perhaps he doesn't remember."

Ada seemed annoyed, as if dementia were no excuse for rude behavior. She threw her hands up in the air, then plunged them down in a gesture that said, *I am so finished with you.*

We said *grazie* and *buona sera* and followed her back to the car.

"That's okay," Ada said. "My cousin has a copy. You call me. I will give you her address."

We drove Ada back to her home, and she asked us to let her out at the bottom of the hill instead of driving up to her door. Mila argued. Ada insisted. We shared brief hugs. Then, instead of following the curved road, Ada climbed straight up the darkened knoll, easily navigating uneven rocks and steep terrain in those impossible shoes. She paused long enough to wave goodbye.

"Will she be all right?" Robert asked Mila.

"She's been doing this all her life. She'll be fine," Mila said as we drove away.

I turned to see Ada, pushing on one flexed knee for added power to reach the crest. If I hadn't seen that spectacle, I wouldn't have believed it possible.

"Where are we going?" I asked, as Mila followed switchbacks cutting into the mountain.

"We have to go to Piazza di Brancoli. The book is there," Mila said.

"The book? What book?"

"It has something to do with your Cecchettini [Che-ke-*tee*-nee] family," Mila said.

I recognized the village we had visited two years ago, where we'd met the woman with the photo of my family in her attic. I had no idea why we had returned to Piazza di Brancoli. Mila parked next to the short wall, and I stepped out of the car into the central courtyard. This time, something new caught my attention: a large watercolor poster advertising an art show in Lucca, signed by Marjorie Werner Picchi.

"Oh, that's the American," Gabriella said. "She still has a house here, but now she stays in an apartment in Lucca."

I gazed at the painting—the evocative turn in the road, golden houses with subtle hues of red tiled roofs, tucked with greens against a blue mountain.

"This is enchantment; she's captured the magic of Brancoli," I said to Robert. "We've missed her reception, but the exhibit is still on in Lucca. I'd love to see more of her work." Robert snapped the image as I jotted down the address in my notebook.

Gabriella led the way as we climbed up steep curving steps in the hillside, the same path that led to her daughter's house. This time we turned toward a light-yellow stucco home a short distance away. Gabriella knocked on the carved wooden door.

A tall, slender man answered. He was about our age, with handsome features and kind eyes.

"*Signore Cecchettini?*" Gabriella asked.

"*Sì, Ubaldo Cecchettini.*"

"Tell him your story. Show him *foto*," Mila said to me.

"My husband and I are here from the United States to find my family," I said in Italian. I retrieved my little picture album from my purse and pointed to the sepia photo of a beautiful woman. "This was my *bisnonna*, Marianna Fambrini. Her mother was Maria Annunziata Cecchettini. I hope to find information about her people."

"Come in, come in," he said.

The four of us entered a small but tastefully decorated living room, with neatly arranged pillows on the couch and upholstered chairs. We remained standing.

"I heard that you had a book about the Cecchettini family," Gabriella said.

"*Sì, sì.* It has been some time since I last looked at it. Perhaps I can find it."

Signore Cecchettini walked over to a large desk, bent down to the cabinet below, and opened the double doors. He moved to one side to allow lamplight onto its contents. His right thumb riffled through papers wedged in at odd angles and traveled down one stack. With his other hand he lifted magazines, paused briefly, and moved on. He repeated the process along the top shelf and moved to the lower level. His fingers tapped along papers as if they were playing piano keys. They danced all the way down the stack, stopped, moved back up, and paused at a clump of white pages. Ubaldo reached in with both hands, steadying papers above while he pulled out a booklet.

"*Eccola!*" Here it is!

He handed me the bound sheets of paper. "Cecchettini Family" was printed in English on the top. The name of the author appeared at the bottom of fifty-six pages: Eugene J. Cecchettini; December 15, 1998.

I opened the document to the first entry, also written in English.

First Generation:
1. Gio. Domenico Cecchettini was born CA 1650.
He married an unknown person.
Gio. Domenico Cecchettini had the following children.

I scanned through names in the second and third generations and stopped at the next list.

Fourth Generation:
Giovanni Domenico Cecchettini and Lucia Gaddi had the following children:
49. ii. Ma. Annunziata Cecchettini was born in P. di Brancoli Feb. 7, 1806. She married Domenico Fambrini in P. di Brancoli Apr. 22, 1841.
Domenico was the son of Giulio Fambrini.

"Oh! It's them! It's Marianna's parents!" Tears filled my eyes. I could barely speak. Marianna had lived here in Piazza di Brancoli. No wonder there was a photo of her in the attic of the reluctant neighbor we met two years ago. Time was dissolving. Marianna had found her way into this place, this night. "I'm holding my great-grandmother's family history!"

"*Per favore, Signore, possiamo fare foto?*" Please, sir, may we take pictures?

"*No, no,*" he answered. My hopes sank deep into a new ache in my chest.

"You must take this book to Lucca, where you can make proper photocopies," he said.

"What? I can take this book with me?" I repeated. Ubaldo Cecchettini was handing over his ancestral tree, this treasured document, to a stranger.

"I won't be able to return it tomorrow," I said.

"Keep it as long as you like," he answered. "Bring it back when you are finished."

How do you thank a person when words fail? Once again, "*Grazie, grazie mille,*" was all I could manage.

"I can't believe it. How is it possible? This would have taken months of research. What a find!" I babbled.

We found our way back to Mila's car and followed the winding road down the mountain toward the Serchio River.

"We want to buy you dinner," Robert announced as we approached Lucca's lights.

"No, no, impossible," Mila answered.

"You and Gabriella have done so much for us. Please let us do this," I begged.

Mila argued. I insisted.

"We'll go to a pizza parlor," Gabriella said.

"No! We want to find a place to dine in the heart of the city—you deserve more than pizza."

"But we like pizza. We will order beer. We stop here." Mila swerved with sudden conviction into a parking lot, giant umbrellas dotting the patio full of customers. "This is the perfect spot for three crazy women and one very patient man."

We found a table for four, the last available seats. Robert took his first bite, closed his eyes, and groaned. "Italian pizza is like nothing else in the world."

I tasted the delicacy, a thin crust of whole wheat kneaded with an ancient yeast, the rich creamy flavor of water-buffalo mozzarella, melded with savory tomatoes patiently simmered with Italian seasonings, and baked in a wood-fired oven.

With the miraculous key to my family history in my purse, I filled my senses with food and friendship. I remembered the flash mob in Pontestazzemese, the giant pizza party that filled the restaurant, empty one moment, packed to the rafters the next. There, we were outsiders, vicarious observers sidelined on the fringe. This time the camaraderie and the heady joy of celebration were ours.

31

Images of Lucca

The next morning, Robert paced in the kitchen. "We can't go on like this," he said dramatically. "We're out of olive oil, pasta, tomatoes. Situation critical. Time to *fare la spesa*—shop for groceries."

As we left the building, I saw the old white-haired woman sitting across the small piazza, the indirect sunlight illuminating the aluminum rails of her walker.

I said "*Buon giorno,*" just as I had each morning since our arrival two weeks before.

She turned her face away as if she hadn't heard and began talking with a friend. On the days when she sat alone, she kept her face averted. She had never spoken to us.

We returned after lunch with armloads of pasta and produce. I saw her again in her favorite chair, her stare fixed on flowers in a window down the street.

"*Buona sera,*" I said, and turned toward our door.

"*Sera,*" she said to my back.

I froze, almost dropping the groceries. I set down the bags and turned back to her as Robert fished for the key. "*Che bel giorno,*" I said. What a beautiful day.

"You do computer work?" she asked in Italian.

I answered in Italian, "Yes, we are here in Lucca to find my family, and I use the computer in my research. We are renting this apartment for the month."

"I thought so," she said. She probably would have said that if I had answered I was an artist, or a nuclear physicist, or a housekeeper.

"*Buona sera, Signora*," I said.

"*Sera*," she answered.

Robert turned the key to our door. "I wonder what came over her. She spoke!"

"She probably thought we were here to stay. She might be a little friendlier now that she knows we're just renting. Maybe the Lucchesi are sick of all the expats moving in, threatening to change the culture of the place."

Robert nodded. "Remember that guy grumbling about Lucca selling off parts of itself? People move here for the charm, the unique quality of Italian life. And then they want to open a genuine Greek restaurant, or one with Tunisian cuisine, or a McDonald's."

"I think there's a law against new foreign food restaurants in Lucca," I said.

"That's smart. Too bad there's no such law in Florence. Remember what we saw at the train station? One entire city block across the street is a McDonald's, so now the city boasts the Duomo and the Golden Arches of fast food. Doesn't seem right."

That afternoon, we strolled into the heart of Lucca and stopped at the Church of Santa Caterina. Locked up for twenty years, today the building was open to the public to garner financial support. One look inside, and it was clear that its beautiful sculptures and paintings needed restoration and repair.

"A grand old lady with torn and dirty hems," I murmured.

"Please sign this petition to save the church." A woman with a clipboard was waving a pen at us. She handed us a pamphlet.

"We don't live here," I said in Italian. "We're just renting an apartment for a month."

"*Perfetto!*" she said. "Please sign here." Robert picked up the pen. Somewhere in Lucca, our names and rental address are on a petition to save the Church of Santa Caterina.

We browsed through the pamphlet and spotted a painting of the church by Marjorie Werner Picchi, the same artist who had signed the poster in Piazza di Brancoli.

"I'd like to see more of her work," I said. "Didn't Gabriella say she has an apartment here in Lucca?" I pulled a memo pad from my purse. "I copied her address from the poster. Let's see if we can find her."

Dusk descended as we ambled along cobblestone streets in search of the artist from Brancoli. The familiar tones of apricot and amber stucco reflected a rosy glow, just as they did most evenings. Lucca was wearing her pink veil. The white walls of San Martino Cathedral blushed a faint red hue. Clouds above echoed crimson colors. Robert snapped a photo, our strange surroundings preserved in pink pixels.

At Via Battistero, addresses were elusive, numbers missing. A window display featured paintings by local artists. An antiques dealer stood nearby in his doorway.

"*Buona sera.* We're looking for the apartment of Marjorie Werner Picchi," I said.

He gestured. "It's across the way. Just ring the bell."

"Where is the bell?"

The proprietor walked across the narrow street and pressed one of three wafers in a bronze rectangle. I didn't recognize that strange object as a doorbell.

Moments later, a woman's head popped out of an upstairs window.

"*Buona sera!*"

"*Buona sera!*" the proprietor answered. "These people are looking for you."

"We were in Piazza di Brancoli and saw your poster," I said. "We can visit another time."

"Come up. I will buzz for you," she said in English.

32

Brushstrokes of Brancoli

The buzzer blared, and Robert pulled open the thick wooden door. In the small lobby, rough stone steps in irregular forms wound skyward, most tilted at odd angles, all pockmarked and misshapen.

"Looks like something the Romans left behind," Robert murmured.

A melodious voice echoed down the rock walls. "Mind the stairs. They were built by the Romans, you know."

We followed the spiral up to meet Marjorie Werner Picchi. Tall and slender, in flowing cream-colored evening pants and top, a shawl draped over her shoulders, she was the picture of grace and elegance. Her shoulder-length white hair glistened with strands of gold. We introduced ourselves and apologized for our drop-in visit.

"We saw your art in the poster. It's wonderful. You captured the magic of Brancoli. We had to see more," I said.

Marjorie led us on a tour of her small living room. Easels of watercolors were propped in one area, and walls were covered with framed artwork; the landscapes and houses of Brancoli villages dominated her paintings. I couldn't take my eyes off one: bold swaths of blue and gold capturing the sky, light bouncing off sunlit hills, shadows cast on upper walls beneath a tiled roof, a beckoning twist in the road, treetops blurred with the warm wind of summer, a partially open iron gate inviting exploration. I was stunned by her simple strokes and complicated undertones, all of which amounted to artwork we couldn't afford.

Marjorie served a plate of cheese and crackers and poured goblets of white wine. We perched on a small settee by a cube table.

"What brings you to Lucca?" she asked.

"A search for my mother's family," I said. "I wonder if you could tell me something about the history of Piazza di Brancoli."

"Ah, yes. My husband and I moved into the house in Piazza almost three decades ago. I have Italian citizenship, and I speak Italian fluently, but neighbors still call me the American. My husband passed away two years ago, and I moved here to Lucca Centre to be closer to the art community. I find the city to my liking. Now I rent out the Brancoli house to tourists."

"We saw renovations in progress in several old homes. Did your house in Piazza need work before it was livable?" Robert asked.

Marjorie laughed. "Oh my, yes. The house was a disaster. It had to be totally redone: plumbing, wiring, support beams, new roof—you name it. The big kitchen fireplace had kept animals alive in the winter. I wouldn't be surprised if they had milked a cow in there."

I pictured an empty woodbox on a stone floor by a cold hearth, a vicious blizzard raging on the other side of the door, ice crystals in a bucket of water in the corner, steam rising from the nostrils of a cow. As fierce winds howled and snow smothered the hills, perhaps the warmth of the animals kept a family like mine alive in that kitchen while they waited out the storm.

Marjorie continued her story. "My husband, Fosco, was eleven years old, living in America, when his parents took him for a visit back to their first home in Piazza. They were caught there when the Germans invaded and occupied the Brancoli villages in World War II. The villagers were confined by house arrest. Fosco slept upstairs with his mother and father while the Germans slept downstairs near the front door."

"I thought the Germans and the Italians were on the same side," Robert said.

"None of it made sense. Mussolini and his Blackshirts were crazy. The Italians here didn't want to fight that war. The German soldiers said to the villagers, 'For every one of ours killed, seven of yours will die.' Imagine that!"

"My grandmother had emigrated to America long before the war began," I said. "But she still wrote to family members and friends in the Brancoli villages. The letters must have stopped when war broke out. She must have felt so helpless, so afraid for them," I said.

"What happened to your husband?" Robert asked.

"One day the soldiers told the villagers they had twenty-four hours to gather their proof of citizenship along with what they could carry and meet in the plaza the following morning. My husband's family had American passports. They not only feared for their own lives, their presence threatened the survival of the entire village."

"My people must have been there, terrified. How did your husband stay alive?"

"During the night, Fosco and his parents escaped out an upstairs window and hid in the mountains. They lived for days on chestnuts gathered from the forest floor and water cupped in their hands from a nearby stream. Finally, they ran into an American Army regiment, all Black men, who fed and protected them. They were saved from starvation by those brave soldiers. My husband suffered with stomach problems most of his life because of that ordeal."

"I heard the radio message when the war ended," I said. "I was just five years old, too young to understand. But the man on the radio kept yelling the same sentence again and again, 'The War Is Over! The War

Is Over!' We heard the sirens blaring in Healdsburg, nine miles away. My Italian grandmother gripped the edges of her American table, tears streaming down her face. 'Thank God,' she said. 'Thank God.' I didn't know it then, but her nephew Andrew Albert Marcucci was a casualty, an American Army lieutenant. His plane was shot down in Europe during that terrible time."

The conversation drifted to family connections, and I related the strange story of finding my Cecchettini roots in Piazza in a book written by Eugene Cecchettini.

"I know Gene well," Marjorie said.

"You know him?" I repeated.

"You should have no trouble finding him. He lives just outside Sacramento."

"This is really bizarre," I said. "We follow your trail from a beautiful poster in Piazza to your home in Lucca to see your paintings, and find out, *oh, by the way*, you're a friend of the American who discovered my ancestral roots. And he lives less than three hundred miles from my home in Oregon. You enriched our lives with your art, and now this. Amazing!"

Robert and I strolled hand in hand through meandering streets back to our apartment, our heels clicking on cobblestones under Lucca's dim light. Safely tucked in my bag were two gifts—postcard reproductions of the Brancoli villages—their watercolor brush strokes by Marjorie Werner Picchi.

33

La Guerra—The War

Tuesday morning, we embraced the sun at our door and called out a warm *buon giorno* to the old woman seated across the small piazza.

"*Buon giorno!* Where are you going today?" she asked in Italian.

"Amazing! She's moved from ignoring to interrogating," Robert whispered.

"We're on our way to the museum, and we have tickets for the Puccini concert tonight."

The old woman launched into a compare-and-contrast discussion of Lucca versus Rome museums. Of course, Lucca won out as being the best, in her eyes. Then she told us her history. Her late husband was a well-loved physician in Lucca; they lived inside Lucca Centre, not outside the walls, which implied a distinct social advantage.

"When do you go home?" she asked.

"Soon. We don't want to leave, but we must—early next week." I felt a sense of loss just saying those words.

"I hope I see you before you go," she said.

"Me too. *Buon giorno, Signora.*"

How very Italian—she had finally lowered the barricades to communication, making this hard-won connection closer than it could have been with a casual exchange from the start.

We strolled into Piazza Napoleone to the sound of 1940s American big band horns blaring joyful notes. My parents had called it GI Jive. As a little girl, I heard this same toe-tapping music played on their radio. Today, one side of the plaza was decorated with Italian flags and about two dozen military jeeps. Some olive-drab hoods displayed a large white star within a circle and the stenciled letters USA. American flags fluttered in the breeze. Clusters of tourists chatted with uniformed soldiers and women dressed in forties-style dresses. We had wandered into the recreated story of World War II and the Allied military occupation of Lucca.

One "soldier" spoke to us in Italian. "Where are you from?"

"*Gli Stati Uniti*," I answered.

"We will never forget what the Americans did for Italy," he said. He described a passion to keep that history alive through his organization, Associazione Linea Gotica. It took its name from the Gothic Line, the last major Axis line of defense along the summits of the Apennine Mountains. Just below were the villages of Brancoli, my family villages. In the last stages of World War II, the Allied forces had broken through and liberated Italy from Nazi-Fascist control.

"How can I find out more about your organization?" He jotted down their website on a small piece of paper: www.lineagotica.eu.

A short distance down a little alley, we located Museo Storico, a small museum that featured an old printing press near the front door. Poster reproductions headlined "Lucca Liberata!" I translated the text for Robert.

Citizens! The Nazi-Fascist tyranny is collapsing—the Allied troops are at the doors of our city. In this hour in which they stand to shed the shackles of our city, after long years of oppression, sacrifice and blood, we join together for the ultimate fight in the name of all of those fallen for an ideal of liberty. *Long Live Free Italy! Long Live The Allies!*

The story of wartime Brancoli, as told to us by Marjorie Werner Picchi, took on new meaning, and I felt a stronger bond with this land and its people.

34

Ancestral Connections

We prowled Lucca for thank-you gifts for Ubaldo Cecchettini, Ada Motroni, Mila Antonini, and Gabriella Gabrielli, plus a spare in case we forgot someone. That's a lot of *vino* and *cioccolato*. We splurged on a light evening meal in a hidden garden. Rich with aromas of fennel, oregano, rosemary, and thyme, the delicious offering included gnocchi, pecarino, pumpkin, and pine nuts. The Puccini concert featured a hometown version of *Tre Tenori*—three tenors—whose performance brought the boisterous audience to its feet for *Bravo! Bravo!* and three encores.

Grand operatic sounds, delicious sweet and savory flavors, magnificent paintings and sculpture, majestic mountains—all of which had been experienced by my ancestors and now Robert and me. Unforgettable.

Mila arrived with Gabriella the next day to transport us once more to the villages north of Lucca. Robert and I carried bags of wine and chocolate and placed them between us in the back seat. I had tucked the *Cecchettini Family Tree* into my portfolio. We drove through the mountains to Piazza di Brancoli and made our way to the house of Ubaldo Cecchettini. Gabriella rapped on the door, and we waited.

"We should have called ahead," Robert murmured.

"I didn't have his number," I said softly.

"Mila probably had it. She knows everything."

Just then, a beautiful, dark-haired woman opened the door, in slim skirt and coordinated soft floral blouse, looking like she was expecting important company. She said her husband, Ubaldo, was out and that he would be sad to have missed us. I returned the coveted *Cecchettini Family* booklet with a large box of chocolates and my profound thanks.

"Where to now?" I asked as Mila drove west through the alpine foothills above Gignano.

"We are going to Rosa's house. Ada gave me her number, so I called and made an appointment. Ada said Rosa has a copy of the Motroni chart." (I've given the woman a common name to conceal her identity.)

I reached into the bags of gifts and pulled out a large box of chocolates, the extra we had purchased in case we forgot someone. Mila parked at the edge of the road. A few feet down the steep mountainside, stone steps flanked with flowers stopped at a short landing, then dropped another few feet to the front door of a lovely home, Tuscan gold with a red tile roof.

A short woman answered the door, auburn hair framing her round face. She peered at me through tortoise shell glasses. Rosa appeared to be in her forties and was carrying some extra pounds. We made the appropriate greetings and introductions in Italian, and I offered the beautifully wrapped box of chocolates. Rosa didn't smile.

"Just what I needed," she said in Italian. "I'm trying to lose weight." We were not off to a great start.

Rosa led us into a large, enclosed sunroom with a spectacular view of the valley. A long table pushed against the wall offered three sides for seating. Rosa settled in at the head, a bulging folder between her and the wall.

I showed her my Motroni family tree and the photo of my grandfather, Giovanni Motroni. She pulled a paper from her folder labeled "*Albero Motroni*—Motroni Family Tree." At the very top was listed my distant ancestor, Domenico Motroni, and his son, Agostino Motroni.

"We have a match!" I exclaimed as I retrieved an 1815 census record from my portfolio. "Look, this mentions Domenico's father, Lorenzo Motroni," I said, pointing to the entry.

Rosa peered, nodded, thumbed through her stack, and took forever to tease out another paper. This one made me gasp. Rosa's Motroni family tree listed two earlier generations, dating back to about 1650. I quickly sketched additions into my chart to be confirmed later: *Giovanni* (my grandfather), *son of Costantino, son of Agostino, son of Gio. Domenico, son of Lorenzo "alfiere," son of another Gio. Domenico, son of another Lorenzo Motroni.*

Wives weren't listed, nor were there dates of birth or death, just names of paternal lineage.

"What does that mean, *alfiere*?" I asked.

Mila translated, "Military leader, standard bearer."

"This is wonderful information," I said. "Is there any documentation showing the source?"

Rosa riffled through papers and pulled out a couple of sheets that appeared to be photographs of parish death records. Written in Italian in a priest's hand, one was dated 10 Sep 1786: *Alfiere Gio. Lorenzo, son of Domenico Motroni, age 64.*

Now I had an approximate date of birth for Gio. Lorenzo: 1722.

"This is wonderful. We have a date," I said. "It's unfortunate that wives aren't listed, just fathers and sons. *Per favore*, could we take photos?" I asked.

With Rosa's nod, Robert began capturing images while Gabriella and Mila stood and moved to the corner of the table next to me to see the records. Rosa fished back in her folder and slowly pushed out another paper, a chart penned on graph paper, with "Motroni, Lorenzo" at the top. In all subsequent generations, wives were listed by birth name. Some confusing lines were hard to follow, and dates of birth were hit and miss, but most were there, and most were understandable.

"This is fantastic! Wives are named. This is a very important document."

Rosa looked in her folder, shuffled through pages, and slowly teased one more into view. "*Ricordi del cimitero*," she said. Cemetery records.

I peered at hard-to-read handwriting. The paper listed cemetery plots, by number and name, of Motroni family members and their spouses. Writing on the opposite side of the paper had bled through, forming blurs that obliterated some of the listings, but I could make out most. While I pored over the cemetery listings, Rosa retrieved more papers. Robert took more photos.

"*Casato Motroni*," the "Lineage of Motroni," was a gold mine of information. Three typed pages listed each Motroni family member with years of birth and death, name of spouse, and village of residence. I saw the top corners numbered 62 through 64 and wondered where the other pages were stashed.

"This is fabulous information! Look, there's Costantino Motroni, my great-grandfather, born in 1829." I stared at his wife's name: Anastasia. Costantino was listed with the wrong wife.

"This is odd." I leaned forward.

Rosa leaned back. "What do you mean, odd?"

I reached into my portfolio, pulled out copies of census from 1861 through 1881, and pointed to the listings for the family of Costantino Motroni. "On all three of these records, Costantino's wife was Maria Pieroni. See here? Maria's unmarried sister, Anastasia, was listed as a servant, living with the family and helping with the care of eight children."

Rosa studied each census sheet. "Maria died." Her voice was abrupt. "After 1881, Costantino married Anastasia."

"Was that unusual? Marrying a sister-in-law?" I asked.

Rosa's back went rigid. Mila intervened. "No, not at all. It makes perfect sense."

Rosa closed the folder over a bulge of papers. "I don't want to show you these."

Then she launched into a rapid-fire monologue. I understood about every tenth word, but none of it made sense—a terrible injustice that American relatives had done; a package sent to her as a little girl, containing a woman's dress . . . how could they have done such a thing! With a frown, Rosa backed away from the table, chair legs grating against large square tiles. She stood, reached out to scoop up scattered papers, and pushed them into her folder.

I looked at Mila for guidance. Mila gave a slight nod toward the door. We rose, said our brief *grazie* and *arrivederci*, and climbed back up the hill and into Mila's car.

"Wow! What happened back there? Did I insult her?" I asked Mila.

"Don't worry about it; you didn't do anything wrong. Let's go get something to drink."

What had set Rosa off? Was she insulted that I offered chocolates? or that her ancestor Anastasia was listed as a servant in census records? or that I asked about in-laws marrying? or that an ugly American relative had dashed her hopes for a new dress decades ago? Whatever the reason, her door was closed.

Robert must have noticed my look of distress. "We have it all," he said, patting the camera.

I exhaled and gripped his hand. "I couldn't do this without you."

A short distance away, we turned into Gignano's central piazza, parked at the edge of the drop-off, and climbed the steep, winding stairs to Trattoria Tosca for celebration toasts and a breathtaking view of the valley surrounding the Serchio River. Once more, Mila had located clues to my ancestors.

The young barista disclosed that the owner, her father, had the last name Micheli. I wondered, *Are you my ancestral link? Do your branches unite with mine in some ancient family tree?* It was too far in the distant past to contemplate, and I didn't pursue it further.

35

The Festa di Santa Croce

On Monday morning, Lucca teemed with tourists. Some held maps as they backed into the streets to gawk at buildings. Others moved in herds, led by a red hat or a baton with a yellow pom-pom. We listened in as tour guides explained the Festa di Santa Croce.

According to legend, the Santa Croce, the Blessed Cross, was carved from wood and inspired by Nicodemus. The figure on the cross is called Volto Santo—Holy Face. Hidden for centuries, it survived a perilous journey across the Mediterranean Sea and reached the beach of Luni in AD 742. The Santa Croce was then placed on a cart and pulled by oxen that headed by divine will toward its destination of Lucca. Each year at nightfall on September 13 the Volto Santo is pulled on a cart through candlelit streets in a mile-long devotional procession.

All afternoon, huge boom trucks lifted workers, who seated candles in glass cups and placed them in metal receptacles along roof eaves, window ledges, and door frames. We followed their meandering one-mile path through Lucca Centre's medieval maze from the Basilica of San Frediano, where the procession would begin, to its endpoint at the Cathedral of San Martino.

At sunset, I dialed Mila's number. "*Pronto,*" she answered. Ready.

"We're near the *catedrale,*" I said. "Where should we stand?"

"Find a high spot, not on stairs or in front of doors. Look for a nook in the wall," she said.

Ciao, ciao . . . ciao, ciao, ciao. Italians were quick to say hello and slow to say goodbye.

Within view of the cathedral, we found an elevated stone niche. A friendly German couple joined us in a space just wide enough for four, just high enough to raise us above the growing crowd. How odd, and strangely disconcerting, to be in their company here in Italy, near the hills where deadly battles were once waged.

At sunset the trucks returned, inching forward. Again, mechanical lifts moved men up and down to light the candles—a difficult job, as a light rain had begun to fall. Most stayed lit, thanks to lids partially covering the glass jars. We raised our umbrellas to form an awning, metal spokes resting against the wall. Lucca was dark except for thousands of candles and their reflection on wet stone.

Drums and horns heralded the procession before we saw it. From around the corner of a building appeared a great glow of rippling light. It approached and spread to reveal its source: white-robed men, each holding a three-foot-long flickering white candle. I watched the spectacle through the eyes of my grandmother, Amabile Rossi. Perhaps she had once stood in this very spot.

An enormous painted banner of the Santa Croce led men in crimson satin robes, followed by hooded gray costumes. My family history marched by. First-century coarse woolen garb gave way to luxurious colors and art of fourteenth-century Renaissance. Clusters of tall gold crosses were interspersed with filigreed staffs, banners, and flags. The parade continued into the twentieth century with Puccini student singers honoring Giacomo Puccini, who had once lived in Lucca. They were followed by marching bands and one elaborate floral cross borne by ten men in jeans.

Some of the pomp and circumstance held little meaning for me, a non-Catholic. But my ancestral roots were tied deeply to the Catholic faith, their rites and rituals carried forward through the ages. If not for the records penned by priests, my family history would have remained sealed in darkness.

An archbishop passed. Several groups of robed cardinals, bishops, priests, and nuns filed by, each section singing or chanting. Lucca and all other regions of Italy were represented by clusters of civic and military officials; by the time they reached us, they were struggling to keep their giant white candles lit beneath an undulating canopy of bobbing umbrellas as rain poured down on the parade.

Following this group came the sons and daughters of emigrants, *Lucchesi nel Mondo*—Lucca People of the World—in clear plastic ponchos, their white banners held high to announce cities, states, or countries of current residence in no particular order: Pittsburgh, Sacramento, Ireland, Australia, San Francisco, Florida, Buenos Aires. Each group was greeted with a roar of approval from the sidelines. Not everyone cheered, though; one disgruntled man near me shouted in Italian, "*Bravo* for you, but we stayed!"

The Volto Santo, with its gold adornments, had reached its destination inside the cathedral, but festivities were far from over. Rain or no rain, fireworks followed outside the wall. Hours after we returned home, our bedroom was still lit by reflected bursts of colored light. The celebration ended with a final boom at one thirty in the morning.

As I drifted off to sleep, I wondered if my mother knew that she was born on this special day of celebration, September 13, the Festa di Santa Croce. We hadn't experienced the terrible hardships of our ancestors, but that tenacity, that perseverance, were ours.

The following morning, Robert and I browsed through an open-air market of vendors' tents extending through city streets. Piazzas featured the Lucchesi, clad in elaborate costumes, still celebrating the festa with bands, skits, and precision flag tossing—this time without the rain.

We ambled along a gray brick street, Via Vittorio Emanuele II, and stopped to gaze through a black wrought iron fence to the golden Ducal Palace. A mass of ivy nearly obliterated the iron spires and engulfed a large section of the attached building. We moved in for a closer look at a small painted rectangle attached to the mottled pink wall.

"Museo Paolo Cresci," Robert read.

I translated the rest of the sign ". . . for the History of Italian Emigration."

36

Leaving Italy

We stepped through the open door of Museo Paolo Cresci and into a large hall. I gaped at walls filled with floor-to-ceiling murals—gigantic photographs of Italian emigrants. The display continued through a portal into an adjacent three-story cylindrical tower, the Chapel of Santa Maria della Rotonda, where more large photographs covered angular room dividers. Display cases brimmed with maps, postcards, letters, and other memorabilia, hundreds of personal and public documents from the late 1800s through the early 1900s. A video in Italian gave voice to the forgotten people. "A bundle, a suitcase, a passport, a ticket—just a few things to start their life journey . . ." I stared, overwhelmed by the enormity and impact of sepia images that could have been my grandparents.

At a train station, women and men each lugged one sack on their shoulders or in their arms, their belongings encased in a white sheet or large basket. Free hands held tightly to small children. They lined up on the platform before a uniformed ticket agent, who handed out boarding passes. They wore layers of clothing, hats, scarves—everything they could carry.

At the harbor they stood together on a raft without rails, pulled by heavy ropes across choppy water toward the waiting steamship. We looked into the haunted eyes of Italians as they left their families, their homes, their traditions. Plagued by overpopulation and unemployment, the prospect of starvation was a strong motivator. Theirs was a story of strength and hope.

Pamphlets provided to the emigrants bore a powerful message: *Do not be afraid of the sea—the worst crossing is through your door.* Those words brought tears to my eyes. My family members were among the twenty million people in that mass exodus from 1895 to 1915. Aboard the ships, they faced horrific overcrowded conditions wedged in stacked bunks as they pitched and swayed through stormy seas to an unknown land an ocean away.

We packed for the flight home as images of my family swirled in my mind. Last night we had walked in my ancestors' footsteps along the Luminaria as we followed the journey of the Volto Santo. Today we saw them leave Italy, their courage etched into my soul.

37

Orzali Family Reunion

"You will hear them, our ancestors, whispering in the church and in the forest. You will hear them." A chill lifted the hair on the back of my neck and danced down my spine.

Maria Bruna, the sixty-something woman seated across the outdoor table, had spoken with a sure voice and a persuasive smile. She styled her hair like Princess Diana, each strand perfectly placed, golden streaks in darker blond brushing her tanned forehead. Her handsome husband, Pasquale Naccarati, beamed and nodded, his thick, white hair glistening in the afternoon sun.

We were back in Lucca Centre after a four-year absence.

Behind the couple, people ambled through an arched entrance in the curved yellow walls of Lucca's Roman Amphitheatre. Instead of belted robes and flowing gowns, they wore khaki pants and loose summer dresses, like time travelers who showed up in the wrong century.

"The Orzalis had endured religious persecution as Catholics here in Lucca," Maria Bruna said. "But they escaped, away from city crowds, away from the plague, to the Brancoli region, where their lives were spared." She pulled her five-foot frame higher in her chair. "I am proud to be an Orzali!"

Her hands danced in the air as Maria Bruna described the Who's Who of the Orzali ancestral line: an archbishop, several architects who designed beauty into buildings in Lucca and Genoa, and *Pinocchio* author Carlo Collodi, with a mother named Orzali. And the crest, the Orzali crest. I wasn't sure when or why that was introduced, but a scroll dated 1171 mentioned a castle on Orzali Island. The conversation was moving too fast for questions. "To the Orzalis!" she said.

We raised our goblets of Prosecco in unison. "To the Orzalis!"

"You know," Maria Bruna added, her goblet descending abruptly, "your Susanna is a strange name. There is no Susanna Orzali in our family tree." My stomach turned. "And Mario said he couldn't find your Maria Domenica Orzali," she went on. "The Maria Domenica in our family was a nun."

She was talking about my relatives, the two names I had emailed to Mario Orzali, the names with offspring in my family tree, two names that guaranteed admission to the Orzali international family reunion less than one week away. Big mistake—no match.

In a relaxed mood, Pasquale and Maria Bruna rambled on about life in Lucca, leaving me flooded with anxiety. I imagined showing up as uninvited guests—the party crashers from America—exposed by whispers in the trees: *Imposters!* One thing was clear. Robert and I needed to find another bona fide Orzali connection, or this reunion could turn into the biggest social blunder of my life.

Four months earlier, I had Googled the surname Orzali, from my incomplete ancestral chart. Up popped the Orzali crest with the following message: "From the official website of all the Orzalis in the world. A yearly meeting of all the Orzalis is organized in Brancoli, a [region] that has great importance in the story of our family, on the hills near Lucca . . . You will have the opportunity to meet many of your relatives. We wait for You!! Mario Orzali, Brescia, 2014"

The website Orzali.net opened a photo album, and clusters of smiling Italians popped up on the screen. In the background, I recognized the same sites Robert and I had explored in Lucca. Faces and places in the photos changed annually, with people who streamed in from Europe, the United States, and South America for the Orzali reunion. I longed to join in their celebration of *la famiglia*. I stared at the message on top of the computer screen, "We wait for You!!"

How could I possibly have resisted? That seductive invitation had led me to an email address, where I left a brief description of my two Orzali relatives. Days later, Mario Orzali had answered and attached a family tree that branched into ten dozen names, all relating back to Nicolao Orzali, born in the late sixteenth century. I'd scanned for a match, searched again and again, and found a possible connection. I couldn't find my Susanna Orzali, but Maria Domenica Orzali appeared in Mario's chart. I was missing dates of birth and had no proof that his Maria Domenica and mine were the same person. But Mario's website photo of the Church of San Giorgio gave me hope of finding missing links. That same church was located near the Brancoli village where my grandfather was born and raised.

In a flurry of emails, Mario explained that he lived about three hours away from Lucca and wouldn't be able to search the archives for my relatives before the reunion. No problem! Robert and I would visit Lucca's archives, and we'd find my connections in baptismal records. Of course we could do it. Why not? The doors had been locked on our last visit. This time we'd have no trouble finding my family.

Mario provided the name of our Lucca contact, Maria Bruna, who would make all our reservations.

Tuscany again. This time, June. I began planning what I'd wear to the Orzali family reunion.

38

Archivio Diocesano

There we were, on a hot and steamy Monday morning in June, standing once again before the massive carved doors of Archivio Arcivescovile, the mother lode of parish records for Lucca and the surrounding area. In our four-year absence, the name had changed to Archivio Diocesano, now registered in UNESCO Memories of the World.

On our first visit, we had only a couple of hours to explore records. Two years later, the building had been closed the entire month of our stay. Maybe this third time would spell success, and we'd find the Orzali connection. Today, a few people milled near the entrance, then more. I counted a dozen.

"Uh oh," Robert said. "Last time, there were seats for eight. Maybe there isn't room for us."

With a loud clang, a bolt was pulled from its mooring, doors opened, and we all filed in. Most headed for the marble stairs. Robert and I chose the elevator and squeezed in with two other people. The doors closed slowly, and we waited. With a moan, the elevator made a slow climb up two levels. With a bump and a groan, the doors finally opened.

We signed the register in the central area and entered the research room to find ten seats already filled. Additional seating was arranged across the hall in the original library area. Two young women improvised a study area for us by carrying a couple of chairs to the registration table. We gave our passports to an assistant, who scurried away to get them copied. I placed my incomplete family trees on the table—one for my grandmother, Amabile Rossi, one for my grandfather, Giovanni Motroni—and began chasing down ancestors. We browsed through the index of vital records by dates and names of Brancoli villages, and I filled out retrieval requests in Italian for four thick volumes filled with stiff yellow folios.

A dozen churches studded the Apennine Mountains in the Brancoli region northeast of Lucca. Each church kept parish records. Priests who recorded births, marriages, and deaths also entered the same information in archbishops' records, now piled in stacks for us to review line by line.

Slowly, tediously, we examined each chronological entry. Penmanship of priests varied as time and location changed, but all handwriting had one thing in common: it was hard to read. An "*S*" resembled an "*f*" with its long stroke below the line. Numbers 1, 2, and 7 were strangely similar; "*7bre*" translated to *Settembre*—September, "*8bre*" for *Ottobre*—October, and "*9bre*" for November. Cursive entries varied from barely legible to marginally better, with occasional ink blots from an over-exuberant quill pen. One priest's spiky letters were written in Latin. Another priest listed only the bride's first name in marriage records, and he didn't bother to write down the mother's name on baptism records. Who was she? Who were her parents? Forget the ink smudges and loopy letters in a foreign language. If a priest hadn't recorded a mother's last name, our search became a nightmare as we plowed through yellowed pages for clues to her identity.

"I hope he spends his time in eternity writing all the women's names he omitted, over and over," Robert muttered.

Each time we found a match for any name in my family tree, I jotted new information in pencil on my ancestral chart and ordered an email copy of the source document. We were thrilled to find a flood of new information for Motroni, Pieroni, and Cecchettini family members, but the Orzali connection remained elusive. Four hours later, the library closed.

"This doesn't look good," I said. "The library is open Wednesday and Friday. Two mornings. That's all we have." I didn't want to face those ancestral whispers.

39

Exploring Tuscany

Back at our rented apartment, the doorbell rang, and we raced down forty-four steps to meet Mila Antonini. Shouts of joy and hugs melted away a four-year absence. We chattered in a combination Italian-English that everyone understood.

"Oh, I love your hair!" I said. Mila's silvery white locks framed her unlined face. She hadn't lost her big smile, her dancing blue eyes, or her bubbling enthusiasm.

"Do you like it? I finally found someone in Gassano who does what I ask."

I wondered how we looked to her—more gray in Bob's curly hair, more silver streaks in mine, my frame about ten pounds lighter, both of us sporting new laugh lines. Conversation quickly turned to our frantic search for Orzalis.

"Ridiculous," I said. "A six-thousand-mile trip to my family reunion, but wait, first we have to find out if I'm related."

"What can I do?" Mila asked.

"Nothing," I said. "The library is closed today, or we'd be back there poring over the books."

Just like old times, Mila took charge. "Worry does no good. You should take a break. We should get out into the country. Would you like to go to Barga? I think you would find it interesting. What do you think? Who knows what will turn up? We'll drive along the Serchio River into the mountains." She took a breath and a pause.

"Will we drive by Ponte Rotto?" I asked.

"Yes, yes!" Mila said, as we climbed into her car. "We should see what happened while you were away."

Mila drove us through a portal, out the walled city of Lucca Centre, and north toward Barga. About twenty minutes later, I recognized the town of Piaggione.

"Look! There's the pink church and the monument with my family names." I watched the right-hand side of the road for the hamlet of Ponte Rotto.

"There it is!" Mila said. "Do you want to stop?"

Without waiting for a reply, she parked a short distance beyond the main building, the home of Noni's parents, Marianna Fambrini and Agostino Rossi. I craned my neck out the side window to stare at three refurbished units, honey shades of stucco crowned in pristine red. The fourth was still in shambles: broken and scattered ash-colored roof tiles, ugly gray and black rock walls, holes exposing rusted metal support rods.

"Oh! Look at the end wall," I said.

"Where?" Robert pivoted in his seat to peer out the back window. "I don't see anything but gray stones."

"I know. They're gone," I said. "The letters are a blur. 'Ponte Rotto' has completely disappeared. Oh, Mila, if you hadn't seen those letters six years ago, we'd never have located my family's lost village. You found it just in time, before the letters vanished. I wonder if they'll reappear when the restoration is finished."

We followed the twisted road to Bagni di Lucca for iced espresso, then wound through the foothills of the Apennines to the hilltop town of Barga, a medieval village capped with the inevitable red tiled roofs. Mila told us that numerous Scottish people had settled here, and that the annual festa was a big dinner of fish and chips.

A merciless sun beat down as we climbed through the village along steep stone steps and slanted brick walkways. By the time we reached the hilltop cathedral, I was gasping for air. We slipped through massive carved doors and cooled off in the silent limestone interior of Chiesa San Cristofero. In the dim light, I gazed at the twelve-foot wooden statue of St. Christopher, the patron saint of travelers. In an irreverent moment, my mind sent a message: "Well, what do you think, Chris? Can you help this weary traveler find some elusive Orzalis?"

A few minutes later, we reopened the church doors to a blistering Tuscan sun. At the edge of the walled piazza I shielded my eyes to gaze at sharp, rocky protrusions of the Apuan Alps across the green Garfagnana valley.

"That crag with the hole through the top is Monte Forato," Mila said.

"We've seen that one before, from the opposite side," I said. "That's the mountain we saw from our hotel room in Pontestazzemese. We rode a scary little blue bus through those Alps to find my great-grandfather's birthplace in Farnocchia."

"Why didn't you call me? I could have driven you," Mila said.

Mila was busy meeting the needs of her granddaughters in Lucca Monday through Friday, and weekends were devoted to Rino Mariani in Gassano. Yet she generously carved out time to help us with her enthusiastic support.

"What is that?" I pointed to a mansion on the top of a nearby knoll.

"That's Daniela's *palazzo*," she said.

"Daniela? Our Daniela?"

"Yes, yes. She owns the Lucca property, too."

We had rented an apartment in Daniela's Lucca villa six years earlier. In a city of eighty-four thousand people, she was the woman who had suggested an interpreter, her friend Mila, one of 7,500 residents inside the walls of Lucca Centre. If Daniela hadn't introduced us, none of this amazing adventure could have happened.

As we trudged back down the hill, Mila stopped and chatted with the locals. She mentioned to us that she had once owned an antique shop here. No wonder she knew this place so well.

We wound our way back toward Lucca, this time exploring the opposite side of the Serchio River. "There's the bell tower of Diecimo," she said.

"Yes, that marks the spot where my great-grandmother, Marianna Fambrini, married her first husband, Domenico Marcucci. We know so little about him; we have just a photo of a man in a military uniform. Why would a perfectly healthy person die or disappear at age forty? I wonder if it was service-related."

"Maybe you can find the answer in Lucca," Mila said.

"Oh, we tried," Robert said. "The archivists told us that records for Diecimo are stored in the village of Borgo a Mozzano."

"I'm tempted to go there," I said.

"We need to find Orzali first. Right? Right?" he said.

"*Calma, Roberto, calma.* I didn't mean today."

Twenty minutes later, Mila joined us in our apartment inside the walls of Lucca, where we prepared an American dinner. Well, it wasn't entirely American because we were limited to available groceries. And what is American food anyway? It's international, which is what we served. We started with *Prosecco* and little Swedish crackers topped with a swirl of herbed cheese from France. Robert grilled wild Atlantic salmon and served it with a colorful array of Lucca's fresh vegetables seasoned with Cajun spices we had packed for just this occasion. We topped off the meal with a dollop of gelato and biscotti.

Mila approved. "I would have been disappointed with an Italian meal."

She scanned the living room, tastefully decorated with antique furniture. High ceilings soared above the upstairs balcony and bedroom. "Do you know the history of this place? It was once a bordello!"

"Perfect!" I laughed. "I can say we entertained guests in the red-light district of Lucca."

Tuesday morning found us at Archivio Storico, where the three wise women greeted us with smiles and hugs, faces touching cheek to cheek: Maria Chiarlo, the gray-haired woman who had given us a fabulous book and whose letters had opened doors to Archivio di Stato; Cristina Marinari, the young woman who had doggedly followed leads and provided us with copies of source documents; and Mariella Morotti, who had personally escorted us through bureaucratic barricades in Lucca's municipal offices.

Cristina smiled and said, "The last time you were here, I was . . ." she ran her hand in a curve around her abdomen. "Now she is three years old!"

In Italian, I described the upcoming Orzali reunion and our frantic search for my family connections in Archivio Diocesano.

Mariella said, "That's odd. I'm researching the Orzali family for a gentleman from Milan. So far, we haven't found anything that connects him to this group of Orzalis. I would be interested in what you find." There it was again, that heavy, sinking feeling in the pit of my stomach. If Mariella, the super sleuth, couldn't find Signore Orzali's missing links, how could we possibly find mine?

We requested the 1815 index of parochial records, which listed members of each Brancoli household. Heads down, we pored over names. We used yesterday's archival finds to search for more family members—full names of parents, their offspring, and an occasional mother-in-law with a different last name living in the house. Their ages would provide clues to more baptismal and marriage records. We left the office with four copies of new information and a promise to return. None of the copies mentioned the Orzali clan.

We took a leisurely route back to the apartment, with a stop at the Forno for *panino cereale*—a dark whole grain roll bursting with flavor—and Italian lessons from the baker. He didn't remember me, but he finally recalled the incident from four years ago when, after several tries, I had finally said, "*Buo-NISS-imo!*" He flashed a big grin and said, "Ah, yes! I remember now!"

This time he spoke in perfect English of his recent visit to New York to find his American relatives. He reminded me that to learn Italian, I needed to speak the language. So Italian it would be, every morning at the Forno, for our entire four-week stay in Lucca.

That evening we walked the wall, a 2.6-mile circuit, forty feet high, with a commanding view of city lights. To our surprise, we ambled into a Renaissance revival, complete with compositions, costumes, and cannon fire. Musicians played ancient instruments on the lawn as red-caped rascals with feathered hats gathered on the balustrade. They began firing cannons amid cheers from a growing audience. I assumed they were blanks; nothing was toppling over in the direction of the shots. Lucca was playing with my mind, luring me back to the sixteenth century and Nicolao Orzali.

I couldn't relax on my emotional roller coaster. I stewed about the search for family links. If only Lucca libraries were open at night. Crazy, that's what it was, worrying about paper chases on a beautiful evening in Tuscany. I willed my thoughts into the now.

We strolled down a ramp and into the lush green arboretum to the receding sounds of cannon blasts. Warm breezes carried the fresh scent of redwood and cedar trees imported from California and Oregon. We stood beneath the giants as we savored gelato by lamplight.

40

Orzali Search

On Wednesday morning, we sweated over ledgers in Archivio Diocesano in Lucca's oppressive heat wave; it was 92°F with 95 percent chance of rain. In a gesture of optimism, research assistants opened the windows, but the air was dead still. Our damp clothes plastered to our bodies, we hunched over ancient registers as the temperature climbed.

A clap of thunder sent the archive staff scrambling to the windows. Loud noises broke the library silence with thuds, scrapes, and screeches as librarians closed shutters, slid window frames, and secured latches. Four hours later, drained and bleary-eyed, we peeled ourselves out of our chairs and turned in a request form for copies of six source documents—births, marriages, and deaths—to be emailed to us. One of them was a baptismal record of my prolific ancestor, Maria Domenica Orzali. She definitely was not the nun named Maria Domenica in Mario's chart. We needed to find another Orzali record, and we were running out of time.

We'd stumbled into other last names I recognized, neighbors and friends in the California valley where I was raised: Bacigaluppi, Puccinelli, Buonacorsi, Micheli. That last one was the name of the boy I'd dated in high school, the one we had met at my class reunion eight years before.

"I think all those Italians in Brancoli moved to Healdsburg," I said to Robert as we headed down the marble stairs. The door clanged shut behind us. Only one morning left.

We skirted San Martino Cathedral to the roar of thunder and darted down a curved alley. Just as rain fell, Robert pushed the key into our apartment door at 8 Via della Dogana.

"I'm ready to call Maria Bruna. This two-day reunion is a pipe dream. We need to cancel our reservations," I said as we climbed the forty-four steps to our apartment.

"Not yet," Robert said. "We still have Friday morning."

That night a storm raged outside our door. Lightning flashes lit up the room, followed immediately by explosive thunder that vibrated everything not nailed down. Fierce winds peppered hailstones against windows and skylights. I expected to hear the crash of broken glass above the bed.

In a disturbing place between waking and sleeping, I imagined the nightmare of attending the reunion without solid proof of my family connection. The ancestors would whisper in the wind, *Imposters! La famiglia* would turn and stare at us in dulled surprise. We'd be escorted to a Brancoli kiosk to wait for a scary bus ride back to Lucca while the Orzalis would drive off in joyful celebration singing zippy Italian songs—*finiculi-finicula*.

The next morning Pasquale called. As head of the foundation at Lucca's arboretum, he had been summoned to assess storm damage. One tree limb had fallen on the roof of his office. He would have to move to different quarters. The arboretum was now closed, barricaded from public access. The damage was so extensive that clean-up might take weeks. Pasquale's voice wavered. I could almost see tears running down his face. This loss had affected him in a very personal, profound way.

Later that morning, Robert and I walked the wall and looked down into the chaos at the arboretum. The storm had toppled some giant trees, exposed long-buried earth-encrusted roots, sheared off limbs, and left enormous spikes of wood pointing skyward. We heard chainsaws clearing more rubble outside the walls. I wondered how the storm had affected the forested Brancoli region, where the Orzali reunion was scheduled to take place in two days.

We found seats in a bar and sat sipping espresso. Robert was immersed in newspaper headlines about the latest *calcio*—soccer scores. I pulled documents from my portfolio and studied my grandfather's ancestral chart. Who was Pasqua? My three-times-great-grandmother sat suspended like a leaf with no last name, no stem in my family tree. Several other branches were missing connections, but for some reason, Pasqua commanded my attention. What was her birth name? I didn't dare hope, but in the back of my mind I wondered, could she be an Orzali? Was she my missing link to the reunion? She was married to a Carli, and they had a daughter in the late 1790s.

"We need to go back to Storico this morning," I said. "They close at one."

A brisk walk and a half hour later, we met with Mariella, who suggested Archivio di Stato for the 1809 census. "I will make an appointment for you for tomorrow morning," she said. How could we have managed without guidance from the wise women of Storico?

Friday morning we waited at the entrance to Archivio di Stato, the nest of the Hawk. Doors opened at eight o'clock, and we climbed fifty-four steep steps to the third floor and the reception room. No Hawk today. A well-dressed woman with curly brown hair appeared from a side door. She looked vaguely familiar. We spoke in Italian. She asked if we were waiting for a tour that was scheduled for later. No, we were here to search for records.

"All the staff is quite busy with the tour. I'm afraid there is no one here to help you."

"Mariella Morotti from Archivio Storico said she would call to schedule an appointment for us. She told us to ask for Dotoressa Busti," I said in Italian.

"I am Dotoressa Busti."

"Oh! I'm so glad to see you again. We met several years ago when we were researching my family here."

"But this is not Archivio Storico. This is Archivio di Stato," she said.

"Yes, I know. We only want to look at one register: the 1809 volume for the Sesto region."

"But no one called for an appointment."

"Perhaps she tried and couldn't reach you."

"Everyone is so busy with the tour."

"We have traveled so far."

"It's highly unusual." She paused, narrowing her eyelids.

"It should only take a few minutes."

She pursed her lips, furrowed her brow. I held my breath.

"Let me see what I can do. You won't have copy service. If you find records, you will have to photograph them yourself."

"*Grazie, grazie.*" The Director of Archivio di Stato, this very busy woman, had just agreed to retrieve census records for us. We found seats at a library table and waited. She returned shortly with a large volume.

We turned powdery yellow pages written in 1809 and soon found the entry: the Carli Family. Lorenzo, age forty, and Pasqua, thirty, had three children: Margherita, ten; Pietro, eight; and Anna Maria, six. By calculating birth years, maybe we could find baptism records for the children and a marriage record for the parents. Any one of those documents might reveal Pasqua's birth name. All we had to do was search line by line through hundreds of pages of handwritten loopy letters and ink blots in parochial registers at another archive office. Robert clicked camera images of the census record, and we left the building at eight thirty.

An hour later, we waited with a growing group at the massive carved doors of Archivio Diocesano. Agonizing minutes ticked by. Several people grumbled that the doors should have opened fifteen minutes earlier. I paced. Finally the bolt clanged, and we scrambled into the building and took the elevator up to the library. A researcher recognized us and carried in an extra chair so we could sit together. The tomes we had previously requested were already stacked on the table, ready for our review.

"Grazie. Grazie," we said in unison. Robert and I each grabbed a book and, heads down, began to search for Orzali.

What a difference this was from our first attempts to find any of my ancestors. Every discovery back then was a celebration as we struggled through priests' penmanship to find even one name. Now, with full access for three half-days this week, and more experience translating pages, we were overwhelmed with information as familiar last names flooded in. I had penciled several generations of names and dates, new leaves in my family trees.

An hour passed, two, three, but still no new Orzali link. One o'clock. The library would close in thirty minutes.

"Forget the males," I whispered. "Look for a female named Orzali."

Heads down, pages turning rapidly, we searched frantically for that elusive woman.

One-twenty. I closed my last volume. I felt drained, energy zapped, exhausted.

"That's it. It's over," I murmured.

I looked at Robert, still hunched over, his attention riveted to an open book.

"It's over," I repeated. "I need to cancel our reservations."

Robert turned to face me. "I think I found her," he said.

"What? Where?"

He pointed to the center of a page. "Right there. And you'll never guess her last name." He slid the volume over to me and pointed to a record of baptism for my great-great-grandmother, Margherita Carli, born 8 April 1799.

"But she's not an Orzali," I said.

"Keep reading," Robert said.

Margherita figlia di Gio. Lorenzo di Luciano di Domenico Carli, e di Pasqua di Pietro dell' Alfiere Domenico Micheli . . .

Margherita, daughter of Gio. Lorenzo, son of Luciano, son of Domenico Carli, and of *Pasqua*, daughter of *Pietro*, son of the Standard Bearer Domenico *Micheli . . .*

"Pietro Micheli!"

"We saw him in Mario's chart," Robert said. "He was married to an Orzali."

"Pasqua Micheli's mother was an Orzali. Pasqua Micheli *is* the missing link!" My heart was racing. I turned to look at Robert. "How did you remember that? How did you remember the name Pietro Micheli?"

"How could I forget the last name of your old boyfriend?"

I put my head in my hands and laughed. "I don't believe it. I absolutely don't believe it."

I wanted to throw my arms around Robert and shower him with kisses, right there in the middle of the Most Holy Library.

I spoke in Italian to the research assistant. "I know this is very unusual, but I need these record images for the Orzali reunion tomorrow. Could you possibly email them to me today?"

"I'm sorry, we need more time to prepare them," she said. "It is not possible."

"Oh . . ." I looked at Robert, who smiled and shrugged his shoulders to say it would be okay. "I'll update the ancestral chart. Maybe that will be enough. *Grazie, grazie.* We will be back *lunedì*—Monday. Can you believe it? He found Pasqua Micheli! *Arrivederci. Grazie.*"

I was still babbling in two languages as Robert escorted me out the door.

We found a little trattoria for a celebratory lunch—a little vino and a few gnocchi, finished off with *insalata caprese* in the colors of Italy's flag: green basil, white mozzarella, and red tomatoes, with a drizzle of olive oil.

Nearby I spotted a kiosk displaying Pinocchio string puppets, magnets, and postcards.

"I never noticed it before, but Pinocchio is everywhere," I said. "Who knew the author's mother was an Orzali!" Even the carousel in the central piazza featured the famous characters.

Back at the apartment, I transcribed penciled notes into my laptop. With a thumb drive in my pocket, we walked about a mile to get paper copies of my updated family trees—just in case Mario needed to see what we had found.

"I still can't believe it. We're going to the reunion. The weekend is packed with events," I said. "Tomorrow we get to meet my family."

41

Meeting Relatives

On Saturday afternoon, we waited just outside of Porta Elisa, one of the six portals into the walled city. Maria Bruna had phoned to say that she and Pasquale would meet us there. It was impossible to stand still. I peered over the bridge into slow-moving green water. I tried to focus on the dome of a church outside Lucca's walls, on the numerous Vespa scooters buzzing by, on the classy way Italians dressed. Minutes dragged into a quarter hour as I paced.

Finally, a silver-gray sedan approached the portal, made a U-turn, and drove by as I strained to see the occupants. Maybe it was our hosts; I couldn't be sure. Just ahead, the car pulled over and parked. Out stepped Maria Bruna, arms wide for *buona sera* hugs. Relieved, we slid into the back seat and, as prearranged, Pasquale and Maria Bruna drove us a short distance to Stadio Comunale, the soccer stadium. The parking lot was packed.

"Look at all these cars! They can't all be Orzalis," I said.

"No, no. There's an event at the stadium. This is just our meeting place. We go to Montecarlo from here," Pasquale said as he double-parked, half of his car sticking out in the roadway.

"Monte Carlo?" I murmured to Robert. "The only one I know about is the one I once visited on a cruise. Monte Carlo is on the French Riviera."

We clambered out and waited. A few minutes later, another car arrived and double-parked. A handsome man stepped out of the car wearing a big smile and introduced his beautiful brunette wife.

"I'm Mario Orzali," he said in English.

"Oh! I'm delighted to finally meet you," I said, grasping his hand. We had emailed so often, he seemed like an old friend. He was young enough to be my son.

Another car arrived, and another young, good-looking Italian male stepped out of his car with his stunning blonde wife. This was Fabio Orzali from Milan. He also spoke English.

Soon a taxi arrived with another attractive couple, a distant cousin named Andy from California. Discussion seemed to focus on how he spelled his name: Orzalli with a double L. I wondered if Andy had struggled like us to find a legitimate reason to be here, but Mario cleared up the mystery. He had confirmed Andy's lineage online through American census records.

"Where is your brother?" Maria Bruna asked Andy.

"Rick and his wife are coming by car from Lucca," he replied. *What an odd statement*, I thought. Lucca Centre's walls were less than a hundred yards away.

"There they are! That's Rick!" Andy pointed to an approaching white car.

Pasquale loped over to Rick and his wife for introductions. Then he added, "We're not staying. We're going to Montecarlo. Follow us."

Andy and his wife scrambled into Rick's car, and we were on our way. Pasquale led the small caravan through the city, constantly checking his mirror, pulling over to wait several times when our other drivers were caught in traffic. We finally turned off the main highway and began to climb a narrow serpentine road into the Apennine foothills. Pasquale paused and sounded the horn at every blind turn. Several times he stopped to wait for the other three cars to catch up. The taut muscles in my arms and legs began to relax as I realized that Pasquale was a very good driver.

We turned onto a dirt road, and Pasquale parked the car in a clearing near dense woods. He and Maria Bruna climbed out of the car, and Robert and I followed. There wasn't a house in sight, and Pasquale didn't offer an explanation for the stop. The other three cars arrived, and we waited for all to gather.

Pasquale pointed to a tree and said, "Have you ever seen anything like that?"

I stared at a massive oak standing alone, surrounded by yellow grass, its ancient limbs so long they were supported by wooden props. Miraculously, it had been spared by the recent storm. In fact, there were no broken limbs on the road, and none of the surrounding trees seemed damaged.

"This is the oak tree where the fox and the cat lured Pinocchio to steal his money," Maria Bruna said. We each approached to get a closer look. I touched a low branch and wondered how this particular tree had been designated as "the one" in the story of Pinocchio.

Maria Bruna said, "Let's gather around the tree and hold hands."

We all complied as if this were a normal, everyday event. Twelve adults formed a circle, arms outstretched, holding hands around the huge trunk.

"To the Orzalis!" Maria Bruna said.

We lifted our clasped hands high and shouted in unison, "To the Orzalis!" Such a simple ceremony, a child's game. A slight breeze rustled the leaves and gave me goose bumps.

Next stop was the other Montecarlo, not on the French Riviera but perched high on an Italian hill, with a commanding view of the valley below. The twelve of us climbed to a medieval fortress, where the current owners led us on a tour through the castle's brick-paved rooms, connected by irregular stairs and stone arches.

Our guide gave us a brief history in English. "The castle was built for Charles IV, who freed Lucca from Pisa in 1368." Seven centuries—that's a long time to hold a grudge with a neighbor just eleven miles away. But even now, Lucchesi citizens tended to bristle at the mention of Pisa's twenty-six-year reign.

We learned that the castle was under Florentine control in the late fourteenth century, and a fortress was later constructed around the castle by the ruling Medici family. This was the perfect site to spot approaching hostile armies, even those pesky Pisans. My Orzali family had traced their lineage back to Nicolao Orzali, born in 1580. He and his two sons had survived perilous times of warring factions, thanks to fortresses like this one.

We followed the leader to the original exterior door, formidable timbers anchored in place with iron bars. This opened into a small chamber with an interior door of the same design. Strategically placed directly overhead, a hole in the stone roof may have allowed men to pour boiling oil on assailants.

Within the castle grounds, we crossed through a maze between double rows of low-growing, sculpted boxwood. Arranged like four square frames, a corner of each one intersected a smaller central frame. Each of the two dozen corners was topped by a large knob of greenery.

"These shrubs will grow tall," Robert said. "One day it won't be easy to find the right path." I thought of our search for my ancestors. We had followed one blind alley after another, only to retrace our steps and try again, time after time. Today we had a clear view above the maze.

We emerged at the base of one of the towers. Treacherous stairs were steep enough to slow down any advancing army—even one from Pisa. I pushed myself up the stairwell by using my hands on the surrounding rough rock walls. Robert reached down and grasped my hand to help me up the knee-high top step. The climb was worth it. The Lucca Plain formed an impressive backdrop for medieval houses clustered below the fortress walls.

We left the castle to join more Orzalis in a small piazza in the center of town, eighteen of us sharing bruschetta and wine before dinner. Light rain fell as we moved downstairs into the Ristorante Osteria Del Vecchio

Olivo, to be seated at a long table before a wall of windows. Flowering plants filled large pots on a narrow strip of suspended patio with guard rails. The balcony ran the entire length of the building and hung above a steep hillside. Spectacular views extended a few miles across the green Lucca Plain to blue mountains.

Mario leaned across the table. "Did you ever find your Orzali connection?" he asked.

I reached into my purse and pulled out my updated ancestral chart. I had typed *Pasqua Micheli* in red. Mario brought out his tablet and unfolded it to form a screen and keyboard. He studied my family tree, then searched for a match in his. I held my breath. I'd included dates, but I didn't have copies of the baptism record.

"Ah, there she is, Pasqua Micheli," he said. He smiled and handed back my ancestral chart. I exhaled. Maria Bruna overheard and smiled, then turned to her husband and murmured, "Pasqua Micheli."

I leaned over and whispered in Robert's ear, "We're staying for dinner."

Dark clouds hovered, and bursts of lightning moved closer across the valley, followed by a deluge of rain.

"Oh, good! There's Father Cesare and Father Ottone," Maria Bruna said. We stood as two drenched, plain-clothes priests entered the room and announced they had to change. A short time later they reappeared in dry clothing. I wondered if it was customary for priests to pack an extra set of streetwear whenever they mingled with the masses.

People on each side of the table parted in the middle like the Red Sea to make a central place for each priest to dine with us. Father Cesare sat by me and began chatting with a British accent.

"I feel bad for Pasquale. That storm did terrible damage to the arboretum," he said.

I had no opportunity to continue the conversation. Tonight's tempest built to a crescendo as orders were taken, fierce rain slashing against the glass, dizzy dances of light and thunderous roars. The raging storm seemed to say, "You want celebration? You want spectacle? How's this?" Bursts of lightning flashed across the valley.

I was served first and sat, hands in my lap, waiting for the inevitable prayers that would precede the meal.

Father Cesare said, "You must eat, or your food will be cold and terrible." Was he joking? I scanned the faces of my Orzali cousins.

A few joined in. "*Mangia, mangia!*" Eat, eat!

Amid smiles of approval, I plunged my fork into *ravioli radicchio rosso* with flakes of *pecarino* cheese. Bits of pasta rolled in my mouth and filled my senses with memories of my childhood. Wine, crisp local vegetables, more wine, strawberries swirled with cream on a square of cake. I had waited a lifetime for this moment—to be seated among chatting and laughing family members, safe from the storm, savoring the spices and stories of my ancestors.

The rain settled into a sprinkle. People leaned into their chair backs to chat. Across the table, Maria Bruna bent forward and said, "Our son is arriving tonight from Milan, and we have to meet him at home. You'll have to get a ride down the mountain with my cousin Chesie." Who was Chesie? I couldn't remember meeting anyone by that name.

Someone collected the money, a modest sum of thirty-two euros for both of us.

The two priests stood and said, "*Buona sera.*"

Maria Bruna said, "They are leaving now." I gave her a blank stare. Of course they were leaving now.

"You must go now with Chesie," she said. "We'll pick you up in the morning at Porta Elisa." Robert and I stood up, still waiting for Chesie to appear.

Father Cesare said, "It's raining a little. Do you have an umbrella?"

"No," I said. "It's in Pasquale's car."

"We'll have to hurry so you don't get too wet."

Robert and I and the two priests were the only ones standing, and Maria Bruna was waving goodbye. It finally dawned on me. *Priests.* We were leaving the party with the two priests. Father Cesare wasn't just an honored guest; he was Chesie, my very distant cousin by marriage about a hundred and twenty-seven times removed.

Rain splattering on our heads, Robert and I chased the two priests through dimly lit village streets, around a retaining wall, down a hill, up a knoll, to a little car tilted with two wheels against the hillside. Our two companions dove into the front seats; Robert and I, in our damp clothes, slid into the back. The headlights did one last fan-shaped sweep of Montecarlo, and we began the twisted descent through the Apennine foothills.

We clipped along the slick one-lane road for two-way traffic, and I left indentations in the padded door handle as we rocked side to side down the mountain. Robert had braced himself between the door and the back seat, as usual. I reminded myself that headlights might signal oncoming traffic. Rough sections of road might prevent the car from watersliding over the edge. Maybe Chesie had divine intervention on his side.

"Maria Bruna said you've been to Lucca before," Father Cesare said.

"Yes, we looked for my family in all of Lucca's archives."

Father Ottone said, "Just use the records from Diocesano. You can rely on them for fact." He probably hadn't read the marriage records scrawled by a priest who consistently left out the last name of every bride and her family members. That's when we'd relied on census records.

"Yes. We spent a great deal of time at Archivio Diocesano," Robert said. "We found my wife's Orzali relatives in those records."

"And what did you think about the reunion dinner?" Father Cesare asked.

"Beyond my wildest dreams," I answered. "The food, the kindness of the Orzali family—it was fabulous."

We made a couple of hairpin turns at warp speed. I gripped the edge of the seat.

"What do the Americans think of our Pope Francis?" Father Cesare asked us, the non-Catholics in the back.

"They love him," I said. "He fills headlines with surprises. He refuses to live in the Vatican palace, travels in a compact car, and mingles in the streets with all the people, Catholic and non-Catholic."

"Yes, he has interesting new ideas," Father Cesare said.

We arrived at the valley floor and eased into traffic. Our windshield wipers thwacked a metronome beat as we drove on in uncomfortable silence.

"Do you live in Lucca?" I asked.

"No, we don't. Father Ottone is here just for a little while. He's a missionary in Africa. He's standing in for me tomorrow because I have a service near Pisa."

I didn't understand what "standing in" meant, but I didn't have time to ask. The walls of Lucca loomed ahead. A few minutes later we stopped just outside Porta San Pietro, the engine running, a clear signal that this was the end of the road for us.

Maybe Father Cesare couldn't go any farther because he didn't have Mila's decal on his window. Whatever the reason, with a *buona sera* and a couple of *grazies*, we stepped out into the warm summer rain and raced the six blocks for home.

42

The Reunion

Islipped into the outfit I'd packed for the event, a carefully chosen, dramatic little number in black and white. It had to be just right for me to blend in, to look like I belonged to an Italian family, most of whom paid close attention to *la bella figura*.

I stared at my reflection in the mirror. "It's all wrong! I'll die of heat stroke." I rummaged through tops and finally settled on my black slacks and a cream-colored cotton jacket I'd purchased the day before for ten euros from a street vendor.

A brisk walk and twenty minutes later, we stood outside Porta Elisa, our faces to the morning sun. We didn't have long to wait for our hosts to arrive.

"There you are, elegant as always," Maria Bruna said as we climbed into the car.

One glance at Pasquale's open-collared shirt, and Robert slipped off his tie and folded it into his pocket.

"Today we go to Chiesa San Giorgio," she said. "Father Ottone is standing in for Chesie."

Now I understood last night's conversation with the two priests. Father Ottone would be conducting today's mass. This much I knew: Chiesa San Giorgio—Church of St. George—was located near Gignano, perched high in the western foothills of the Apennine Mountains.

Maria Bruna said in perfect English, "Of all the families we have hosted, you are the first who bothered to learn Italian."

My heart skipped. Eight long years ago, I had peered into a microfilm viewer at Giovanni "John" Motroni's birth record, impossible to read. Now here we were, chatting with his Orzali relatives in Italian, headed for the very church where he was baptized.

Pasquale maneuvered easily through steep inclines and sharp bends on the same route Robert and I had traveled with Mila. This was Via Pieve di Brancoli, the road to my grandfather's home. I could almost see him as a young boy skipping and jumping along the stone path from his house, around the retaining wall, and down the narrow road about a half mile to Chiesa San Giorgio.

Wild, jumbled forests gave way to terraced orchards of olive trees and precise rows of grapevines. We climbed through high terrain above honey-colored stucco houses with red tile roofs, clustered around churches. Just ahead, on the valley side of the road, stood the gray bell tower of Chiesa San Giorgio, the church I had spotted on Mario Orzali's website. We joined two other cars in the parking lot and clambered out for introductions.

Near the stone wall overlooking the valley, a bilingual sign declared, "Even though certain sources claim that this parish existed as far back as 772, the most ancient reference dates from the year 1097." That gray brick building had witnessed baptisms, marriages, and funerals for more than nine hundred years.

Beside the church door, a small sign stated that although the church was closed, donations would be appreciated for volunteers who cared for the building and its contents. Dozens of village churches in this region had closed due to poor attendance, a story repeated throughout Italy. Yet, ironically, thousands of pilgrims and visitors streamed into St. Peter's Square in Vatican City each week for a blessing from Pope Francis.

We pushed open the thick wooden door and stepped onto marble tile surrounded by ocher stone walls. The musty scent of old wood mingled with the odor of furniture polish. As my eyes grew accustomed to the dim light, I listened to whispers and murmurs from other visitors, shadows moving between granite walls. I remembered Maria Bruna's prediction: *You will hear them, our ancestors, whispering in the church and in the forest. You will hear them.* My grandfather must have heard whispers like these as he entered this very sanctuary.

Objects inside the church became visible as my eyes adjusted to the muted light. The apse was divided by rows of stone columns with ornately sculpted supports. Two fierce marble lions guarded the pulpit. Straight ahead was the altar, a freestanding stone table with six legs, supported by a raised platform. Above it hung a cross-shaped painting of the crucifixion, illuminated by second-story windows and suspended by chains from the ceiling.

Between the front door and the altar, a marble wall divided the church on both sides of the aisle, with seating in front and behind each barricade. Three stone steps led up to the front seats and altar within the light-filled rotunda. I sat briefly behind the wall in one of those dim back seats, completely out of view of the people in the front section, and I wondered who was consigned to those isolated back rows.

A gold-embellished, white-glazed sculpture of San Giorgio, the patron saint, filled a polished blue recess in the wall. Cape flying, he rode a rearing horse, and his spear was plunged into the mouth of a greenish-beige dragon. A sculpted young woman watched him from a distance, her hands clasped in gratitude. She probably represented the damsel St. George had just saved.

To our left, a large octagonal stone baptismal font seemed intended for total immersion. I placed my hands on the sculpted stone surround, where my grandfather and multiple generations before him had been baptized, symbolically dying to darkness and rising to new spiritual light. In that moment I felt a strong connection to my ancient family roots, grateful for the privilege of being invited into this sacred place, opened today for this special occasion—the Orzali family reunion.

We left the sanctuary and stepped into bright sunlight. Jolted out of reverie, I searched for Maria Bruna.

"Why the separation in that church?" I asked. "Who sat in the back?"

"The women," she answered.

"You're kidding. Do you mean that only the men could be up front near the priest?"

"Of course," she said. "That's the way it was in those days."

We were distracted by introductions to new arrivals as more cousins clustered near the door. Father Ottone joined us, and Orzali family members followed him into the church, along with a few residents from the nearby village.

We approached the marble walls that had separated men and women. I stopped. Maybe it also separated Catholics from non-Catholics. I stepped aside to let the others pass. Mario leaned in close to my ear. "It's okay. You can go up," he said.

I saw other women take the stairs to the best seats in the church, and I followed. I'd love to have been there on the first day women were allowed into the front rows. Did the men shake their heads and mutter their disapproval? Were there protests? Did it seem like an unholy act? Or did the men accept the Supreme Voice from the Vatican and say, "Well, okay then; this might work." And were the women happy with this outcome? Or were they more comfortable with tradition after centuries of the old arrangement, thank you very much? I smiled as I took my seat next to Robert, grateful that the walls of separation belonged to ancient history.

Father Ottone welcomed us, and Maria Bruna stood near the altar to read Bible passages, which were followed by audience response—rituals that linked these people to their spiritual world. Father Ottone followed with another Bible passage. He announced that he would deliver the homily twice, the second time for the English speakers in the audience. Then he began in Italian.

He spoke rapidly, too fast for me to comprehend. Some of my Italian progenitors must have had a similar experience with the mystery of Latin just beyond their grasp. I closed my eyes as unfamiliar phrases resonated from the curved ceiling. Words melded and echoed in rhythmic repetition. As I sat, lost in listening, beyond understanding, surrounded by light and mesmerizing sound, something ancient stirred within my soul: a conversation with the divine. I felt raw energy, the powerful presence of my ancestors. Unimpeded by distance and time, they surrounded me, cradled me in the mystery of eternity. Unexplained, unimaginable, they had found me.

The service over, I found it hard to stand. Robert pulled me to my feet, and we moved slowly in total silence through the church, out to the courtyard, and into Pasquale's car. In full sun, we joined a caravan through tight turns to our next destination. The leisurely two-mile drive to San Giusto di Brancoli offered just enough time to reenter the now.

As we crested the hill, Ristorante A Palazzo seemed to rise to greet us. The stone structure held four levels of small windows.

The Orzalis now numbered more than thirty. People gathered in small groups to greet each other before we filed into the restaurant, redolent with the sweet scent of Italian seasoning and old wood. The rustic interior held a large banquet hall with stone walls and dark beams. Potted philodendrons and succulents spilled from windowsills. In one corner, green globes resembling winter squash hung in a staggered cluster from the high ceiling.

Pasquale said the thousand-year-old building was once a prison. A man's voice in the crowd boomed out in Italian, "I'd gladly go to jail here if I could eat their food every day."

Polished wooden chairs scraped against the stone floor as people took their places on both sides of a long L-shaped table covered in white linen. Wine was poured, "chin-chin," and lunch was served.

Crostini—small, toasted bread rounds—held exquisite little pieces of edible art: pine nuts cradled in a tiny nest of wilted greens, or finely diced tomatoes with basil, or a swirled bean concoction topped with a parsley leaf, or bits of paper-thin prosciutto. We took our time to savor the delicacies and to commune with one another in friendship and fellowship: slow food, Italian style. The right place, the right time; this was where I belonged.

Plates were cleared, and chatter resumed with a little more wine. Then another course arrived—*gnocchetti agli asparagi*—plump little stuffed potato pillows with bits of asparagus in a cream sauce.

Basta—enough. More discussions, more laughter, and servers carried away the dishes.

We were well into the second hour of lunch when, surprise, more food arrived—a delicious combination of nutty grains and wild mushrooms seasoned with Italian spices. That course took another hour of small bites, a little more wine, livelier small group conversations: Lucca's recent soccer win; restoration efforts at the arboretum; the *bambini*, so adorable.

I gazed down the table at the youngest Orzalis: a four-year-old girl and her twelve-month-old brother. He eagerly munched a spoonful of mashed beans offered by his mother and made a funny face when he took a sip of watered-down red wine.

Mario approached from across the room. "I have a surprise for you." He bent down to show me a crumpled brown parchment with uneven edges. "This copy is dated 1171. It's written in Latin and comes from the state archives in the Macerata region of Italy. It was stored with other scrolls, twenty-six mentioning Orzali, all closed in special trunks." He placed the document into my hands. "It's the first mention of Orzali, a castle on an island at the confluence of two rivers. This is for you."

I gasped. *What did he just hand me?* This looked like an original fragment of a scroll. I quickly glanced at the reverse side, relieved to see modern ocher-colored paper. This was an astonishingly good copy of an ancient manuscript—right down to the thick, crumpled parchment. Mario must have spent a great deal of time creating that extraordinary reproduction.

"This—this is fantastic. Thank you," I stammered.

Then he handed me typewritten pages labeled *Symposio Orzali 2010*. "These contain the Latin transcription and an English translation of the scroll. There is also a family tree of the Counts of the Castle Orzali from the tenth and eleventh centuries," he said.

The date 1171 swirled through my mind, and I wondered about daily routines in the Orzali castle more than eight centuries ago. Perhaps it was a prototype for the stone castle we had visited in Montecarlo—drafty and dangerous. I had wondered why we'd visited that castle last evening. Now it was clear. What better way to set the stage for Mario's gift!

He straightened up and smiled. Then he carried other sets of copies to the two Orzalli (with a double L) brothers from California. I couldn't wait to read the summaries, but I reluctantly filed the papers in my purse as dessert arrived.

Panna cotta metà fragole metà cioccolato featured flower petals fashioned from strawberry slices, a center of creamy *panna cotta*, and a thread of dark chocolate drizzled in wavy lines over the dessert and onto the white plate. I savored each small berry slice slowly, hoping to remember this sweet ending long after we left the Orzali family reunion.

Feeling fulfilled on so many levels, we rose with others as the event came to a close. We gathered our belongings, and I wandered over to a long sideboard draped with a banner of the Orzali Family Tree. The gigantic chart covered two table lengths with more than 140 names.

We assembled outside the restaurant for photos, Mario and his wife on the top step. Others found places on stairs and the piazza to form four rows, Father Ottone with one knee on the piazza on the front left, Pasquale and Maria Bruna down on one knee in the front, and me, standing in the center between them.

Members of the Orzali clan were all Caucasian, but there the similarity ended. From twelve months to eight decades old, they could have been a cross section of random people we passed every day on the streets of Lucca. Engineer, pathologist, botanist, researcher, teacher, farmer, university student, manager—these people represented a wide range of occupations, a microcosm of diversity. Father Ottone, who wasn't related to any of the Orzalis, blended right in.

No one seemed ready to leave. People chatted in clusters, and Robert snapped photos. Pasquale and Maria Bruna stood with Barbara, their vivacious daughter-in-law. Both she and her husband, Alessio Naccarati, were doing postdoctoral research for the Human Genetics Foundation in Torino. Her business card read, *Genomic Variation in Human Populations and Complex Diseases Unit.* The three were deep in conversation.

I seized the opportunity to dash back inside the building and approached the hostess.

"*Mi scusa, per favore.* Could you tell me if there is a woman in this village by the name of Ada Motroni? She's my distant cousin. I visited her here in San Giusto four years ago, when she was ninety-six years of age." I remembered chasing Ada through darkened yards and watching her climb steep hills in impossible open-toed sandals with wedge soles. "I wondered if . . . if she's still alive." I was afraid of the answer.

"Oh, yes," the waitress answered in Italian. "She used to be quite active, walked all over these hills, frequently dropping by to visit us. Recently she has been more confined to her house. We don't see her very often, but there will be a huge dinner party in her honor here at A Palazzo in July, when she turns one hundred."

Her words brought a smile to my heart. "Amazing," I said. "I would love to send her a birthday card and some photos. Do you know her address?"

"No, but you might try contacting her son. He lives here in San Giusto. I don't know his address, but I will write down his name." With a *grazie mille*, I folded the scrap of paper into my coin purse. Once more, I planned to request Mila's help. If anyone could locate that gentleman, she could.

I emerged into the Tuscan sunshine. Cousins were still milling about, hugging, making plans for future meetings. As with telephone calls, "hello" was quick, and "goodbye" took forever. I found Robert near the edge of the piazza, and we gazed down over the wall at a stunning panorama of the Serchio River far below.

"She's still alive," I said. "Ada Motroni is headed for birthday number one hundred, and I believe she'll make it."

"Of course, she will," he said. "Do you want to see her?"

"I'd love to. But it sounds like she spends most of her time confined to her house. I don't want to barge in with a surprise visit if she's ill. Mila told me that the last few times she called, Ada didn't answer."

"Maybe the time isn't right to see her now." Robert said. "I think I'd like to remember that spirited woman the way she was four years ago."

Pasquale and Maria Bruna were among the last to leave the party, and we followed them to their car. The road circled below Ada Motroni's driveway, the house just out of view. I nudged Robert and pointed up the steep embankment that Ada had scaled on our last visit. He smiled.

Tears welled bittersweet. "Happy birthday, Ada," I whispered. I was grateful that she was still alive, sad that I might not ever see her again. I had done what I was compelled to do. My work in these hills was finished. We drove down the mountainside and out of the Brancoli region for the last time.

43

The Search for Domenico Marcucci

"We did it! We found your family. Mission accomplished." Robert was beaming as he bounced around our apartment. He gathered up pamphlets, leafed through brochures for a final keep-or-toss decision, and packed a carton of books to ship home. "I wonder how much this weighs."

I was staring at my little album, assembled back in Oregon and carried with me through all our Tuscan adventures. I tapped on the open page. "There's just one more thing . . ."

I pointed to the sepia photo of Domenico Marcucci in uniform. His picture had traveled with us on three separate trips to Italy.

Born in 1841, Domenico had married Marianna Fambrini, my beautiful great-grandmother. Their wedding was held in Diecimo. Names and birthdates of their family members had been provided by the researcher at Window #5 in the Ufficio Comune, but from there the paper trail for Domenico disappeared. No census record, no death record, no parish record; Domenico had vanished about 1880. Four years later, Marianna gave birth to a little girl, my grandmother Noni, but the newborn's father was Agostino Rossi, not Domenico.

"I wonder what happened to Domenico," I said.

Robert shook his head and smiled. "Looks like we need to visit the wise women of Storico."

A brisk walk across the city, and we stood at the open gates of Archivio Storico. I pressed the buzzer, and Cristina Marinari smiled and waved through the glass. The doors slid open, and we stepped onto the stone floor of the library. Cristina's cheeks touched both sides of mine, then Robert's, and we caught up on recent events.

I pointed to Domenico's photo. "We have a mystery. This man disappeared without a trace about 1880. I'm hoping his uniform will tell us something about his military service. I found a similar one in the illustrated *Guide to Archivio Storico.*"

Cristina retrieved the book from a back room and opened it to a colored drawing of a military man in the *divisa della guardia daziaria*—the uniform of a customs officer. She studied my sepia photo and said, "They are similar but not identical. The uniform in the sketch is blue and green. Your photo appears to be a dark top with light-colored pants."

"But look at that strange hat." I pointed to an inverted bucket topped with a small sphere the size of a ping-pong ball. "They're the same in both pictures, and the chevrons on the sleeves are very similar. Is it possible that the color of uniforms changed over time?"

"I'll go look for the original sketches," she said.

Cristina soon returned and placed the original on the table before us. "I'm sorry, this is the only sketch of a customs officer." It was the same one I'd found in the illustrated guide.

"In the 1870s, those guards were stationed at each of Lucca's six portals," Cristina said. "They collected taxes on items brought into the city, and on purchased goods when people left. The man in your photo may have been a customs officer, but I can't verify that he worked in Lucca. Did he live here?"

"I believe the family lived in Diecimo," I said.

"That's under the jurisdiction of the town of Borgo a Mozzano," she said. "Maybe you can find something there."

We gathered our things, thanked Cristina, and headed home.

Early the next morning, we boarded the northbound bus and threaded along the banks of the Serchio River, stopping at various villages. Forty minutes later, we stepped down on the side of the highway at Borgo a Mozzano. "No bus station," Robert said. "No help available to get us back to Lucca."

We approached a roadside building with an *Informazione* sign over the door. The woman at the counter spoke Italian and fielded our questions about the location of municipal archives. She also suggested several good restaurants for lunch. We settled on dining with a view, and Robert found a business card for an *osteria* with a map on the back.

"Do you have a schedule for the bus back to Lucca?" I asked.

She pointed to a kiosk across the highway. "There's a poster of departing times."

"I want to find the archive office." I said to Robert. "The kiosk can wait."

We dashed across the busy highway. Our feet crunched on gravel by the side of the road, and we inhaled the pungent odors of oily pavement and sweet yellow grass. We followed an empty street up the hill, through a tunnel barely wide enough to accommodate one car, a blind turn at the other end. We raced about three car lengths, made the turn, and stopped outside the tunnel to give each other a high five. Another steep climb, then we padded along gray pavers flanked on both sides by three-story buildings in shades of pink and gray. Little shops advertised shoes, flowers, toys, and garden tools.

On top of a sixteen-foot-tall archway Robert spotted an oval sign: *Municipio—Borgo a Mozzano*. Through the open door we entered a lobby two stories high and large enough for ballroom dancing. A woman approached from a side door, fresh-faced, dark-haired, midtwenties.

I retrieved my little album and pointed to the photo. "We're looking for this man, Domenico Marcucci." My voice echoed in the great hall. "He was born in 1841 in Diecimo and vanished about forty years later. Do you recognize this uniform?"

She shook her head. Domenico probably wasn't a regional legend.

"May we look in your census records for Diecimo? Something around 1880?" I said in Italian.

She smiled and said, "I speak a little English." She led us down a narrow corridor into a small room holding two gigantic drop-lid desks with slanted tops, school desks for giants. She pointed to forms on a counter, and I filled out papers as she searched through a card file in the first desk.

"Oh, it is here!" She seemed to be excited, surprised to find a record for Marcucci. "I will call for the supervisor."

Moments later she returned with a slender, fifty-something man with dark hair and steel rimmed glasses. He muttered in Italian as he prowled through a cabinet, retrieved a book, thumbed through its pages, and placed the open ledger on a table.

"*Eccola,*" he said. Here it is.

Robert and I peered at the Marcucci family listing: nineteen people in the same house in Diecimo. That implied very crowded living conditions. I concentrated on Domenico's nuclear family and ignored his cousins, in-laws, and children of other relatives.

Two people in the list (**) were buried at Olive Hill Cemetery in Geyserville, California.

Marcucci, Domenico Born 12 Jan 1841, Diecimo
*Fambrini, Marianna** Wife Born in San Giusto di Brancoli*
Marcucci, Regolo [Orlando] Son Born 31 Aug 1867, San Giusto
*Marcucci, Lorenzo** Son Born 22 Dec 1868, Diecimo*
Marcucci, Pietro Son Born 07 Jun 1871, Diecimo

Near the bottom of the page I spotted one more familiar name, Marianna's father: *Fambrini, Domenico Born in Brancoli.*

"He must have moved across the Serchio River to live with his daughter in Diecimo," I said. "There's a cross by his name. What does that mean?"

The archivist answered in Italian. "It means he died, probably after this census was taken."

"What is the date of the census?"

"We're not certain. This is our only census for the period, and information may have been gathered over several years."

How did they keep track of anything without a date? I glanced at the last entry, number nineteen, the birth date of a child, 30 August 1882. The same loopy handwriting ran down the entire length of the page; odds were good that this census was completed after that date.

So Domenico Marcucci was probably still alive in 1882, but two years later, Marianna was with a different man, and gave birth to my grandmother. Nothing I saw made any sense.

Robert asked the archivist to move the ledger near the window for better light, and he began snapping pictures without a flash.

"I'd like to look for a death record for Domenico Marcucci," I said.

The archivist closed the desk lid. "They are in another room." We followed him down the corridor, across the wide expanse of the lobby, and into an office, where a woman worked at a computer screen.

"There was a wedding today, and she must record the marriage and list the witnesses," the archivist said.

Near her desk, upright ledger cards stood at attention in a large open box the size of a hope chest. The archivist thumbed through them, repeated the process, and shook his head. "I'm sorry. There is no card for Domenico Marcucci. It's not unusual for death records to be missing."

I pulled out my little album and pointed to photos. "This is Domenico Marcucci and his wife, Marianna Fambrini." I looked into the eyes of the archivist. "*La mia famiglia.*" My family.

I have no clue why I did that. Maybe I was hoping records would materialize just by showing those photos. The archivist smiled and nodded as if this were normal behavior. I was desperate to find something, anything. Maybe we could find Domenico through one of his relatives.

"Could you look for his son, Pietro Marcucci? He may have died around 1888."

He thumbed through the card file again. This time the archivist said, "*Eccola.*" Here it is. Once more, he cross-referenced a ledger. We returned to the little room down the hall. He retrieved the book, turned several pages, and held it open for me to see. I leaned in close to read the death record of Pietro Marcucci.

"He died in his teens. Too bad the cause of death isn't listed," I said.

"Oh, you'll never find that information in these records," he said.

"Are these names listed alphabetically?" I asked. "Is it possible to find other Marcuccis in this register?"

He nodded yes.

"Could you please look for Domenico Marcucci in this book?"

His index finger crawled back through the page corners. He flipped leaves of paper back and forth. Then he stopped and stared.

"What's wrong?" I asked.

He didn't answer right away. "This is unusual. Highly unusual."

I moved to his side to see the open ledger. This wasn't a brief note. Both pages were filled with information about Domenico Marcucci.

"This is the transcribed medical report sent here from a doctor in San Francisco, California," he said. "Domenico Marcucci died there in 1880."

"San Francisco! That's impossible," I said. "Could I see that Diecimo census record again?"

The approximate date of the census record was 1882, two years after Domenico had died in San Francisco. Why was he listed in the census record?

The archivist placed his index finger on line number 3, Domenico Marcucci. He ran his finger to the right along the line and continued across the blank page on the opposite side. He stopped at the last column, where something was written in tiny script. I hadn't noticed it before.

"What does it say?"

"California."

"Domenico Marcucci was supposedly away in California at the time of this census," I said, "but there's no cross on the ledger page. No one back home knew he had died there two years before."

The archivist moved the death register to view it in better light, and I translated a summary of the second page aloud for Robert:

> *Certificate of Death – Department of Sanitation, Office of Vital Statistics – Book 7, Page 71*
>
> *11 O'Farrell Street, San Francisco, California, United States 9 July 1883*
> > *Name: Domenico Marcucci; Sex: Male*
> > *Place of birth: Italy; Age: 40 years*
> > *Date of death: 28 December 1880*
> > *Place of death: St. Mary's Hospital*
> > *Cause of death: Peritonite*
> > *Place of burial: Calvary Cemetery*

"*Peritonite.* He died of peritonitis—maybe a ruptured appendix," I said. "Domenico's death wasn't registered in Borgo a Mozzano until 1884, four long years after he died in California. My God. All that time Marianna was in limbo here at home. Three boys to feed under the age of thirteen, no word from a missing husband thousands of miles away. What a nightmare."

This discovery had revealed that Domenico was the first to sail to America. The rest of my family eventually followed his trail, but Marianna was the last to leave Italy. Three decades after Domenico's death, and two years after the death of her second husband, Agostino, Marianna had boarded a ship in Le Havre, sailed across winter's stormy seas to New York, and took a three-thousand-mile train ride west. She must have endured weeks of terror, but what a glorious ending when she was finally reunited with long-absent sons and daughters and grandchildren in San Francisco.

Robert snapped photos of the death register as I gave my *grazie mille* to the archivists for solving the mystery of Domenico Marcucci.

We stepped out of the building and up the street in search of our café. We hadn't gone more than half a block when Robert murmured, "Someone is following us." We stopped and turned to see the young woman approaching from the archive office. She hurried to narrow the gap.

"Excuse me," she said. "I don't think you understand how extraordinary is this discovery. Many people come for a death record, and we are disappointed, because many are turned away without information. Deaths were not always listed in the 1880s, and census was done when there was time and money for someone to do it. We can thank the doctor in San Francisco for mailing his report to Borgo a Mozzano. We are excited to find this. You are lucky today. Very lucky. I thought you should know." I gave my sincere thanks.

We followed meandering streets up steep hills to the *osteria* with a view. Over lunch we celebrated our find. I pulled out my little album and browsed through family photos.

"Domenico was tall and handsome, an officer and a gentleman," I said. "You could see it in his clothes, in his eyes, in the way he held himself. I questioned why Marianna ended up with Agostino, a rough-cut miner from Farnocchia." I pointed to my album. "This is the only photo of him, a short guy with a cigar, an ill-fitting jacket, and a hole in one of his shoes. I wondered what Marianna saw in him. But from what we discovered today, I have a different impression of Noni's father," I said.

"What do you mean?" Robert asked.

"Marianna was a widow, nine years older than Agostino, with three young sons and no means of support. Her immediate family—father, mother, both siblings—all dead; no word for two years from a missing husband in America. Think of the agony she must have endured. She must have been frantic. How could she raise her boys alone with no source of income? Agostino must have offered a solution: his home across the river in Ponte Rotto."

"Marianna couldn't remarry without proof of Domenico's death, but she couldn't survive without Agostino," Robert said. "Then they had two daughters, two more mouths to feed. It couldn't have been easy. Food must have been scarce. No extra money for new shoes."

"I have enormous respect for Agostino. He rescued Marianna," I said. "This discovery has changed everything I thought I knew about the man."

According to immigration records, Agostino's last known occupation was as a proprietor in Ponte Rotto, during a time when no one could pay for goods or rent with money. Trades would have made it very difficult to support a family of seven, but he persevered as long as he could.

One by one, Marianna's four surviving sons and daughters, Lorenzo and Orlando Marcucci, and Amabile and Argentina Rossi, managed to emigrate to the United States. Eight years later, Agostino Rossi followed them for a promise of a better life in California. According to immigration records, Marianna stayed with Agostino's brother, Santi Rossi, and his family in Ponte Rotto. Agostino died ten months later of heart disease at age fifty-nine, before he could send for his wife.

His physical being could withstand no more stress. Agostino Rossi was my hero.

After lunch we ambled back down into the heart of Borgo a Mozzano. The village was silent, streets vacant, shops closed for afternoon naps. The archive doors were locked.

"Spooky," Robert said. "I'm glad we didn't take the afternoon bus; we'd have missed everything."

We headed down the last hill to the valley floor. The *Informazione* building was closed. A short distance away we found the blue kiosk planted among clumps of dry grass alongside the highway. I looked in the plastic sleeve for the bus schedule. Empty. No arrival or departure times posted.

"We're in big trouble," I said. "What if we missed the last bus of the day?"

"I vote we wait," Robert said.

I paced, peered down the highway repeatedly, ten, twenty, thirty minutes under Tuscany's relentless summer sun. "This is making me crazy. I think we should go to that gas station up the road and call a cab. How can you be so calm? What are you staring at?"

Robert was peering at the ground. "Ants."

"How can you watch ants at a time like this? Here we are, stranded by the side of the road in this sweltering heat, my brain is broiling, and you're watching ants!"

"Watch what happens to that one hauling home a piece of straw," Robert said.

I looked down. The insect struggled to move a stem about the size of his body. With great effort he positioned it over the hole in the anthill and heaved it in, then crawled in after it. The straw popped out of the hole and fell to one side. The ant emerged, located his prize, and repeated the difficult procedure. Once more the object shot out of the hole like a missile. He tried again.

"Reminds me of us," I said. "Hammered by scary roads, locked churches, language barriers, lost records, and train strikes."

Robert smiled and reached for my hand. "We didn't give up."

"I couldn't have done this without you," I said. "You stayed the course when it seemed impossible."

"We didn't do it alone," he said. "Think of Mila and all the other people who moved mountains for us."

I don't know how the ant's story ended. I heard the engine whine just before the blue bus pulled up to take us back to Lucca.

44

Amici—Friends

That night, we shared stories and photos with Mila at her new apartment outside the walls of Lucca Centre, this one with a real elevator. Mila had found an address for Ada Motroni's son, so I could send a birthday card and photos for her centennial celebration.

Gabriella joined us. She had guided us through Piazza di Brancoli on previous visits. She was with us when Mila found Ada Motroni in a little stone church with two pink balloons waving in the wind. She had led us to my family tree, in a book stashed in the home of Ubaldo Cecchettini.

We were just leaving for dinner in the valley when Mila's partner, Rino, called and said he'd come along. The five of us ended up in Mila's car, Rino driving and complaining bitterly with wild gestures about the danger of parts that might fly off the old car at any moment. He didn't know that this old car was the magic coach that had carried us to the homes of my ancestors.

Our time together was filled with good food and wine, and lots of laughter. Mila was like a sister, and I adored her. When we started this journey, I had no idea that my quest would produce an amazing link of friendship strong enough to last a lifetime. I hated for the evening to end.

"Our work here is finished," I said sadly.

Mila answered, "Ah, but your journey has just begun."

45

Dinner and Discovery

The next morning, our last day in Lucca, Pasquale, our Orzali host, surprised us with a phone call and an invitation to dinner at his house. That afternoon, he picked us up at the usual spot just outside Porta Elisa, and we drove about a half hour east to the town of Gragnano.

Pasquale pointed downhill from the road. "That's it. The house is hidden by the forest."

He parked in front of a large iron gate, where we left the car. He keyed in a code, and we entered a botanical paradise. Trees of every description surrounded the villa, specimens from all parts of the world. Shrubs made up the inner tier, many in huge pots. Within that boundary, an explosion of colorful flowers lined the walkways. A blue metallic tag caught my eye, and I leaned down for a closer look.

"They're all labeled," Pasquale said. "Each tag is inscribed with the Latin name of the plant."

Maria Bruna greeted us on the brick patio. She invited us to tour the property with Pasquale while she put finishing touches on dinner.

He led us through a tropical zone, glossy dark leaves and exotic floral colors surrounding a pond. Then we climbed a few steps to a terrace filled with desert plants—succulents and cacti stretching barbed and bulbous arms skyward. Nearby, a greenhouse was filled with labeled trays, green shoots emerging from pods on white cotton pads. Countless vials of seeds waited to be planted.

"How is this possible? How do you keep them all alive?" I asked.

"We have two seasons here: what you see now, and the other half year when the plants are moved into greenhouses." Pasquale pointed to another large structure and to a sunroom running the length of the house.

"But so many plants. And the pots are enormous!"

"Yes, it's quite a job." Pasquale was a master of understatement. He described his daily walk through the property, manually turning on water where needed, checking his nursery, tending to hundreds of specimens.

Now I understood Pasquale's reaction to the storm damage in Lucca's arboretum. Plants were his passion on a scale I couldn't have imagined without walking these grounds.

Candlelight flickered on the patio table, where we shared a delicious meal prepared by Maria Bruna. I was amazed by the kindness of these people, honored to be invited into their home. After dinner, we moved indoors for a video of their recent trip to the United States.

"I love your music, I love your cities, I love your country," Pasquale said. He raved about the enormous sacrifices made by brave men and women to free Italy from Fascist control. "I love your country more than you do! We will never forget," he said.

The telephone rang. "*Pronto*," Maria Bruna said. She turned to us, her hand over the receiver. "It's my cousin from California. He wants to know how the reunion went." She continued the conversation in Italian, then handed the phone to me. "He wants to speak to you."

"*Buona sera*," I said.

"It's probably better if you speak English," said a male voice.

"No problem. You're calling from California?"

"Yes. Maria Bruna tells me you lived in Healdsburg. That's what I wanted to ask you. Where was your home?"

"About ten miles out of town in Alexander Valley."

"Near Alexander Valley Winery?"

"The winery wasn't there when I was growing up, but yes, it's just down the road from the property. How do you know about that winery?"

"I live in Healdsburg," he said.

"Really! What is your address?" He rattled off the number and the name of a road that meandered west of Healdsburg.

"I don't believe it!"

"Yes, you must come and visit me."

From the discovery of seven unmarked graves in California, Robert and I had started the strange journey to find my family. Now here we were, eight years later, at my cousin's house in Italy. A relative just happened to phone while I was here, and he was calling from my hometown of Healdsburg.

"We've come full circle," I said to Robert. "He lives less than eight miles from Olive Hill Cemetery, where this all began."

46

Tombstones in the Yard

Back in Oregon, I pulled the chart of seven names for Olive Hill and penciled in Lorenzo Marcucci's birthdate, verified in the records at Borgo a Mozzano, but I still needed more information about my step-grandfather, Vincent Mortara, and his brother Frances.

I placed a call to Vincent's stepson, Elias Hruska, who invited Robert and me to his California home. Heads down over his dining room table, we pored over Vincent's diaries, all written in Italian. Elias, a former Italian instructor, helped me translate. His wife, Maria, born and raised in Italy, assisted us with clarification of troublesome text.

Elias was still in contact with Vincent's family in Italy, and they emailed a copy of his birth record. I left the home of Elias and Maria Hruska with a bulging portfolio of notes and copies of Vincent's diaries. Back in Oregon, I sent for a copy of his brother Francesco's California death certificate. His date of birth matched information gleaned from Harry Bosworth's records in Geyserville, California.

The chart for Olive Hill finally finished, we dove into the problem of financing tombstones.

"It's not just the cost of gravestones," I said. "Add in transportation and placement, and that jacks the price into the thousands. This project seems impossible."

Robert said, "I'll call a granite company to see what we can work out."

Eight short miles from home, we entered a well-lit showroom with a high ceiling and a wall of windows on the south side. Scattered around the perimeter, multicolored stones ranged from charcoal gray to forest green to reddish brown, some with magical marble swirls, others with iridescent mica flecks infused into granite. All were polished, and most were inscribed with names and dates of people who had recently died.

We met the manager, a soft-spoken man with an air of formality more suited to funeral parlors than to stone works. He guided us through a side door into an avocado-green office with a big desk left over from the seventies, then through a passageway and into the production area. We walked on concrete pockmarked from heavy use and avoided the puddle surrounding the stone-cutting saw. One large work in progress was covered with a Lucite template, letters and numbers carved into the hard surface beneath. Layered grit covered everything.

"You mentioned you were concerned about costs. Understandable with six stones to do, but I may have a solution." The manager pointed to several blank ones lined up along two-by-four wooden runners. "Those remnant blocks are suitable for smaller headstones. We could polish and engrave them to your specifications at a reasonable cost."

I gazed at five chunks of nondescript gray stone. The sixth one had been polished, its dull surface transformed like a mineral mass of iridescence seen under water.

"Would they all have to be the same kind of stone?" Suddenly overwhelmed, I said, "I don't know what I'm doing. I don't even know what size to order."

The manager's voice dropped just above a whisper. "This would depend on the length of the name and what you want on each stone. We could help you with that." Over the decades that reassuring, respectful voice must have guided hundreds of bereaved people through tough decisions.

Robert pointed to a remnant. "That stone over there. What would that cost with an engraved name and years of birth and death?" The manager said it would depend on the length of the name. He suggested a price around $150.00, but that didn't include a base for the gravestone and transportation to Olive Hill. I knew the estimate was reasonable and affordable, but the added costs were still too high for our budget.

"Could we set them in concrete bases ourselves?" Robert asked. I looked at him to see if he was joking.

"I guess that's doable," the manager answered. "We could call you each time a remnant becomes available, and you could decide whether or not you want to purchase it for engraving. There isn't a rush on this, is there?"

"No, no, not at all. Take your time." I was relieved with the possibility of stretching payments over several months, but how would we manage Robert's construction project?

Back home, Robert outlined his plan for building tombstones in the back yard. It seemed crazy, but he convinced me it was worth a try. We huddled over our household spreadsheet of projected income and expenses.

"Our budget doesn't include tombstones. Are there any expenses we could eliminate?" I asked.

"Like food? Clothing? Lights? What do you have in mind?"

"What about television? If we cancel cable, the savings in one year would almost pay for the project. Could you live with that?"

The next day found us unhooking cables and re-hooking TV ports to a couple of devices from Radio Shack, two sleek little boxes resembling transistor radios. As we flipped through channels, we picked up ABC, CBS, NBC, FOX, and three PBS choices. We found a couple more: a sci-fi channel, one featuring movies, and one playing reruns of M*A*S*H and other old shows from the sixties and seventies.

Our task finished, Robert paused to reconsider the option of canceling cable. "I've never been thrilled about throwing all that cash at ridiculous programs." He sounded hesitant, then declared, "Television for tomb-stones—works for me."

We returned to the monument showroom every time we received a call, sometimes in rain and snow as winter blew in, and selected the best stones to be engraved before we hauled each one home. Slowly, inscribed marble and granite gravestones piled up in our garage.

In the spring, Robert began the task of setting each engraved marker into concrete in our back yard. First he constructed a two-by-four frame of wood large enough for a three-inch collar of concrete to surround each stone, with drilled holes in the wood for slanted rebar supports so the stone would tilt at its upper edge. He poured concrete into the form and onto a blue plastic tarp beneath the wooden structure. Then he wrestled each rectangular grave marker, average weight fifty pounds, onto its slanted rebar grid, and filled the collar form to the top with the remaining concrete. Once it cured, he unscrewed the wooden supports and knocked them away from the block. As summer went on, our landscape began to resemble a graveyard. The gnarled and twisted branches of late November's bare trees made a spooky backdrop for the bizarre collection.

The following March ushered in a wild profusion of cherry blossoms, with blue hyacinth, white daffodils, and pink bleeding hearts framing our flagstone paths. In the fence corner, stationary since their creation, six tombstones sat on a big blue tarp.

The forecast promised clear weather, and TripCheck web cameras showed bare pavement between walls of snow on the highest summit of Interstate 5—the perfect time to move our homemade headstones south over the mountain pass from Oregon to Olive Hill Cemetery.

Robert placed a large sheet of cardboard on the floor of our small sports utility vehicle, nearly covering the entire cargo space. I followed him into the back yard.

"I'd like to get these loaded tonight so we can leave early tomorrow. Do you think you could help carry this?" Robert asked as he pointed to one of the engraved blocks.

"Um, I don't know. How much does it weigh?"

He pulled on his yellow gloves. "I can walk backward; that'll help."

"Really? Backward? Can't we use the hand truck?"

"Across bark chips and flagstones, all the way out to the driveway? I don't think so. Can you carry forty-five or fifty pounds?"

"Yes, I can carry forty-five pounds. But that's not the issue. I'm worried about you tripping over backward into the daffodils. You'll take your last breath under somebody else's tombstone."

Robert handed me a pair of leather gloves. "Let's do it." He bent his knees and grasped the stone. "On the count of three. One . . ."

"Wait. I have to get my gloves on. I can't hold ninety pounds of rock if you fall."

"One, two . . ." Knees bent, my hands tightened over the lower edges of the gravestone . . . "three." Lifting the stone seemed like lifting a car. It took much more effort than I thought it would.

"This weighs more than ninety pounds," I grumbled.

We inched along the side of the house, Robert blindly tapping his toe behind him before planting his foot and sliding the other leg backward. I couldn't see my feet either because a chunk of granite and concrete was in the way. I moved in time with my partner, watching his eyes in a strange slow dance. Tap-tap-step-slide, out the gate, around the corner to the driveway and the waiting open door of our SUV.

"We'll have to lift it in sideways," Robert said as he backed alongside the rear bumper.

With one last burst of effort, we lifted the stone into the cargo space, and Robert shoved the block toward the front of the car. When he couldn't reach any farther, he climbed in, and with a mighty groan he pushed the headstone the remaining few feet to the back of the driver's seat.

He uncurled from cramped quarters grinning, his whole face glowing. "I told you we could do it. One down, five to go."

As we repeated the process, I realized that the first stone was the lightest, and "five pounds or so" was a much bigger struggle than I had first imagined. My fingers ached and my muscles twitched as we fought against gravity. Every time we pushed a marker into the car, the bumper dropped ever lower toward pavement. We had five of the gravestones loaded when we tried to lift the last one. That particular granite block was identical to another in length and width, but it was thicker, and much more of the stone was concealed in concrete. I reached down to pick up my side but it wouldn't budge. I tried again, but it seemed glued to the ground.

"How much does this weigh?"

"I think I might have underestimated the weight on all of these," Robert said. "I used one bag of Sakrete for each gravestone. That means about seventy-five pounds of concrete plus the weight of the stone for each one."

"Well, I can't lift this."

"Yeah, I used a bag and a half on this one. Add in that thick slab of granite, and I'll bet it goes about 170 pounds. Where are you going?"

"To take a hot bath. Now."

Robert phoned one of his brawny friends, explained the dilemma, and planned for Aaron to meet us here early the next morning. When the two men finally wrestled that last monster into the car, the back end sank even lower. I watched Aaron's taillights disappear around the corner and wished we could take him with us. We managed to find room in the cargo space to jockey in a wheeled handcart, garden tools, and two planks for a makeshift ramp. Good thing we were traveling in daylight; with the car's newly acquired tilt, our headlights would have skimmed the treetops.

This was the beginning of spring break, time for rest and recreation. But here we were, taking headstones for a 350-mile ride to Olive Hill. I was worried about the steep ascent to the Siskiyou Pass, a grueling 2,300-foot change in elevation in just seven miles. We joined fully loaded semi-trailer trucks in the slow lane and crept our way to the summit. The engine developed a strange high-pitched whine as we slowed from forty-five to thirty miles per hour.

Once we made it to the top of the pass, the drive across the California border was easy, with ample time on our side for the seven-hour trip south to meet Harry Bosworth in Geyserville. When I'd phoned him the previous day, Harry had offered to be there with us at Olive Hill to help us move stones and to assure that markers were correctly placed. We couldn't do it alone. We'd agreed to meet him at the Bosworth store at three o'clock. Allowing for a couple of stops, we planned to arrive an hour early just to be on the safe side.

Midway into the trip, we turned west on Highway 20, and I breathed a huge sigh of relief. Now we could travel at a slower pace, away from frenetic freeway traffic. Ten miles later, we were stopped by a blockade and two California highway patrolmen. A burly uniformed officer bent down to talk through our open window, "Where you headed?"

I expected him to finish the sentence, *and where ya goin' with all those tombstones?*

"Middletown, then Calistoga," Robert answered.

"You can't get through this way," the officer said. "There's been a tanker explosion in the canyon." Apparently, he didn't spot the cargo. "You gotta go around, detour down the I-5."

"I didn't want to go that route," Robert grumbled as we joined a procession of cars U-turning back the way we came. He let out a groan as we eased onto the crowded freeway, where cars hugged our rear bumper and screamed by at seventy-five miles an hour. I didn't want to think what would happen if we had to make a sudden stop. Even though the cargo was secured to the floor behind us, in a battle between straps and stone, stone would surely win. Seven hundred pounds of granite and marble would hurtle their way forward at deadly speed right for our heads.

We didn't say a word, but there were audible double exhales when we finally maneuvered safely off the freeway. My heart sank as digital dash numbers jumped to three-zero-zero. We were supposed to be in Geyserville by now. We merged into tourist traffic, an agonizing stop-start snail pace through wine country—Napa, St. Helena, Calistoga—then resumed speed for the final segment through the winding valley route of Highway 128.

We turned just past Geyserville Mud Coffee and Catelli's Restaurant and parked a short distance away, in front of the old gray-board building, its big false front advertising "Bosworth & Son General Merchandise." We rushed past "Gents Furnishing Notions" stenciled on its windowpane and opened the front door.

"Harry, I'm so sorry," I said, checking my watch. We were exactly one hour late.

Harry Bosworth grabbed his ledger. "We'll have to hurry. I'll follow you."

We drove northwest a few blocks, past the church and a couple of bed-and-breakfasts, to the outskirts of town, where we turned left and followed Canyon Road to Olive Hill Cemetery.

Marking Graves

We parked on a gravel road just above my family's section and hurried down the hill. Harry seated himself on a nearby graveside curb, pulled a small piece of paper out of his ledger, and began to sketch a map.

"You'll need to know where to place the stones," Harry said.

"You're not going to stay and help us?" I asked.

"My sister is doing a presentation at the Historical Society. I don't want to be late." His pencil skittered across the small page. I couldn't believe what I was hearing. We had come too far, done too much for the project to capsize now. A rush of adrenaline kicked my brain into crisis mode. I gave Harry my full attention.

"Over here, that's Agostino Rossi," Harry said as he pointed to a tangle of poison oak under an oak tree. "Down here, inside the curbing, Marianna Rossi and Argentina Motroni." Harry was moving fast, too fast.

"Wait! Which one is Marianna?" I asked.

"Argentina above, Marianna below."

Moving down the section, Harry pointed to a wide area of dry grass. "Over there, that's Lawrence."

"Lawrence? You mean Lorenzo?"

"Yeah. You'll have to leave a space for the path."

"What path? There is no path. Do you mean he's in front of the pine tree?" I asked.

Robert loped over to the tree and stood in place as a proxy headstone, waiting for further instructions.

"No, at the edge, to the right." Harry waved his hand to the side as Robert changed position. "A little more . . . yeah, that's about right."

Standing on one foot and scraping with the heel of his other shoe, Robert gouged a groove in the dirt to mark the location for Lorenzo's gravestone.

"And over here, between Lawrence and Mabel's headstone, that's for Vince," he said, pointing to the right of Noni's pink granite marker.

"At the brown stake?" I asked.

"Yeah, that's it." Harry was on the move again, continuing down the hill, Robert and I in close pursuit. "And this one, this last one's for Tony," he said, pointing to a grassy area below my grandmother's grave, just to the left of a scrub oak tree.

"Tony? Who's Tony? There is no Tony. Do you mean Francesco Mortara?" I asked.

That was the only name left, the only one Harry hadn't mentioned. Francesco "Frances" would never have answered to Tony, but his full name, discovered on funeral records, was Antonio Francesco Mortara.

"Yeah, that's it," Harry replied, as he handed me the little map and turned to trek up the hill, Robert and I chasing his heels. I was clinging to a thread of hope, a slim chance that maybe he'd change his mind. And then Harry climbed into his car.

I held the map, a palm-sized folded scrap of paper, tightly in my hand so it wouldn't blow away in the wind. We watched Harry drive away, and a surge of nausea climbed its way up from my stomach. The sound of his car faded as it rounded a curve, then just the rustle of leaves and otherwise dead silence. Ominous clouds darkened an already somber mood. We were losing daylight, rain was forecasted for the next day, and we had limited time to get this done. We needed to level the ground for stone placement, weed and rake, trim branches, clean up debris, and dodge poison oak in this pioneer cemetery.

"There's so much to do! Can we move these on our own before dark? And how are we going to move that one?" I pointed to the monster stone on the right side of the cargo space.

Robert said, "We can do it."

He didn't move the monster stone. Instead, he selected a smaller grave marker from the left side and jockeyed it down the makeshift ramp of two wooden planks. I held the board ends in place on the ground and scooted the hand truck under the stone. Together we proceeded thirty yards downhill from the road to the correct gravesite. Our footsteps crunched on a rocky path carpeted with decaying leaves and twigs. Each time there was an obstacle, I bent down beside the wobbling two-wheeled dolly to steady its load so the stone wouldn't catapult down the hill on its own, tumbling and crumbling its way to disaster. Five more times we would weave and bob our way through the cemetery, guiding an over-loaded, teetering hand truck with undersized wheels. We'd stop close to the appropriate site, I'd check the map, and Robert would wrestle each gravestone into place.

With hoe and rake, we clipped and pulled poison oak aside to place the first stone for my great-grandfather:

AGOSTINO ROSSI 1852–1911

Agostino was born in Farnocchia, a forested village perched in the steep Apuan Alps. There he worked as a marble miner, using sledgehammer and wedge to carve huge slabs of stone from a nearby quarry. Agostino saw his way of life disappearing along with the marble, and he set out for Lucca with his brother, Santi Rossi. Together they would purchase a four-unit dwelling in the hamlet of Ponte Rotto.

In the village of Decimo, on the banks of the Serchio River, Agostino Rossi found Marianna Fambrini Marcucci, a beautiful woman with three young boys and a missing husband. In 1882, Agostino took on the formidable task of supporting her and the boys in his Ponte Rotto home at a time when Italy was in economic freefall. Together they would add two girls to their family: Amabile in 1884, and Argentina in 1886.

In 1888, Marianna's youngest son, Pietro, died of unstated cause. Twelve years later, as living conditions worsened, they watched Marianna's surviving adult children leave, one each year, for the promise of a better life in America. In 1910, Agostino paid for his own passage aboard the steamship *America* and traveled alone to Ellis Island. He carried forty dollars and purchased a train ticket to his destination eighty miles north of San Francisco, where his daughter Amabile and son-in-law Giovanni Motroni owned a home and vineyard in Geyserville. His second daughter, Argentina, lived nearby with her husband, Rafaello Motroni. Agostino Rossi had been in California only eleven months when he died of heart disease at age fifty-nine, before he had a chance to send for his wife.

The second stone was inscribed:

MARIANNA ROSSI 1843–1922

Born Marianna Fambrini in a village north of Lucca, my great-grandmother had remained in Italy two years after Agostino died. All of Marianna's grown children—two surviving sons from her first marriage to Domenico Marcucci and two daughters from her union with Agostino—had moved to California.

Marianna's letters revealed how much she missed them, how she longed to see them. My mother had kept one of her postcards in a small box tied with a pink ribbon. Written in Italian, dated 1905, it was addressed to her eldest son, Regalo Orlando Marcucci: *I think of all of you. If only you could come to me—that would be my ultimate happiness.*

But Marianna's sons and daughters couldn't return to Italy. They had made the agonizing decision to break up the family in order to save the family. Poverty, overpopulation, and natural disasters—volcanic eruptions, earthquakes, and floods—all spurred Italian emigration. Between 1880 and 1924, more than four million Italians sailed an ocean away to the United States.

Marianna must have been torn between staying in the country she loved and taking a terrible risk to join her grown children so far away. Both of her spouses had died in America, a bad omen. She knew about harvesting and drying fruits and vegetables for winter. She knew how to cook savory meals, how to turn recycled cloth and thread into a new skirt. She didn't know about placing her foot on a slippery deck to sail to an unknown land.

Nevertheless, two months after her seventieth birthday, Marianna traveled alone by train from Lucca, Italy, to Le Havre, France, where she boarded *La Lorraine* for the transatlantic crossing to New York. According to the ship manifest, she was five-foot-one with gray hair and gray eyes, and she carried twenty-five dollars. It was the last week of November 1913, and the weather was unpredictable, with a high probability of storms at sea.

Eight nights she must have spent pitching and rocking on a narrow bed wedged tightly between other beds, a tier of bunks fastened above and below. Did she lie awake in the belly of the steamship feeling the loud engine pulse in her bones, enduring the sounds of retching coughs and moans? Did she even know the names of the people lying beside her? Did she cover her face to blot out the acrid odor of human distress?

That voyage must have been a terrifying experience for an elderly woman from a small village, traveling alone.

Marianna couldn't speak English. At Ellis Island, an interpreter hung a large white card from her neck by a string, the magic words on the card reading *San Francisco*. Strangers pointed the way to a stairway, to a ferry, to the train terminal. Marianna endured another long trip by rail, then by ferry, arriving in San Francisco the second week of December 1913. What a joyful reunion it must have been for that matriarch, finally, after thirteen long years, to be reunited with all her grown children! I can imagine tears and shouts of joy as this tiny woman stepped down onto the platform and into the arms of her family.

Marianna's son Lorenzo, his receding auburn hair still thick with curls, had boarded a ship for North America in 1900. His brother Orlando had followed in 1901, his six-foot-three-inch frame now slightly bent from a back injury. Orlando's two children, Albert and Iris, once small enough for Marianna to hold in her arms, were now teenagers schooled in California. Marianna's daughter Amabile was barely eighteen when she had sailed away in 1902. And here she was, standing proud and tall, married, with blond seven-year-old daughter Pia—my mother. Marianna's seventeen-year-old daughter Argentina had followed her sister's footsteps in 1903, and now she was filled out, no longer a child, twenty-seven years old and married.

But the four siblings weren't the only ones who had changed. Marianna's dark hair was now gray, her thin face lined by the past thirteen years of hardship. In this new land, Marianna chose to stay for seven years with her son Lorenzo in a Geyserville cottage surrounded by vineyards, then in a San Francisco brownstone apartment with her daughter Amabile for the remaining two years of her life.

~

With loud grunts and groans and a pry bar, Robert somehow wrestled the monster stone into place for Marianna and Agostino Rossi's second daughter:

ARGENTINA MOTRONI 1886–1920

Immigration records stated that Argentina was a "tailoress." She sailed from Le Havre in November 1903 on the steamship *La Gascogne* with twenty dollars in her pocket, her passage paid by her older sister Amabile (Mabel), whom she joined in San Francisco. After their arrival in California, these two sisters married two brothers, Giovanni and Rafaello Motroni. Argentina and her husband first settled in Geyserville.

Rafaello (Ralph) was a farm laborer in the fledgling wine industry. He may have struggled with illness, unable to continue working. The first clue was in the 1900 *La Touraine* ship manifest. On arrival in New York Harbor, Rafaello was not on board at final check. He had jumped ship into bone-chilling waters, perhaps to avoid medical inspection and the possibility of deportation. Two decades later, he was registered in the 1920 census as an inmate, age forty-five, at the Relief Home for the Aged and Infirm, Alms House Road, San Francisco.

That same year, Argentina fell ill with toxemia, now called preeclampsia, during pregnancy. Her illness would have been marked by a sharp rise in blood pressure, followed by seizures and coma. Neither she nor her unborn baby survived. Argentina was only thirty-four years old when she died in Mabel's home in San Francisco. Funeral records stated that Mabel arranged transport to Olive Hill in Geyserville, where family members dug her grave. Argentina's husband, Rafaello Motroni, died five years later.

We cleared the ground of weeds and debris in front of a pine tree, where we placed the next gravestone:

LORENZO MARCUCCI 1868-1944

In March 1900, Lorenzo boarded *La Bretagne* in Le Havre and arrived in New York Harbor eight days later. From there he traveled by train to California and settled in Sacramento, then moved in 1907 to the Geyserville ranch house of his half sister Amabile.

In 1913 he moved with his mother, Marianna, to a small house surrounded by vineyards in Geyserville. His last home was in Alexander Valley, in the outskirts of Healdsburg, where I was raised.

Lorenzo was a kind and gentle soul, quiet, with a ready smile, and he lived a simple life as a farm laborer. I remembered his cottage, its brown interior carrying the pungent scent of old wood and Prince Albert pipe tobacco, which he kept on a shelf in a red tin.

When I was four, I was playing a game with Uncle Lori, trying to prevent him from opening the field gate through a series of tactics which included shouting orders, trying to hold the gate closed, and finally, throwing pebbles at him. One found its mark on his cheek. Horrified, I watched a trickle of blood travel down his face. "Don't tell! Don't tell! Non . . . non . . ." I tried to speak in Italian but couldn't remember the word for tell, and Uncle Lori didn't speak English. I knew that a crime of this magnitude meant big trouble.

Uncle Lori didn't realize that he was wounded and seemed quite puzzled by my anguished behavior. Several days after the incident, my mother gently explained to me that throwing rocks at people was forbidden. I was astonished at her reaction. My mother knew the horrible crime I had committed, but the earth hadn't opened and swallowed me whole. Uncle Lori had related the incident and petitioned for leniency on my behalf.

My grandmother Noni's headstone had been placed here more than a half century before. We had finally found her date of birth in Lucca, Italy. Engraved in rose granite read:

MABEL MORTARA 1884–1948

I'd contacted a California granite company whose workers had righted the tipped stone and inscribed her dates here at Olive Hill. Mabel's birth name was Amabile (Ah-*ma*-bee-leh), a fitting name that means "lovable."

I imagined Noni dressed in multiple layers of clothing on a Genoa pier. It was October 1902, and she had just turned eighteen. She held a passport and boarding pass, and beneath her belt she carried thirty dollars, a gift from her two half brothers in California. With courage and determination, she would endure the hard journey to a new land. She married Giovanni "John" Motroni in 1905, survived the San Francisco earthquake the following year, and gave birth to her only child, my mother, Pia, in 1906. Noni's marriage would not last, but she found love and adoration from her second spouse, Vincent Mortara.

Noni exemplified *la bella figura*—making a good impression—amid pots of bubbling concoctions, steaming vegetables funneled into sterilized mason jars, stacks of laundry to fold, patterns pinned on ready-to-cut fabric, and the house immaculate and clutter-free at day's end. She managed it all with her back straight, her hair arranged neatly in a crown, and always with time for hugs.

Noni doted on me, brushed my hair, sewed my clothes, and taught me to walk tall with a book balanced on top of my head. Her gifts of love, guidance, patience, and elegance by example would last me a lifetime.

We jockeyed the next stone into place for Vincent's brother:

ANTONIO FRANCESCO MORTARA 1881–1965

Known in America as Frances, Francesco was born in Castagnole Monferrato, in the Italian province of Asti. Vincent wrote in his diary that their childhood was rich with affection but lacking in money. When the two boys finished second grade, their parents couldn't afford to send both to school, so Frances gave his third-grade education to his younger brother. Both boys, avid readers, managed their continuing education with independent study. Like all the other people in this family section, Frances had emigrated to America.

In 1906, he followed Vincent to Smithers, West Virginia, where men faced hazardous duty in coal mines. Frances didn't enter the mines, but census records revealed he worked there as a farmer while Vincent traveled around the state as a union organizer. Vincent eventually moved to California, and Frances followed a few years later. He found work farming in the fertile soil of Alexander Valley near Healdsburg. He lived his final years in his brother's home in Redwood City, where he tended their abundant garden. He rode the cross-town bus to a local park once a week to play bocce ball with friends.

During my early grade-school years, Frances raised our vegetables, assuring us the finest bounty pulled from the earth for our daily meals. He made his wine with a primitive press, bottled and aged in green glass in our basement. Each spring he foraged for mushrooms—*porcini* and *coccola*—carried home in buckets. He dried most, but some of his fresh prizes, sizzled in olive oil, topped our pasta. On winter evenings, when the wind howled and the rain blew against the windows, the two of us would sit by the fire to play *Scopa*, an Italian card game.

As dusk surrounded us, Robert and I removed an unmarked wooden stake, and weeded and raked the last plot. We placed the final headstone, for my step-grandfather, Bo:

VINCENT MORTARA 1886–1974

Of all the work that we had done that day, I was most concerned about marking Bo's grave. When a large block of white marble had become available six months earlier, I knew it was meant for him. Bo was a big presence in my life, a source of love and affection in my formative single-digit years. He called me *Topina*—little mouse. We found his story in his diaries.

In 1903, Vincent's path wound from Castagnole Monferrato, Italy, to Ellis Island, to the coal mines of West Virginia, where his brother, Frances, joined him three years later. Bo was shocked by the dangerous working conditions in the tunnels, and he was an outspoken critic of the meager pay that kept miners indebted to the company store. Passionate and unyielding in his campaign for equal opportunity and justice, he became a union organizer, speaking in numerous towns in West Virginia.

Bo was arrested for inciting civil unrest. At his trial, when asked if he believed in God, he answered, "Is this the Spanish Inquisition?" He was found guilty and served an eighteen-month prison sentence. He hated his cell mate and complained to the guard. The sympathetic jailer moved him to the top floor, to larger accommodations usually reserved for women. Bo's days were spent with a self-imposed routine of exercise, reading, and writing. The walls of his large cell were lined with books. The jailer invited Bo into his home, without restraints, where the jailer's wife prepared their meals. Bo's nights were consumed with studying the stars through a telescope provided by that same guard. Upon his release, at his employer's request, Bo changed his name to Vincenzo Costelli (his mother's birth name) and resumed his union activities until it became too dangerous to continue.

By 1915, Bo had traveled by train to San Francisco and found Mabel, the woman of his dreams. He adored her, and he showered Mabel's daughter, Pia, with love and kindness. He changed his name back to Vincent Mortara, probably about 1920.

Ten years later, Vincent dared to do the impossible. He explored for oil on the Alexander Valley property owned by Joe Harry Smith. The 1930

California census, Kellogg Precinct, listed my family members at that site:

Joe Harry Smith (my paternal grandfather) Farmer and Leaseholder
Leonard Smith (my father) Driller
Vernon Smith (my father's brother) Tool Dresser
Vincent Mortara (Bo) Superintendent
Francesco Mortara (Vincent's brother) Laborer
Lorenzo Marcucci (Noni's half brother) Laborer

According to my father's account, all the men were paid in stock certificates, and all were doing other jobs just to survive. I still have my mother's photographs of two non-productive oil derricks and a small vial of oil-covered shale. By dowsing with a string and pendulum, Bo had found oil, but not enough to bring to surface. I was raised on that same three-acre parcel, purchased by Vincent Mortara and later sold to my father.

At the time Vincent's beloved Mabel died in 1949, he bought the gravesite next to hers, twenty-six years before his death. Now we placed his marker by her grave.

My earliest memory of Bo was late one summer evening, when he carried me, bedclothes trailing, to the field behind our home. Bo pointed to the night skies and said, "Look, Topina! Fireworks just for you!" I've seen numerous meteor showers in my life, but none as wondrous as the one I saw in the arms of Bo. On his headstone, above his name, was engraved a shooting star.

Our work completed, I climbed the hill above the graves to gaze down on carefully placed stones. Before we left that day, I wanted to make certain that they were perfectly aligned, the topmost edges of the grave markers even with each other.

Suddenly, I lost touch with where I was. This wasn't just about tombstones. This was about a spiritual connection with my ancestors and family members that transcended time and space. My family had set examples of bravery and resilience and hope. If genetic predisposition is a reality, it had served me well. It carried me through graduate school, one of only two women enrolled in the business program. One of the proudest days of my life was in 1987, when my husband, Robert, and I received our master's degrees, and my son, Don Keck, received his bachelor's degree, all on the same day, all on the same stage, at Southern Oregon State College (now Southern Oregon University). That day was followed by successful careers, mine in medical practice management, at a time when women were seldom accepted as consultants or administrators.

I am grateful for my amazing Italian family members who led the way, none of whom had received more than a third-grade education. They are my heroes.

I found Robert, and we held each other close. "Thank you for this," I whispered. Our long journey had brought respectful closure to unfinished business at Olive Hill Cemetery.

Before I was born, I dwelled in the DNA of my ancestors. They provided a profound positive influence in my life. They left me a paper trail to reclaim my past, a treasure map of clues. They led me to Italy—to village houses, churches, orchards, and vineyards—and provided vivid images of their lives, which touched my soul. Their breath is in warm breezes, their light in the farthest stars, their courage passed down through the ages. This wasn't just about tombstones. My family members found me. They are remembered.